OLD LOUISIANA PLANTATION HOMES
AND FAMILY TREES

A Blue Book of the Louisiana Plantation Country

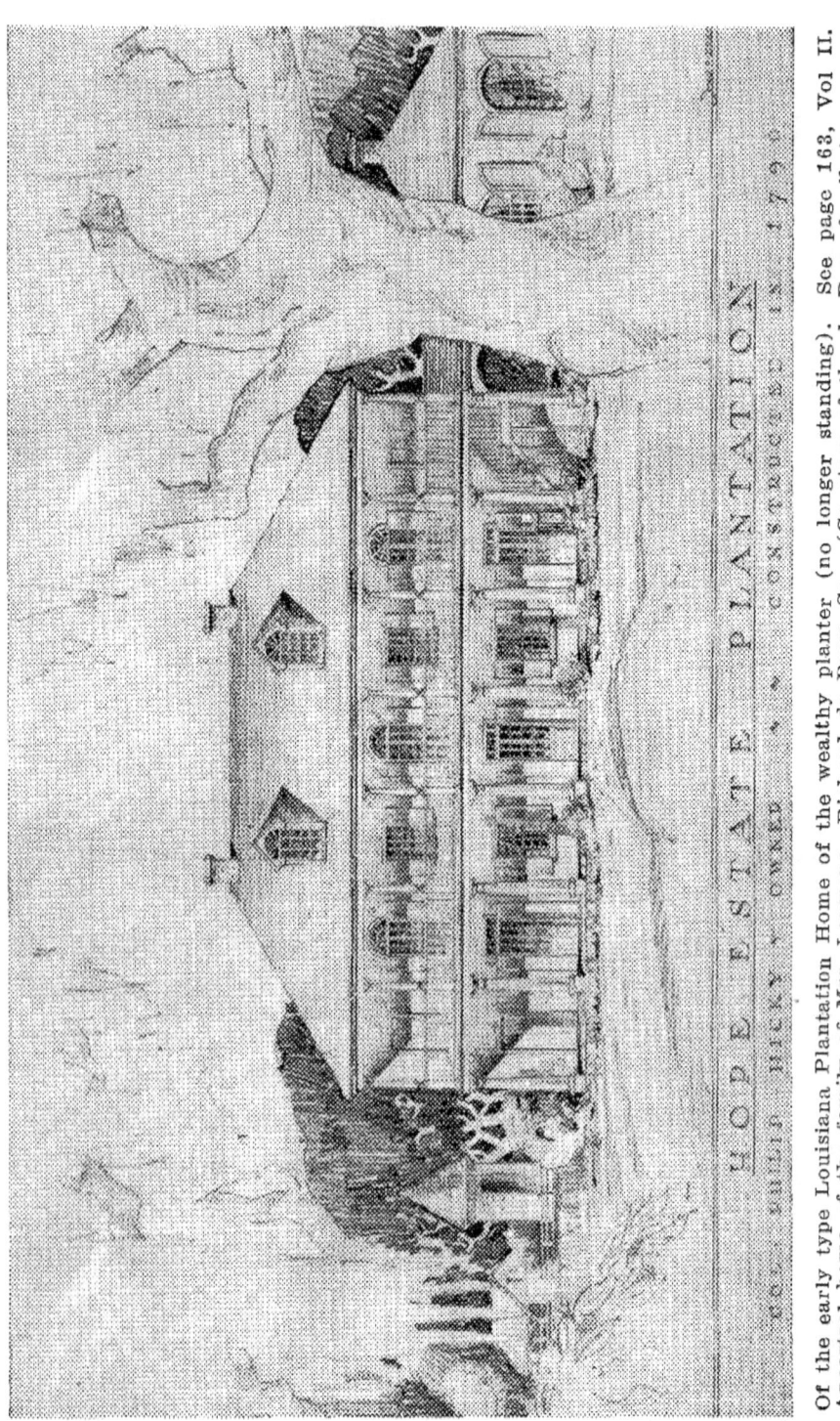

Of the early type Louisiana Plantation Home of the wealthy planter (no longer standing). See page 163, Vol II. Ancestral home of the family of Mrs. Lawrence Richard de Buys, Sr. (Courtesy of the de Buys family.)

OLD LOUISIANA PLANTATION HOMES

AND

FAMILY TREES

By

Herman de Bachellé Seebold, M. D.

IN TWO VOLUMES—VOL. II.

Southern Historical Press, Inc.
Greenville, South Carolina

This volume was reproduced from
An 1941 edition located in the
Publisher's private Library
Greenville, South Carolina

All rights reserved. No part of this publication may be reproduced,
stored in a retrieval system, transmitted in any form, posted
on to the web in any form or by any means without
the prior written permission of the publisher.

Please direct all correspondence and orders to:

www.southernhistoricalpress.com
or
SOUTHERN HISTORICAL PRESS, Inc.
PO Box 1267
375 West Broad Street
Greenville, SC   29601
southernhistoricalpress@gmail.com

Originally published: New Orleans, LA 1941
Copyright 1941 by Herman de Bachelle Seebold
ISBN #0-89308-011-X
All rights Reserved.
Printed in the United States of America

CONTENTS

	Page
CHAPTER I. THE LA FRENIER FAMILY	1
CHAPTER II. THE DE LIVAUDAIS FAMILY AND PLANTATON	3
CHAPTER III. FORSTALL DYNASTY	11
CHAPTER IV. THE FORTIER FAMILY	16
CHAPTER V. DE LA VERGNE — DE ST. PAUL — DE FRENEUSE SCHMIDT — SEGHERS FAMILIES	19
CHAPTER VI. THE MILLIKEN AND FARWELL FAMILIES	28
CHAPTER VII. THE DE TERNANT — PARLANGE — DE BRIERRE — D'HERBIGNY — DE VEZIN FAMILIES	37
CHAPTER VIII. THE DE VERGES FAMILY	46
CHAPTER IX. THE BUTLER DYNASTY	52
CHAPTER X. PIPES FAMILY	59
CHAPTER XI. THE ELLIS FAMILY	65
CHAPTER XII. THE PERCY FAMILY	67
CHAPTER XIII. THE PLAUCHE' FAMILY	72

CHAPTER XIV.
	Page
THE BARROW DYNASTY	75

CHAPTER XV.
BRINGIER DYNASTY
THE BRINGIER-KENNER — DU BOURG — BRENT— TRIST — WOOD — STAUFFER FAMILIES 83

CHAPTER XVI.
THE KNOX — SEMMES — WALMSLEY — RANLETT FAMILIES 104

CHAPTER XVII.
THE SMYTH — SULLY FAMILIES 114

CHAPTER XVIII.
THE DE MARIGNY — DE LA RONDE — ALMONASTER— DE DREUX — VILLERE — BEAUREGARD — LANAUX — RARESHIDE FAMILIES 130

CHAPTER XIX.
THE ALSTON — PIRRIE — BOWMAN — MATTHEWS FAMILIES 152

CHAPTER XX.
THE RATHBONE — DE BUYS — HICKY — DUGGAN — DE MACARTY FAMILIES 158

CHAPTER XXI.
VonPHUL — CADE — DU BROCCA — ALLAIN FAMILIES.. 174

CHAPTER XXII.
D'ESTREHAN DES TOURS — The DE LA BARRE FAMILY 180

CHAPTER XXIII.
THE HEWES — GRYMES FAMILIES 184

CHAPTER XXIV.
THE FROTSCHER — KOCH — MULLER — BRUCE FAMILIES 191

CHAPTER XXV.
THE BOEHM FAMILY 195

CHAPTER XXVI.
Page
THE SEEBOLD — DE BACHELLE' — DE VILBISS — DE BEAULIEU DE MARCONNAY — KONZELMAN FAMILIES 208

CHAPTER XXVII.
THE WALTER PARKER FAMILY — THE PITKIN FAMILY 237

CHAPTER XXVIII.
THE LEVERT — WARE — PRUDHOMME — WILKINSON — STEWART FAMILIES — THE MYRTLES PLANTATION AND OAK GROVE PLANTATION 242

LIST OF ILLUSTRATIONS

                                                                                  Pages

Frontispiece—Hope Estate Plantation Home
Crest and coat-of-arms de la Vergne family................opposite 20
Crest and coat-of-arms de St. Paul family................ " 20
Crest and coat-of-arms de Fréneuse de St. Aubin........ " 20
Entrance of Villa de la Vergne................between 20-21
Fountain at Villa de la Vergne................ " 20-21
Count Pierre de la Vergne................ " 20-21
New Orleans Home of the de la Vergne family............opposite 21
Count Charles de Bony de la Vergne................ " 24
Chateau de la Vergne, near St. Priest Ligouri Haute—
    Vinn Limousin, France ....between 24-25
Madame Henri Landry de Fréneuse................ " 24-25
Garden of the de la Vergne home, New Orleans........ " 24-25
Hall of the de la Vergne, New Orleans home............ " 24-25
Charles Edward Schmidt, fro mminiature................ " 24-25
Mrs. Charles Edward Schmidt, neé Leda Hinks...... " 24-25
Mrs. Hugues Cage St. Paul, neé Leda Helene de la
    Vergne .... " 24-25
Countess Chas. de Boni de la Vergne (Margurite
    de la Vergne .... " 24-25
Interior of the de la Vergne New Orleans home...... " 24-25
Gustavus Schmidt, noted lawyer................ " 24-25
Crest and coat-of-arms of the Dugue de Livaudais......opposite 25
Farwell family crest and coat-of-arms................ " 28
Mr. and Mrs. Richard Allen Milliken................between 28-29
Mr. and Mrs. Charles A. Farwell II................ " 28-29
Mrs. John James Blair .... " 28-29
John James Blair .... " 28-29
Martha Shannon Blair .... " 28-29
Charles A. Farwell I................ " 28-29
Mrs. Charles A. Farwell I, from ivory miniature........opposite 29
Miss Nellie Farwell, from an ivory miniature............ " 29
William Blair .... " 29
Henry Dickinson Blair .... " 29
New Orleans home of Miss Nellie Farwell................ " 32
Charles A. Farwell III. ....between 32-33

	Pages
New Orleans home of Mr. and Mrs. Chas. A. Farwell III	between 32-33
Mrs. F. Evans Farwell as Queen of Proteus	" 32-33
F. Evans Farwell	opposite 33
New Orleans home of Mr. and Mrs. F. Evans Farwell	" 33
de Brierre crest and coat-of-arms	" 36
Madame Avegno neé Melle. de Ternant	between 36-37
Loading sugar cane	" 36-37
Judge Charles Parlange	" 36-37
Walter Charles Parlange, Sr.	" 36-37
Walter Charles Parlange, Jr.	" 36-37
Mrs. Walter Charles Parlange (Paule Brierre)	opposite 37
Mrs. A. A.. Poirson (Evelyn Humphries)	" 37
The Marquis Claude Vincent de Ternant II	" 40
Crest and coat-of-arms of the de Cruzat family	" 41
Coat-of-arms of the de Lino Chalmette family	" 41
Antoine de Cruzat	" 41
Madeline Victoire Heloise de Lino de Chalmette	" 41
Mrs. Pierre Paul de Verges (Madeline de Cruzat)	" 48
de Poupart coat-of-arms	" 48
Chateau Mont L'Evecque, near Paris, France	" 48
Butler family crest and coat-of-arms	" 49
Interior of the home of the Misses Butler, New Orleans	" 49
Mrs. W. A. Fort, by Amand	" 56
Judge Thomas Butler, by Thos. Sully	" 56
James Butler, Second Duke of Ormond	" 56
Adjutant Gen. Robert Butler	" 56
Randolph family crest and coat-of-arms	" 57
Stewart family crest and coat-of-arms	" 57
David W. Pipes in Confederate uniform	" 60
Mrs. D. W. Pipes (Anna Key Fort) at time of marriage	" 60
William Johnson Fort of Catalpa Plantation	between 60-61
David W. Pipes I	" 60-61
Mrs. David W. Pipes (at present)	" 60-61
Beech Grove Plantation manor (D. W. Pipes I)	opposite 61
Mary Johnson, mother of Mrs. W. J. Fort	" 64
Grace Episcopal Church, St. Francisville, La.	" 64

	Pages
Mrs. Walter Crawford (Sarah Pipes)	opposite 65
Gen. J. B. Plauché	" 72
Mary Barrow, by Sir Thomas Sully	" 73
Robert Hilliard Barrow II, by Sully	" 73
Melpomene, city home of the Bringier family	" 80
Marius Pons Bringier	" 81
Mrs. Marius Pons Bringier (Marie Francois Durand)	" 81
Madame Michel Doradou Bringier	" 88
Michel Doradou Bringier, by Amant	" 88
Hon. Duncan F. Kenner	between 88-89
Madame Duncan F. Kenner (Guillemine Nanine Bringier)	" 88-89
Louise Elizabeth Aglaé Du Bourg de Ste. Colombe	" 88-89
Augustin Dominicque Tureaud	" 88-89
Mrs. Joseph Lancaster Brent (Rosella Kenner)	" 88-89
General Jos. Lancaster Brent	" 88-89
Tristford Devonshire, England	" 88-89
Birdwood, Albemarle County, Virginia	" 88-89
Don Estavan Minor	" 88-89
Miss Mary Minor (Mrs. William Kenner)	" 88-89
Concord Plantation manor	" 88-89
"Ma Grande", mammy in the Bringier family	" 88-89
Col. Amadee Bringier, by Amans	" 88-89
Du Bourg family home, New Orleans	" 88-89
Margurite Amand de Vogluzan (Mrs. Pierre Du Bourg)	" 88-89
Madame Francois Charest de Lauzon	" 88-89
Pierre Francois Du Bourg	" 88-89
Madame Pierre Francois Du Bourg	" 88-89
Richard Henry Lee	" 88-89
Mrs. Ludwell Lee	" 88-89
Ludwell Lee	" 88-89
Mary Ann Lee	" 88-89
Robert Blair Campbell	" 88-89
Mrs. Francis Campbell, wife of Thos. Sloo I	" 88-89
Thos. Sloo I.	" 88-89
Nanine Maria Brent, wife of Thos. Sloo II	" 88-89
Thomas Sloo II	" 88-89
Thomas Sloo III	" 88-89

                                                                              Pages
Louis Guillaume Valentine Du Bourg, Bishop of
   New Orleans ....between 88-89
Hore Browse Trist, of Birdwood ....opposite 89
Gen. Hore Browse Trist of Bowden Plantation............ " 89
Marie Elizabeth Rosella Bringier .... " 89
Mary Wilhelmine Trist .... " 89
Major John Wood, born 1770.. " 96
Gen. Robert Crooke Wood, born 1799 .... " 96
Ann M. Taylor .... " 96
Col. Robert Crooke Wood, C. S. A. .... " 96
Seal ring, Taylor family .... " 97
Knox family crest and coat-of-arms................................. " 104
Robert Miller Walmsley .... " 105
Hon. Thos. J. Semmes .... " 105
Mrs. David Cattrell, Jr., below portrait of Mrs. T. J.
   Semmes ....opposite 112
Mrs. S. P. Walmsley (Myra Eulalie Semmes)..........between 112-113
Sylvester P. Walmsley I .... " 112-113
Sylvester P. Walmsley II .... " 112-113
Mrs. Sylvester P. Walmsley II .... " 112-113
Mrs. Thos. J. Semmes ....opposite 113
Mrs. Albert Sidney Ranlett (Cora Semmes).................. " 120
Albert Sidney Ranlett II .... " 120
T. J. S. Ranlett .... " 120
Mrs. Myra S. Curtis ....between 120-121
David Low Ranlett .... " 120-121
Mrs. Cora Ranlett Thomson .... " 120-121
Mrs. Eleanor Ranlett Kantzler .... " 120-121
Adele Ranlett .... " 120-121
T. J. S. Ranlett II .... " 120-121
Cora R. Blankenship .... " 120-121
Albert Sidney Ranlett III .... " 120-121
Cora Semmes Curtis ....opposite 121
Theodora Ranlett .... " 121
Marie Ranlett .... " 121
Eleanor Torrence Thomson .... " 121
Dr. John Smyth .... " 124
McMurtrie, crest and coat-of-arms........................... " 124
Wavertree Manor ....between 124-125

	Pages
Thomas Sully, Architect	between 124-125
Mrs. John Smyth (Jean Sully)	opposite 125
Greene family crest and coat-of-arms	" 128
Katherine Parr	" 128
Self portrait, Thomas Sully	" 128
Chester Sully, by Thos. Sully	" 128
de la Ronde Crest and coat-of-arms	" 129
de Dreux family crest and coat-of-arms	" 129
Baronne de Pontalba	" 136
Baron Pontalba, Sr.	" 136
Baronne Celestin Pontalba	" 136
Baron Celestin Pontalba	" 136
The Duke of Orleans	" 137
Don Andres Almonaster	" 137
Antoine Marie de Marigny	" 137
Bernard de Marigny	" 137
Monogrammed lunette, Pontalba buildings	" 144
Race of the R. E. Lee	" 144
Plantation home	" 145
Evergreen plantation	" 145
de Villere family crest and coat-of-arms	" 148
Mrs. Charles A. Larendon	between 148-149
Miss Laure Beauregard Larendon	" 148-149
Beauregard monument	" 148-149
Army of Tennessee monument	" 148--149
Mrs. John F. Coleman (Valentine Louise Lanaux)	opposite 149
Charles Alfred Lanaux	" 149
Rareshide family crest and coat-of-arms	" 149
Poujaud de Juvisy crest and coat-of-arms	" 149
de Buys family crest and coat-of-arms	" 160
Forstall family crest and coat-of-arms	" 160
Gaspard de Buys	" 161
Henry A. Rathbone	" 161
Mrs. Pierre Charles Forstall	" 164
Mrs. Gaspard de Buys	" 164
Mrs. Henry A. Rathbone	" 164
Mrs. Claude de Jan	" 164
Mrs. Laurence R. de Buys	between 164-165
Dr. Laurence R. de Buys	" 164-165

	Pages
Mrs. Joseph H. Duggan	between 164-165
Miss Edith Duggan	" 164-165
Lopez family crest	" 164-165
Donna Bettie Capomozza	opposite 165
Miss Langhorn	" 165
William Eno de Buys	" 165
Miss Grace King	" 165
James Mather, 1807	" 161
de Macarthy family crest and coat-of-arms	" 168
de Macarthy plantation home	" 168
Mammy Millie Turner	" 169
von Phul family crest and coat-of-arms	" 176
William von Phul	" 177
Mrs. William von Phul	" 177
Mrs. Robert Cade	" 177
Miss Lili Dubroca	" 177
William von Phul, Jr.	" 184
Madame U. S. Dufossat	between 184-185
Dufossat home in Paris	" 184-185
Madame Dufossat and Anna Le Andre	" 184-185
Graves in Pere la Chaise Cemetery Paris	" 184-185
Mrs. Effie Cade Daniels	" 184-185
The Thomas H. Hewes family	opposite 185
Mrs. Richard Frotscher	" 192
Richard Frotscher	" 192
Miss Lydia E. Frotscher	" 192
Miss Mary Frotscher	" 192
Julius Koch, Architect and Engineer	" 193
Richard Koch, Architect	" 193
A corner of the Koch home, New Orleans	" 193
Beautiful ironwork on Koch home	" 193
Crest and coat-of-arms of Boehm family quartered with that of the de Belasyse, Kirkland, and d'Almont families	" 196
Burgomaster August de Belasyse Boehm	between 196-197
Mrs. August de Belasyse Boehm (Magdalina K. d'Almont)	" 196-197
The old von Dalberg castle near Maintz	" 196-197
Mrs. Francis P. Boehm I (Elizabeth D'Aunoy)	opposite 197

	Pages
Anna Maria Boehm (Mrs. Pancratious Swendle)	opposite 197
Mr. and Mrs. Francis P. Boehm II.	" 200
Memorial Tablet von Dalberg castle	" 201
John Charles Fremont	between 207-208
Firemen's Parade	" 207-208
Lisette Boehm (Mrs. W. E. Seebold)	opposite 204
Francis Joseph Boehm	between 204-205
Mr. and Mrs. Peter Boehm I.	" 204-205
The old home of the Boehm family, New Orleans	opposite 205
Dominicque Peter Boehm	" 205
Philip Johnson	" 205
Mantle and over mantle in bedroom Seebold home New Orleans	between 208-209
Crest and coat-of-arms Seebold von dem Brink family	" 208-209
Ancestral home of the Seebold family near Hanover	opposite 209
Burgomaster John William Seebold	" 212
John Frederick William Seebold	" 212
Countess Johanne Henriette de Bachellé	" 212
Sophie Louise Julia Seebold	" 212
Mrs. J. W. H. Seebold (Henriette de Bachellé Munchmeyer)	between 212-213
Rev. J. W. Herman Seebold	" 212-213
Mrs. W. E. Seebold (Lisette Boehm)	" 212-213
W. E. Seebold, Art Dealer	" 212-213
Andres Molinary	opposite 213
Mrs. Andres Molinary (Marie Madeleine Seebold)	" 213
Drawing-room home of Dr. and Mrs. H. deB. Seebold	" 216
Drawing-room front view, Dr. and Mrs. H. deB. Seebold	" 217
Old home of William H. Kinney, Wichita, Kansas	" 217
H. deB. Seebold M. D.	" 220
Crest and coat-of-arms of the MacPherson family	between 220-221
Crest and coat-of-arms of the de Bachellé family	" 220-221
Mrs. John Donald MacPherson	" 220-221
James MacPherson of Iverness, Scotland	" 220-221
Mrs. Geo. O. MacPherson (Stella Lisette Seebold	" 220-221
Geo. Ossian MacPherson	" 220-221

	Pages
Mrs. H. deB. Seebold (Nettie M. Kinney)	opposite 221
Hallway in home of Dr. and Hrs. H. deB. Seebold	" 221
Chateau Fleur-de-lys, Former New York home of Dr. and Mrs. H. deB. Seebold	" 224
Carved door, New Orleans home of the Seebolds	between 224-225
Mrs. Jack Kinney Moore (Noville Mock)	" 224-225
Coat-of-arms of the de Vilbis (de Velbiss) family	" 224-225
Crest and coat-of-arms of the Taylor family	" 224-225
Crest and coat-of-arms of the de Wartegg family	" 224-225
Minnie Hauk (Baronne de Wartegg)	" 224-225
Souvenir post card	" 224-225
Baron and Baronne de Wartegg	" 224-225
Mrs William. Henry Kinney (Jennie Hauk)	" 224-225
William Henry Kinney	" 224-225
Mrs. John Hawkins Moore	opposite 225
Jack Kinney Moore	" 225
Mrs. Gustave von Meyer	" 228
Rev. Gustave von Meyer	" 228
Mrs. F. W. Konzelman (Clara B. de Beaulieu de Marconnay)	" 228
Fred W. Konzelman	" 228
Mary Baronne de Beaulieu de Marconnay	between 228-229
Entrance to the de Beaulieu de Marconnay home	" 228-229
Minnie Hauk as Carmen	" 228-229
Crest and coat-of-arms of the de Beaulieu de Marconnay	opposite 229
Chateau de Beaulieu de Marconnay near Poitou, France	" 229
Elise Antonia Seebold (wife of Baron C. de Beaulieu)	" 232
Baron Charles Philip de Beaulieu de Marconnay II	" 232
Baron Charles P. de Beaulieu de Marconnay III	" 232
Baronne Mary de Beaulieu de Marconnay III	" 232
Baron Charles de Beaulieu de Marconnay I	" 233
Julie Baronne de Beaulieu de Marconnay I	" 233
Albert Baron de Beaulieu de Marconnay	" 236
Baronne Albert de Beaulieu de Marconnay	" 236
William Nichols	" 236

	Pages
Carl Baron de Beaulieu de Marconnay	opposite 236
Mary Elizabeth Baronne de Beaulieu de Marconnay	between 236-237
William L. Hill	" 236-237
Villa Velure	" 236-237
Mrs. Charles de Beaulieu Konzelman	" 236-237
Charles de Beaulieu Konzelman	" 236-237
Albert de Beaulieu Konzelman	" 236-237
Mrs. Albert de Beaulieu Konzelman	" 236-237
Charles de Beaulieu Konzelman, Jr.	opposite 237
Mrs. Marvin Clark	" 237
Marvin Clark	" 237
Mrs. Charles de Beaulieu Konzelman	" 237
Mrs. Christian Schertz (Helen Pitkin)	" 240
William Willings Wells	between 240-241
Cotton for England	" 240-241
Crest and coat-of-arms of the Du Puy family	" 240-241
Walter Parker	" 240-241
Mrs. Walter Parker (Anita Hernandez)	opposite 241
Miss Ester Hernandez	" 241
Andrew Stewart	" 248
A bedroom at Oak Alley Plantation	" 248
Mrs. Andrew Stewart	between 248-249
Mrs. Allard Kaufmann	" 248-249

ILLUSTRATIONS FOR CHAPTER HEADINGS

	Page
Old Spanish water jars, Elmwood Plantation	1
Old iron sugar kettle, Fortier Plantation	16
Crest of the de la Vergne family	19
Crest of the Farwell family	28
Crested monogram from carriage fittings, Parlange family	37
An old plantation home of the de Verges family	46
Crest of the Butler family	52
Magnolias emblem of the Ellis plantation	65
Family tomb of the Plauchés	72
Crest and coat-of-arms of the Barrow family	74
Crest and coat-of-arms of the Bringier family	83
Crest and coat-of-arm of the Du Bourg family	89
Crest and coat-of-arms of the Brent family	93
Crest and coat-of-arms of the Trist family	96
Carnival emblems	105
Solid silver heirloom of the Ranfurley family	108
Artist emblems	114
A cotton picker	129
Crest and coat-of-arms of the Marquis de Marigny family	131
Many families came to the Felicianas in covered wagons	152
Crest and coat-of-arms of the Rathbone family	158
A cane sugar-cane cutter	163
Old Uncle Ned, a typical plantation hand	170
Red Church from an old sketch	180
Front stairway of "Pleasant View Plantation Home"	185
A plantation lantern	190
Military emblems French Army	194
Artist emblems	208
Garden emblem	212
Crest and coat-of-arms of the de Bachellé family	223
Crest and coat-of-arms of the Taylor family (Irish)	228
Crest of the de Beaulieu de Marconnay family	235
Bayou St. John from an old sketch	237
During sugar grinding season	242
Wild water hyacinth	248

Chapter I.

THE LA FRENIER FAMILY

HONORABLE Charles Gayarre (Louisiana Historian) tells us that one Pierre Chauvin, whose birthplace was Aryoa, France, the son of Pierre Chauvin and Catherine Avard de Solesne married Marthe Autreuil and became the parents of: (1) Jacques Chauvin (de Charleville); (2) Joseph Chauvin (de Lery); (3) Nicolas Chauvin (de la Frenier); (4) Louis Chauvin (de Beaulieu; (5) Barbe Chauvin, who married Ignace Robert de Bellair; and (6) Michelle Chauvin, who married Jacques Nepveu.

Their father, who in 1654 had received a Canadian land grant, at their birth named them thusly; Nicolas Chauvin (de la Frenier) married Marguerite Le Seur and had among their children, a son Nicolas Chauvin (de la Frenier) who at the time of the transfer of the Louisiana colony to Spain, became one of the heroic figures in Louisiana history. He was put to death by the Spaniards, and he was one of the first martyrs to Liberty on the American Continent. Members of the Chauvin family married into the most aristocratic families in Louisiana.

The Soniat du Fossat Family

The first of the Soniat du Fossat family to come to Louisiana was Guy de Saunhac du Fossat, descended directly from the noble family of Soniat du Fossat, whose ancient Chateau du Fossat near the junction of the Lot and Garonne Rivers, was taken possession of by Francois Saunhac de Belcastle (Saunhac de Belcastel) in 1538 and has been owned by the Saunhac du Fossat family to this day.

Chevalier Guy de Soniat du Fossat came to New Orleans as a young lieutenant in 1751 with the troops sent by King Louis XV in answer to Marquis de Vaudreuil's appeal for five thousand soldiers. Shortly afterwards, he married Mademoiselle Francoise Claudine Dreux, the beautiful daughter of Mathurin Dreux, Sieur de Gentilly of the Ancient house of Dreux, former Sovereign Due de Bretagne.

The Dreux lands on Bayou St. Jean were classed as princely holdings on account of their value and nearness to New Orleans. Guy Soniat Dufossat was an Alcalde, and in 1778 when he had again returned to civil life, purchased a large plantation tract of land below what later became the Faubourg Marigny, exchanging it in 1805 with the Marquis de Marigny for the planation above the city. The Soniat family later owned a number of plantations in Louisiana. The one in Jefferson Parish obtained from Bernard de Marigny in 1805 was within the area of the old Tchoupitoulas Indian Reservation and was named Tchoupitoulas. The record *"Titles* to the land known as the Jesuit Plantation" is priceless as an historical record, as well as a key to the rightful ownership of this tract was compiled by the late Charles Soniat who died in 1918.

Chevalier Guy Soniat du Fossat was born in the ancient family chateau in 1726, and in 1778 when he had retired from his governmental duties purchased a plantation from the Ursuline Nuns where he erected the ancient plantation home now occupied by the Colonial Country Club of New Orleans.

Chapter II.

DE LIVAUDAIS FAMILY AND PLANTATION

THE first de Livaudais to come to America was Jacques Esnould de Livaudais, Chevalier of St. Louis. He was a son of Jacques Esnould de Livaudais, a native of Saint Malo, and Marie Millette le Jaloux.

Jacques Esnould de Livaudais, when grown to manhood sailed with one Lavigne Voison as an apprenticed seaman, and displayed such marked ability during his apprenticeship that at the termination he secured a position with the Company of the Indies on one of its ships. A born navigator and capable officer, his courage, bravery and general ability being brought to the attention of the Company's directors in the year 1720 before he had reached his twenty-fifth year, he was appointed a First Lieutenant, with a salary of two hundred livres a month on the "La Decouvertre", one of the large vessels. On his return to France further honors awaited him as "une gratification" amounting to two thousand livres—which was a substantial acknowledgment of his value to the company which employed him.

Year after year he continued his East Indian trips, and at the end of twelve years he was appointed to the post of Pilot of the Port of New Orleans, a great honor in the colony of that day.

The Royal Engineer, de la Tour, accompanied by his assistant Pauger, had already proved that a loaded vessel could be brought through the mouth of the Mississippi River to New Orleans.

In 1734 Bienville, Governor of Louisiana, wrote the following letter to the Minister de la Marine in France: "We have had the honor, M. Salmon (the Commissary) and I to write to you in favor of M. de Livaudais, sent by the King of France to Louisiana as pilot. He should be made Captain of the Port". According to Bienville de Livaudais was a nephew of Lavigne Voisin, a famous corsair of St. Malo. A short while afterwards de Livaudais was made Captain of the Ports of Louisiana—bordering on the Atlantic Coast and Gulf of Mexico.

This gallant seaman who time after time had proved his worth by bravery and sound judgment was again in 1760 called upon by Governor Kelerec—who had replaced Bienville—to make a voyage to Vera Cruz for a supply of powder badly needed in the colony at that time. Sailing on an armed transport the gallant de Livaudais left in March and was returning in September, having secured the wanted material, he realized that four British vessels were pursuing him. His vessel, the "Opal", was able to hold a safe distance until the Balize was sighted. De Livaudais, determining not to be outwitted and lose his precious powder, took a desperate chance and slipped his vessel through the dangerous passes in the dark of night even though the water was shallow at the time.

Jacques Esnould de Livaudais, Chevalier of St. Louis, in 1733 married, in the City of Nouvelle Orleans, Marie Genevieve de la Source, who was a "daughter of an honorable family of Mobile". From this marriage issued the numerous branches of the de Livaudais family in Louisiana. Their children were: 1st—Francois Esnould de Livaudais, who was born in 1736 and who married Pelogie de Vaugine. 2nd—Joseph Esnould Dugue de Livaudais who married Jeanne Fleurian de Morville.

The eldest son of Francois de Livaudais and Pelogie de Vaugine was Francois Esnould de Livaudais, who became the husband of Charlotte des Islets de Lery (Chauvin). City records show that this Francois Esnould de Livaudais and de Marigny were the two greatest land owners in the city at that date. The (Chauvin) de Lery holdings in the Tchoupitoulas area were quite extensive. The son of Francois Esnould de Livaudais and Charlotte des Islets de Lery (Chauvin), named Francois Esnould de Livaudais fils, married Celeste de Marigny, a daughter of the immensely wealthy Philippe de Marigny. The land holdings of this couple today, if they were still retained in the family, would be worth a fabulous price. According to descendants, the de Livaudais heirs disposed of their interest in this vast estate over three quarters of a century ago.

Henry C. Castellanos in his writings of old Louisiana "New Orleans as it Was" describes the old de Livaudais Plantation:

> There was but one highway leading above the city along the river, and this was the Tchoupitoulas Road (The French Quarter was the New Orleans of that day). Along this road, commencing about DeLord St., the upper extremity of the Faubourg Saint Marie, (the American section, located between the old city and DeLord St.) and extending towards the magnificent de Livauadis plantation, was a succession of beautifully located villas and agricultural establishments. All along Tchoupitoulas St. there ran a low levee planted with willow trees, and during the season of high water, when the batture then forming was thoroughly immersed, the long Western keel boats and barges, as well as the unseemly flat boats, or charlands, would make fast to these trees and discharge their cargoes. After the receeding of the spring and summer floods, these flat boats, of enormous size construction and unfit for return voyage, would be left high and dry upon the batture front, and then to be broken up for fuel, and building purposes.
>
> The strong side pieces or gunwales, were used in the suburbs as foot paths in lieu of our present brick paved sidewalks. Upon these wooden trails, as it were, pedestrians had to make their way towards the rural precincts through immense vacant spaces, for there were few buildings, on the way leading to the de Livaudais plantation, which constituted that portion of New Orleans which now forms the Fourth District. On the way to that wealthy estate, (The Livaudais plantation), the river was lined with a continuous series of delightful rural residences (plantations) surrounded with orange hedges, orchards, and well tended gardens. The great Macarty crevasse, in the spring of 1816, submerged the rear portion of the numerous plantations, for miles around. The de Livaudais estate was one of the heaviest sufferers from the calamity. This was a great misfortune for Mr. Francois de Livaudais, for the planting of a crop or several hogsheads of sugar, and the splendid residence (plantation mansion) commenced about that time, was never finished, affording until a few years ago the spectacle of an abandoned castle, that went afterwards by the name of "Haunted House" located near Washington St. The value of this plantation became greatly enhanced on account of its being raised several feet by the remaining deposit or alluvial settlement, of the Mississippi water. A company of speculators acquired by purchase a great part of this estate which is now the beautiful Garden District, and which took its rise from this very circumstance of the overflow.

Celeste de Marigny de Livaudais, after the death of Francois de Livaudais, gathered together what remained of her once princely fortune, left Louisiana to live in Paris, France, in which city she used her title of Marquise de Livaudais. Her father, Marquis Philip de Marigny, had entertained Louis Philippe and his two brothers as house guests for a long period, both at his plantation and also at his country home in Mandeville, La. At their departure he gave each of them money, to Louis Philippe a princely sum, M. de Livaudais having contributed freely to the fund. Louis Philippe, now King, did not fail to let social Paris know that the Marquise was a close and dear friend of the Royal Family, and her salon became a prominent social center in the French Capital. Here amid the luxuriant furnishing of her beautiful home she received with open arms her numerous relatives and friends from Louisiana, dispensing a hospitality in keeping with her social position, and in a style which in New Orleans the de Marigny's and de Livaudais demanded.

Of Breton extraction Oliver Esnould de Parme is the first of the family to appear in history—the year 1510, later Oliver Esnould, 1534 and again Francois Esnould in 1559 appear, but according to the family record of Dugay de Livaudais, in 1604 Briand Esnould lived at Saint Malo until 1695, when the continuous family history really begins.

Letters written by Louis Philippe, King of France to the Marquis Bernard Xavier de Marigny de Mandeville and to his Sister, Marie Celeste de Marigny de Mandeville, wife of Count Jacques Esnould de Livaudais.

Claremont August 10th., 1850.

My dear Bernard:—

I did not doubt of the faithfulness of your fond recollections and the constancy of all your good and old feelings for me, and I have received the expression with an intense pleasure. I thank you for the interest that you have felt of the news of the malady that I have just endured; my illness has been long and painful, but thanks to the Lord it has yielded to my strong constitution and to the good care of which I am surrounded.

Notwithstanding the slowness of my convalescence the state of my health is today very satisfying; it allows me to enjoy the presence of my family and of numerous friends who come successively with their comforting consolation as has your letter containing your cordial expressions which I felt very deeply.

My children are not leaving Europe; they will continue to live around me and the Queen, but if some of them should travel in America you must not doubt of the pleasure they will have in meeting you as I have myself more than half a century.

Depend my dear Bernard on my friendly feelings and of those of the Queen for you, for Madame de Marigny and for all of yours.

Your very affectionate,
Louis Philippe.

Letter written by Louis Philippe, King of France, to the Marquis Bernard Xavier de Marigny de Mandeville, now the possession of Count du Suau de la Croix, and certified by him as absolutely authentic, in proof thereof his signature is affixed.

Comte du Suau de la Croix.

The Marquis Bernard de Marigny de Mandeville was the only brother of Marie Celeste de Marigny de Mandeville who married Count Jacques Enoul de Livaudais.

Chateau d'Eu, September 5th., 1839.

My dear Marquis de Marigny:—

Since I am not sure that you will not have left Paris before I return I want at least to wish you a pleasant voyage and a happy return in your new country.

I hope that you will not forget your old country where I will always be charmed to see you again. Tell to your fellow-countrymen of Louisiana how much I have inquired about every one of the families that I have known and how I shall always remember the warm welcome that I have received (more than forty years ago) is still very dear to me.

Good-bye my dear Bernard always rely on all my affection for you and for yours.

Louis Philippe.

Remark:

This was copied from a letter belonging to madame nee Anita Eustis, great granddaughter of Bernard Xavier de Marigny de Mandeville.

Comte du Suau de la Croix.

Paris, September 1st.,
81 Avenue Bosquet.

You desire, Madame, to have my autograph and I am charmed to offer it to you at the same time expressing the great pleasure at seeing you again and also to remind you of how charmed I was at the privilege of dancing in New Orleans forty four years ago with the one that was so appropriately called la Perle (the pearl)

I wish you bon voyage, and I pray you Madam to always depend on my profound friendship for you.

Louis Philippe.

St.—Cloud.
Samedi 19 Novembre, 1842
Madame de Livaudais born de Marigny.

The above is a copy of a letter belonging to and addressed to my great-grandmother de Livaudais born de Marigny de Mandeville.

Count du Suau de la Croix.

Paris, September 1st., 1921.

Madame de Livaudais,

I have received your letter written from Florence on the occasion of the marriage of my beloved daughter the Princess Clementine. I am deeply concerned for your good wishes for her happiness and for the friendly sentiments that you express for me for the Queen and for my sister, may we say that the strong friendship that we have experienced for you for so many long years is most sincere and that it is a pleasure for me to personally remind you of our enduring amity.

Your affectionate,
Louis Philippe.

Neuilly May 23., 1843.

Copy of letter belonging and addressed to my great-grandmother de Livaudais, born Celeste de Marigny de Mandeville.

Count du Suau de la Croix.

Paris, September 1st., 1921.
81 Bosquet Avenue.

Copy of the announcement of the death and invitation to assist to the interment of Mr. Enguerrand Henri Frédéric Emmanuel, Count du Suau de la Croix.

Passed away in Paris, 81 Bosquet Avenue, the 19th of March, 1914, in his 74th year, and of Mrs. Pauline Stephanie Enoul de Livaudais, Countess du Suau de la Croix, died in Paris, 55 Pierre Charron St., on the 26th of January, 1897, in her 83rd year.

You are invited to assist to the Funeral and at the interment of Madame Pauline Stéphanie Enoul de Livaudais.

Comtesse du Suau de la Croix

deceased having received the last rites of the Church January 26th, 1897 at the age of 83 at her domicile 55 Pierre Charron which will take place Friday the 29th at precisely 10:30 at the Church of St Pierre de Chaillet, her parish.

De Profundis

On the part of du Comte Enguerrand du Suau de la Croix, du Baron de Brimont du Baron Dannery, du Vicomte Enguerrand du Suau de la Croix his sons, sons in law and grandsons.

The inhumation will take place in the cemetery of Father Lachaise.

Mlle. de la Grandière, Madame de la Grandière, Prioress du Carmel de Blois, the Count de Kersanson de Pennandref, ancient Officer of the Legion of Honour and the Countess de Kersanson de Pennandref, the Viscountess de Kersanson de Pennandref and her children, Mrs. Fraval Coatparquet and her children, the Countess de Cellart de la Villeneuve, Mrs. Nouvel de la Flèche. The families de Carcaradet, de Beauvoir, de Breuilpont de Leguern, de Rosmonduc, Fleuriot de Langle de Bremoy have the honour to impart to you the painful loss that has just befallen them in the person of

Mr. Enguerrand, Henri Frédéric Emmanuel

Count du Suau de la Croix

While living widower of Mrs. Montigny born de Vincelles. Their father, father-in-law, grandfather, brother-in-law, uncle, granduncle, great-granduncle, first cousin, "oncle-à-la mode de Bretagne" (first cousin of one's father or mother) second cousin, died at his domicile, 81 Bosquet Avenue, on the 19th of March, 1914, in his 74th year, having received the last rites of the Church.

Pray for him.

Havana, January 7th. 1799

The continual delays of the Mississippi have prevented me to answer sooner to your letter of the 20th.

I have spent the greater part of the time in the country since the banks have started to swell, I went to see some new establishments that are being built towards the south of the coast. There are being constructed water mills that the refugees of St. Domingo have made known on that island, they are very well built and they have lavished for their construction the finest timbers from nature. The Country seems to me the most agreeable and the richest one can imagine. I know here a number of individuals who have started with very little means and who are today very rich. In seeing these results I have often thought your telling me of having had the temptation of settling on this Island; I think that if you had realized this project, you would have made an immense fortune but then you would not be among your people and in your country, and in reality you are already too rich to make such sacrifices. Of all the letters that you mention I have received only the one to which I am replying and which was handed me by Captain Maroteau of the Mississippi. The Captain will bring you my answer, and I regret infinitely my inability to accept your most amiable invitation to spend the Carnival with you. I assure you that I would not have to be urged very much if the circumstances permitted one to travel peacefully, but whether in Louisiana or elsewhere we hope of having the pleasure of seeing you again and we wish you to feel that it will be for us a real satisfaction.

We have heard with a great deal of sorrow of the loss you have suffered last summer and we hope you do not doubt how much concerned we are for whatsoever happens to you.

Adieu Sir will you kindly present our compliments to your amiable family and depend forever on our faithful friendship for you.

L. P. d'Orleans.

Copy duly certified as having been written by Philippe d'Orleans, Louis, King of France to Bernard Xavier de Marigny de Mandeville.

Count du Suau de la Croix.

Paris, Sept. 1st., 1921,
81 Bosquet Avenue.

Chapter III.

FORSTALL DYNASTY

In Corda Inim Icorium Regis.

"Into the hearts of the King's enemies"

SO reads the motto of this distinguished family.
Rufus (The Red) King of England, who succeeded William the conqueror, was shot through the heart by an enemy while he was hunting in the forest. The emblazonment of the three pheons (Argent) on the field (sable)—Silver arrowheads on a black background—tells of some service rendered his King by the forester when this tragedy occurred. Like many ancient families the record of the de Forestier, as the name was first written, is one of many notable achievements. In 1066 Guillaume le Forestier crossed the English Channel with William the Conqueror, and became the first ancestor of the English branch of the family. Larry or Laurence le Forestier, nicknamed "Strong-bow", was a companion in arms of Richard de Clare, Earl of Pembroke, in the invasion of Ireland, in 1169. While the Forstalls at that date bore no titles, or displayed no armorial bearings, the family was of the gentry. Of ancient lineage, it was allied to distinguished families, owned vast land holdings and enjoyed the right through heredity to armorial bearings.

The Forstall family in Louisiana, according to the Irish Reggister in the office of the Ulster King of Arms, Dublin Castle, stem directly to Peter Forstall Esq., a direct descendant of Larry or Lawrence le Forestier (Entitled to bear the armorial device, "Three broad arrows argent, field sable.) His wife was Mary Aylward, daughter of the Esquire of Shankhill. They had several children, the oldest son being Edmond Forstall of Rinn Kilkenny, whose wife was Eleanor Butler of Dangan, stemming from the noble house of Ormond. One of their sons Edmond by name became a captain of Dragoons in the Army of Louis XIV, after entering the French military service. He married Elizabeth, daughter of Henry Meade, Esq., of Ballyheale, Kilkenny. Of the several children, one of the sons, Nicholas Forstall, received his early training in Gurteen Castle in the year 1700. Becoming of age he removed to France, settling at Nantes and later went to Pierre on the Island of Martinique where he married Jane de Barry, a daughter of the King's counsellor of St. Kits (Jean du Barry).

The first Forstalls to come to Louisiana was a son of this couple, his name being Nicholas Michel Edmond Forstall who came from Martinique where he was born Sept. 21, 1727. He became commandante of the Opelousas Post, and about 1762 was married to Pelagie de la Chaise, daughter of Jacques de la Chaise and Margarite d' Arensbourg, a grand daughter of the Chevalier Charles Frederick d' Arensbourg. Issue of this marriage were seven children namely: (1) Edouard Pierre Charles Forstall b. Aug. 14th, 1768, who married Celeste de la Villebeuvre and became the father of six children.

(2) Elizabeth Louise Forstall, who became Madame J. B. Poeyfarre, leaving no issue.

(3) Edmond Forstall born July 16th, 1776, married Margarite Adelaide Josephine Melanie de Morant who was born June 6th, 1786 and died Feb. 1831. He died Jan. 18th, 1802; they left no children.

(4) Felix Martin Forstall, born Nov. 24th, 1780, married Marie Celeste Fabre d'Aunoy, and left four children.

(5) Louis Edouard Forstall, born Nov. 28th, 1802, died unmarried.

(6) Emerante Forstall, who married Jacques Montplasir Chauvin de Lery, issue four children.

(7) Melanie Forstall, died unmarried.

At the time Louisiana passed from France to Spain and Count O'Reilly became governor of the colony, he replaced the Superior Council of the French with the Cabildo which consisted of two regidors, six Alcaldes, an attorney-general and a clerk, over whose deliberations the governor presided.

The first regidors were chosen annually on the first day of the year, and, had by virtue of their offices the full power of judges in civil and criminal cases within the city's jurisdiction. During the years from 1771 - 1774, 1801, and 1803 Nicholas Forstall was appointed as an alcalde.

(1) Edmond John Forstall, oldest child of the six children, born of the union of Edouard Pierre Charles Forstall and Celeste de la Villebeuvre, was born Nov. 7th, 1794, and married Clara Durel; became the father of four sons and five daughters.

(2) Francis Placide Forstall, born Sept. 30th, 1796, and married Delphine Lopez.

(3) Felix Jean Forstall, born Nov. 24th, 1800, married Heloise De Jan.

(4) Louis Edward Forstall, born Nov. 25th, 1802, married Mathilde Plauche.

(5) Eliza Forstall, who married Delphine Villere.

(6) Belzire Forstall, married Z. Benjamin Canoge.

E. J. FORSTALL PLANTATION

The Forstall Platnation on the west bank of the Mississippi river, on Norman's Chart of 1858 is shown under the name of E. J. Forstall, and is located three plantations above the immense plantation of Governor A. B. Roman.

Edmond Jean, the owner of the Forstall Plantation, was the son of Edward Pierre Charles, who married Celeste de Lavillebeuvre, daughter of Chevalier de Garros. Edmond Jean Forstall married Clara Durel.

This is another great old Creole family, owning plantations and marrying into numerous aristocratic Louisiana families, forming a dynasty whose reign held sway both in the social as well as the business world for over sixty years, until wrecked by the Civil War. The Forstalls while not quite as prominent now still hold their social position as of yore.

Placide, another of the six children of Edouard Pierre Charles Forstall and Celeste de Lavillebeuvre—married Marie Borgia Delphine Lopez y Angulla de la Candelaria, a daughter of a Spanish Officer of high rank in the Spanish Service, named Don Ramon Lopez y Angullo, and his wife, the beautiful Delphine Macarty. Victor Forstall married Mademoiselle Fannie de Lavillebeuvre; their daughter, Eugenie Forstall, married Valerien Choppin, issue six sons and one daughter. The daughter, Adel Choppin married Robert G. Dugue and they had four children, all still living.

Ninette Dugue became Mrs. Walter G. Cleveland. Amelie Dugue became Mrs. J. Numa Roussel. Robert G. Dugue married Robin Brown of Nashville, Tenn. Maurice P. Dugue married Gladys McDade of Meridian, Miss.

The children of Henry Dugue and Celestine Dreux are: Natalie Dugue, who married Ramon de Gil Tabarado; Lucille Dugue, who married Lucian de Buys; Amelie Dugue, who married Forstall Choppin; Robert G. Dugue, who married Adel Choppin; Adolph Dugue, who married Alice Favre; Randall Dugue, who married Susan Glover.

Charles Edouard Forstall's other children were: Felix Jean, who married Heloise de Jan; Louis Edouard, who married Mathilde Plauche, the daughter of General J. B. Plauche. Nine children blessed the union of Placide Forstall and Demoiselle Delphine Lopez. Anatole Forstall married Pauline Gelpi.

Celeste became the wife of Henry Alanson Rathbone; Emma married Emile deBuys; Pauline married Eugene Peychaud; Laure married Felix Ducros; Julia married Robert J. Taney—a grandson of the Chief Justice of the United States. Detzire married J. B. Canoge—and Delphine remained single.

The union of Mademoiselle Celeste Forstall and Henry Alason Rathbone united this distinguished Creole family with one of equal note of New England parentage. Henry Alason Rathbone being the son of Samuel Rathbone of Stonington, Connecticut, a descendant of Samuel Rathbone, who came to New Orleans shortly after the Battle of New Orleans and married into the then princely house of Forstall. At once the Rathbone mansion in Esplanade Avenue became a center of social activity as was the Forstall home in St. Louis Street. The family noted for its pulchritude, consisted of five beautiful daughters: Mademoiselle Emma, who married J. B. deLalande de Ferrier; Mademoiselle

Pauline, who married Peter Labouisse; Mademoiselle Stella, who married Gaspard deBuys—whose sons are Rathbone deBuys, James Gaspard deBuys, Walter deBuys, and Dr. Laurence deBuys, all prominent; Mademoiselle Alice, who married William Phelps Eno of New York and Mademoiselle Rita, who married Edgar de Poincy.

Chapter IV.

THE FORTIER FAMILY

THE distinguished Creole family of Fortier ranks high among the old colonial families of Louisiana. It has intermarried into prominent old Louisiana families. Many members bearing the name have won distinction in the various professions, in the army, church and in commercial pursuits.

Francois Fortier, a native of St. Malo, Brittany, had a son named Michel Fortier, who was born in 1725. Michel was the first Fortier to come to America. Shortly after arriving in 1740, he established himself as "armurier du roi" in New Orleans. He married the daughter of a distinguished Creole family, a Mademoiselle Perrine Langlois.

In his establishment he not only made arms for the soldiers of his majesty, but he also fitted himself out with weapons, for history tells us he accompanied Galvez in his campaign against the English and aided the Spanish Governor replace the Union Jack over the fort at Baton Rouge with the emblem of Spain. Michel Fortier held the rank of Colonel with the Spanish troops. Michel Fortier died in 1785. By his marriage with Mademoiselle Perrine Langlois he became the father of seven sons: Michel, Jr., Jacques, Honore, who was lost at sea; Norbert, Eugene, Adelard and Ludger Fortier. Michel, Jr., and his brother, Jacques, married two sisters, the Mademoiselles Durel. Mademoiselle Louise Fortier, his daughter, married Michel La Branch. Michel Fortier

II, born in Louisiana in the year 1750, died Sept. 19th, 1819. He was the husband of Mademoiselle Marie Rose Durel and became a wealthy merchant and ship owner. When the double transfer of Louisiana occurred in 1803, from Spain to France and France to the United States, he was appointed a member of the municipal by the French prefect, M. Laussat. He had two sons, Michel Fortier III,, and Edmond Fortier. His only daughter became the wife of Francois Aime, a prominent Louisiana planter, their son, Valcour Aime, becoming one of the richest planters in the state. In their palatial home they entertained on a scale of magnificence equal to that of the Kings of France. Valcour Aime had the Jefferson College put in perfect condition and endowed it with a princely sum when he presented it to the Marist Fathers of Convent, La. Edmond Fortier, the second son of Michel Fortier, was born in 1784, and died in 1849, became a prominent sugar planter. His oldest son named Edmond, married Mathilde LaBranch; three of their sons died during an epidemic of yellow fever in 1858. One son named Michel M. LaBranche Fortier resided in New Orleans.

After the death of Francois Aime, his widow married Adelard Fortier. Michel M. de Blanc Fortier married Mademoiselle Eugenie Garcia, issue three children, Francois Fortier, another son of Edmond Fortier, married Mathilde LaBranche, who died in 1885. He married Louise Augustin, a daughter of Donatien Augustin. Marie Micaela Fortier, a sister of Francois Fortier, married a brother of Louise Augustin, who was Judge Donatien Augustin, and were blessed with eighteen children. Among them were James M. Augustin and George Augustin, both noted writers and journalists, in their time; George Augustin being associated with the Orleans Parish Medical Society for many years.

Florent Fortier, second son of Edmond Fortier and Felicete LaBranch, and brother of Edmond, Jr., was born in St. Charles Parish, on his father's plantation in 1811, and died in 1886. He married a daughter of Valcour Aime and established a plantation in St. James Parish, which later when fortunes were lost, sold the plantation and then resided in New Orleans with his son, Alcee. His son Louis Fortier, entered the Confederate Army at the age of 17, and died shortly after peace was declared. One daughter, Mademoiselle Natalie, became the wife of Neville

Leboeuf, Dr. Louis Leboeuf being their son. Amalie, another daughter, married Edward Roman.

Alcee Fortier was born on the great plantation of his grandfather, Valcour Aime. No longer wealthy, the father saw that his children became well educated. Alcee Fortier began his college career at the university of Virginia, but owing to ill health, had to discontinue his studies. Later, with the aid of private tutors, he finished his education. He became an instructor and then principal of the preparatory department of the University of Louisiana. Always a diligent student, Alcee Fortier was later professor of French in the University, and when the University became the Tulane University, he was appointed professor of Romance languages. He is classed as one of the three great historians of Louisiana. He died Feb. 14th, 1914. He married Mademoislle Lanauze, a daughter of a prominent French New Orleans Merchant; issue four sons and one daughter, Mademoiselle Jeanne Fortier, who married Paul Cox; Edward Jos. Fortier married Miss Tricou. (He became a professor at Columbia University, New York City. He died 1918); James Joseph Alcee Fortier, born July 15th, 1890, married Mademoiselle Marie Rose Gelpi, became a New Orleans Attorney, and president of the Continental Bank; Gilbert Fortier, a New Orleans business man.

de la Vergne

ARMS—D'or a la Rose de gueule—surmounted by a Count's helmet and a Coronet. Motto—"Houneur et Valliance".

CHAPTER V.
DE LA VERGNE—DE ST. PAUL—DE FRENEUSE SCHMIDT—SEGHERS FAMILIES

de la VERGNE.

THE cradle of the de la Vergne family is the Château de la Vergne at St. Priest Ligoure, Haute Vienne-Limousin, France. The grounds of this estate have been in the de la Vergne family since the year 1200.

The first de la Vergne to come to New Orleans was Count Pierre de la Vergne—Chevalier de St. Louis, born at Brive la Gaillarde, France—son of Seigneur Jean de la Vergne and Margarete de Billeran de Jan. He came to New Orleans in 1767 and married Elisabeth du Vergier.

Their son, Hugues Jules de la Vergne—born in 1792, died in 1843—was Major on the Staff of General Andrew Jackson at the Battle of New Orleans. He was Secretary of State in 1820, and President of Consolidated Association of Planters of Louisiana. He married Marie Adèle Villére—daughter of Major General Jacques Phillipe de Villére—second Governor of Louisiana. To this union was born in 1818 Jules de la Vergne, who died in 1887. He was active in public affairs, a member of the lower house of the Legislature in 1844, and of the Senate in 1856. He served as an Aide-de-Camp on the Staff of Governor Thomas O. Moore, during the War. He was a lawyer and a planter, and was the owner of the "Concorde" Plantation. His wife was Emma Joséphine, daughter of Judge Joaquin and Emma Joséphine Troxler

Bermudez. Emma Joséphine Troxler Bermudez was the widow of Charles Meloncy Saunhac de Fossat—their four children Joseph, Edouard, Emma (wife of Théodore Saunhac de Fossat, a cousin) and Amelie (wife of Judge Charles F. Claiborne). The Bermudez were a Grandee family of Spain.

Col. Hugues Jules de la Vergne, the son of Jules de la Vergne and Emma Joséphine Bermudez de la Vergne, was born in New Orleans in 1867. His education was acquired in the schools of his native city and he was graduated from the Jesuit College in 1885 with the degree of A. B. His Alma Mater conferred the degree of A. M. in 1887—Ph. B. in 1893. He was graduated from Tulane University with the degree of L.L.B. in 1888, appointed Major and Aide-de-Camp on the Staff of Governor Blanchard, July 1904, and promoted to Lieutenant-Colonel in 1905.

Hugues de la Vergne married Marie Louise, daughter of Charles Edouard Schmidt and Léda Hinks. Charles Edouard Schmidt was one of the outstanding Lawyers of his time, and for years was Professor of Maritime Law at the Louisiana State University. Hugues Jules de la Vergne and Marie Louise Schmidt had seven children: Marguerite, wife of Count Charles de Bony; J. Hugues; Charles Edouard; Léda, wife of Hugues Cage St. Paul de L'Echard; Jules Kristian; Jacques Philippe and Pierre Renaud.

Colonel Hugues J. de la Vergne died November 28th, 1923.

While the first of the de la Vergnes to come to Louisiana was as stated Count Pierre de la Vergne, he was not the first ancestor of the American family of de la Vergne to come to this country. As far back as 1539 Vasconalles da Silva, a Portuguese, came to Florida with Hernando de Soto. Jules de la Vergne's wife was Emma Josephine Bermudez, whose great, great, grand-father was José Antonie Bermudez—who had married Canolanos Gomez da Silva. Then in 1718 Mathurin Dreux de Bréze came with Bienville to help select the site of the City of New Orleans. He was descended from Robert de France, the fifth son of Louis VI, le Gros—King of France, and left a number of descendants in Louisiana. Mathurin Dreux de Bréze had two daughters, Claudine, from whom the Landry de Freneuse descends; and Charlotte, who married René Gabriel Fazende—father and mother of Jeanne Henriette de Fazende, wife of Governor Villere, whose daughter Adel de Villere, became the wife of Hugues de la Vergne, the great grand-parents of the present de la Vergnes.

DE LA VERGNE—DE ST. PAUL—DE FRENEUSE

Crest and Coat-of-Arms of the de la Vergne family. Arms d'or a la Rose de gueles surmounted by a Count's helmet and a coronet. Motto—Honeur et Valliance.

Crest and Coat-of-Arms of the de St. Paul family. (de Saint Pol). D'argent, a deux pals de Gueules, au Franc Canton d'argent charge d'une Croisette de sable.

Crest and Coat-of-Arms of the Landry de Freneuse de St. Aubin family.

Entrance of Villa de la Vergne, Country Home of the de la Vergne, Landry de Freneuse and de St. Paul families.

Fountain in front of Villa de la Vergne.

Count Pierre de la Vergne, first of the de la Vergnes to come to America. From an oil portrait in the home of Mrs. Henri Landry de Fréneuse.

Beautiful New Orleans Home of the de la Vergne family.

DE ST. PAUL

(de SAINT POL)

Coat-of-Arms of the de St. Paul family:
D'argent, a'deux pals de gueules, au franc canton d'argent charge'd'une croisette de sable.

de St. Paul or Saint Pol as it was sometimes spelled—this family goes back to 1247, at which time Count Hugues de St. Paul sold some land to the Count de Forez. Many notable alliances were made by members of the Saint Paul family, among them the names de Rochefort, de St. Colombe, de la Riviere, de Beaulieu de Lombara, de Besset de Vesc, etc., are prominent.

The first St. Paul to come to America was Henry. Paul André St. Pol de l'Echard, born in Marseilles, France, married Emilie Barbe Angelot, who was born in Havre de Grace. Their son, Henry Honore St. Paul, born in Antwerp, Belgium, during the occupation of that city by Napoleon Bonaparte, spent his early life in Paris and came to Louisiana in 1838, where he married Amanda Eugénie Pucheu, who was born on the Island of Martinique, the daughter of Jules Pucheu of Paris, France, and Louise Marchand of the Island of St. Domingo. She came to Louisiana at the time of the revolution on the island, with her parents while still a child. Their children were Regina St. Paul, who married John Rapia of Mobile, Ala.; Stella St. Paul, who married Louis Phillipe Labarthe of New Orleans; Oneida St. Paul, unmarried; Alba St. Paul, who married George Russell of Mobile; George St. Paul, who married Alice Allain of New Orleans; and John St. Paul, who married Florence Gertrude Townsley of Mobile. John St. Paul, Sr. was born Jan. 9, 1867 in Mobile and married Jan. 6, 1891, Florence Gertrude Townsley who was born in Mobile, Jan. 17, 1868, the daughter of Mary Elisabeth Barclay and Louis Oscar Townsley. There children were: Jerome Meunier, who married Marie Deady of Port Arthur, Texas; John, Jr., who married Nadia de la Houssaye; Marie Regina, unmarried; Louise Helene, who married Edward Gaspart Williams of New Orleans; Amanda Eugénie, unmarried; Hugues Cage, who married Léda Hélène de la Vergne; and Florence Elizabeth, who was unmarried.

Mary Elizabeth Barclay was the daughter of Captain Henry A. Barclay, her brother Henry A. Barclay, Jr., was captain of the English vessel "Pride of the Ocean" who went down with his ship off the coast of Herwich, England. Louis Oscar Townsley was the son of Thomas Finley of Kentucky and grandson of Don Miguel de Eslava, governor of Mobile under the Spanish rule. They were married in April, 1852. Their children were Coralie Townsley, second wife of Waller M. Broun; Louise Helene, first wife of Waller M. Broun; Thomas Finley Townsley; Lilian Townsley; Edmund Gaines Townsley; Isabelle Townsley; and Florence Gertrude Townsley.

de FRENEUSE

Charles Alexander Landry de Freneuse de St. Aubin, born at the Château St. Aubin in Normandie in 1784—came to Louisiana where he married Miss Peytavin de Garan of an aristocratic family of Provence. The Château de St. Aubin—The Château de Freneuse and the Manor de Landry were in their family since the year 1678—all three being situated on the shores of the river Seine in Normandie, at a short distance from each other. The family of the Landry's de Freneuse de St. Aubin can be traced to the year of 1233. Quite a number of the members of this family made aristocratic alliances. One of the daughters married a Tournbut, who was a companion in Arms of William the Conqueror, when he invaded England. Another daughter married the Count de Beaupoel, whose family furnished a French Ambassador to England. Still another married the Marquis d'Abzac. Several members of this family were lieutenant Generals to the French King. Another daughter married the brother of Bonnet, who was "Fermier General Aux Armees du Roi" and who had the honor of receiving Louis XV at his chateau. Charles Alexander Landry de Freneuse de St. Aubin, married Leontine Bouligny. The oldest living member of this family is Henry Jacques Landry de Freneuse de St. Aubin, who married Marie Louise Schmidt, widow of the late Col. Hugues J. de la Vergne.

The original of the Bouligny family was Bolognini. Francis Bolognini changed his name to Bouligny when he married Cecilia Germain, in March, 1649, through pique, because his family opposed the alliance. The Bologninis married three times in the Ducal family of Visconti of Florence and Milan. They are also related to the families of Chevalier Vincent Guillaume de Senechal Dàuberville and the Dukes of Noailles.

The Boulignys descend from Mathurin Druex de Bréze, who was a direct descendant of the fifth son of Louis VI, King of France.

Joseph Hincks, great-grandfather of Mrs. Henri Landry de Freneuse, had a sister named Eleanor who married J. Waters and had two children. Sophie married Mr. Lemonnier; one of their children (the second) named Josephine, married Warren and were the parents of Sophie Newcomb who died at the age of 16 years, her mother founding the Henrietta Sophie Newcomb College for women, which since has become a part of the Tulane University of Louisiana.

GUSTAVUS AND CHARLES EDWARD SCHMIDT

Gustavus Schmidt was the father of Charles Edward Schmidt. Both achieved eminence in the practice of law in the Courts of Louisiana. Gustavus was born at Mariestad, Sweden, June 16th, 1795, and died at Old Sweet Springs, Monroe County, West Virginia. He was a distinguished linguist, speaking and writing seven languages. The Summer of his death—while in West Virginia, he occupied his leisure, studying Chinese. He was the author of very valuable law books—Civil Law of Spain and Mexico—Schmidt's Law Journal—Legal Opinions, etc. The Civil Law of Spain and Mexico was written after a long stay in Mexico, where he had been sent by the United States Government to defend a law suit.

Gustavus Schmidt was the son of Hans Kristian Schmidt, born in the Province of Scania, and who was Secretary of the Prefecture of Skaraborg, and afterwards Judge of the Aulic Court for the South of Sweden. His mother was Sigrid Katharina Mork, a family who owned large iron mines in Sweden. The eldest brother of Gustavus Schmidt was Karl Kristian Schmidt, editor and owner of the legal journal of Sweden, and who occupied the highest judicial position in Sweden. He was also private Councilor of King Oscar.

Gustavus Schmidt, after receiving private instructions, attended the public classical school of Joukoping until he reached sixteen. He then entered the Swedish Military Navy, which he left at twenty to try his fortune in America. He landed in the

City of New York and from there went to Maryland where he was employed as private teacher in the family of General Emory, and also of John Lee Gibson. About 1820, he moved to Richmond, Virginia, where he read Law, was admitted to the bar and practiced his profession. In 1829 he moved to New Orleans and in 1831 married Mélanie Seghers, daughter of Dominique Seghers an eminent attorney and Marie Anne d'Otrange, daughter of Count Bertrand Joseph d'Otrange, who was Ambassador from the Principality of Liège at the Court of Brussels and also Councilor of the Grand Order of the Teutonic Knights. Dominique Seghers was one of the most brilliant lawyers of his day and acquired from the practice of his profession of law, a large fortune.

Charles Edouard Schmidt, son of Gustavus, was born in New Orleans February 29th, 1832, and died in Capon Springs, West Virginia, August 20th, 1891. He was educated at Spring Hill College, Alabama, and St. Xavier College, Cincinnati, and later received a degree of L.L.B. at the University of Louisiana. In the practice of law, he rose rapidly and acquired a large and lucrative business. After a career of more than thirty years, he died at the age of fifty-nine—full of honors and public regard—one of the most learned and profound lawyers of the Bar. He married in 1862, Louise Hélène Léda Hincks, daughter of the late Hon. John W. Hincks and Louise Hélène Lambert. Mrs. Charles Edward Schmidt was educated at the Convent des Oiseaux in Paris, and returned to Louisiana at the age of eighteen, speaking French like a Parisian, and a perfect musician, so gifted that she often accompanied Gottschalk in his concerts. She was a woman of beauty, distinction and charm.

From this union only one child survived, Marie Louise Schmidt, who married Hugues Jules de la Vergne. They had seven children. At the death of Hugues Jules de la Vergne, his widow married Henri Jacques Landry de Fréneuse.

Mrs. de Freneuse has two daughters—Countess de Bony de la Vergne, born Marguerite de la Vergne, who resides in France, and Mrs. Hugues Cage St. Paul, born Léda Hélène de la Vergne. Both are lovely young women, Mrs. St. Paul possessing the patrician beauty of a blonde Creole, as charming as rare. Inheriting much of her mother's and grandmother's personal traits and charm—she has become a leader in the younger set. Always

Count Charles de Bony de la Vergne.

Chateau de la Vergne, near St. Priest—Ligoure Haute—Vinn Limousin, France.

Winding walks about the garden grounds of the de la Vergne home, St. Charles Avenue, New Orleans.

Madame Henri Landry de Fréneuse

Spacious Hallway of the de la Vergne Home, New Orleans

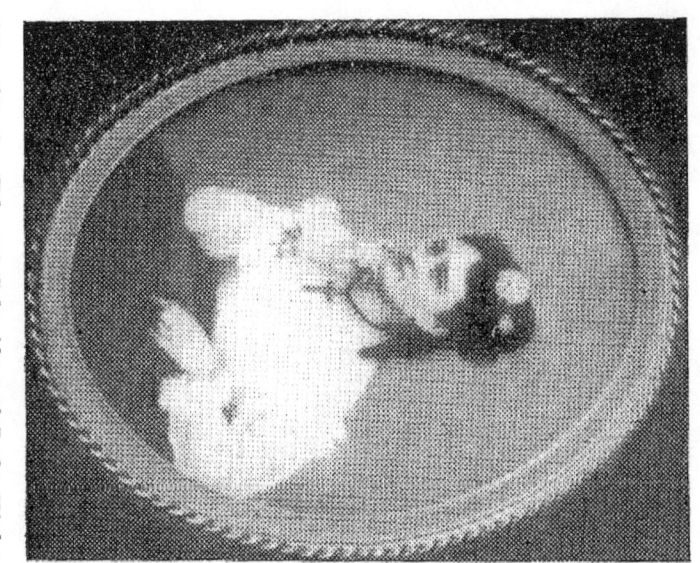

Charles Edward Schmidt   Mrs. Charles Edward Schmidt neé Leda Hinks

(From ivory miniatures in the de Freneuse Collection.)

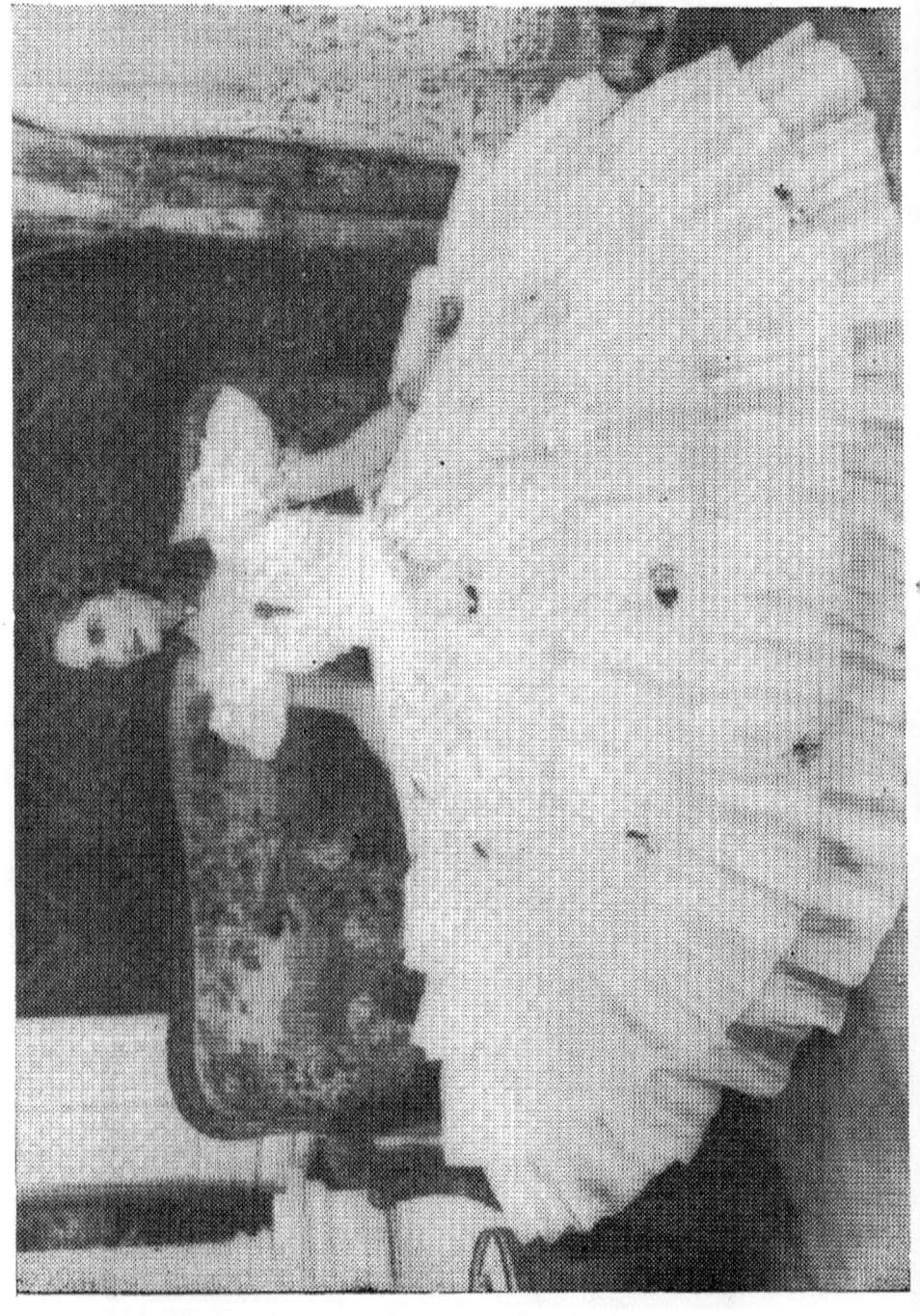

Countess Charles de Bony de la Vergne (neé Marguerite de la Vergne.)

Interior of the beautiful de la Vergne Home, St. Charles Avenue, New Orleans.

GUSTAVUS SCHMIDT
Noted Lawyer.
(Illustrations courtesy of Mrs. Henry Landry de Freneuse)

Crest and Coat-of-Arms of Esnould Dugue de Livaudais family. Courtesy of Mr. and Mrs. Robert Dugue (de Livaudais). See page 3.

sought after at distinctive affairs, her beauty is an asset in any receiving line, and in costumed pageants she appears as if she might have stepped out of a Romney or Nattier Canvass.

SÉGHERS FAMILY*
Of Louisiana.

Dominique Seghers, the first of the name to arrive in New Orleans, with his wife, Marie Anne Dotrenge Seghers, and their seven children—were all born in Brussels. The names of the sons and daughters were: Julien, Edward, Victor, Theodore, Adolph, Melanie and Euphrosine Seghers. This family sailed from Antwerp for America in September, 1807 because the head of the family declared no son of his should grow up to fight for Napoleon Bonaparte. On reaching our shores, he at once applied for citizenship and it is said he never recrossed the ocean tho' some of his sons did, Théodore dying in Paris and Edward in Brussels.

Only three of the family of "first arrivals" left descendants, viz: Julien Seghers, who married Virginia Duffel; Adolph Séghers, who married Elizabeth Duffel; and Mélanie Séghers, who married Gustave Schmidt. The de la Vergnes are descended through their mother, Marie Louise Schmidt, who married first, H. J. de la Vergne from Mélanie Séghers; the Francois Séghers and Dominique Seghers II families are descended from Julien and his wife, Virginia; the Adolph Seghers family from Adolph Seghers and Elizabeth Duffel. The children of these last were: Edward D. Seghers I, Amelia and Virginia. Amelia married John Trasimond Landry; Virginia married Jacob Haight Morrison I; Edward D. Seghers I, married Clara Duffel Williams, who was a daughter of Henry Threlkeld Williams of Virginia and of Margaret Bruce Boyd of England.

The name Seghers in Belgium goes back to the Battle of Courtrai—1302. Anthoine Seghers de Capelle received a patent of nobility in 1618 from Albert, Archduke of Austria and Duke of Burgundy. In this patent was recited the fact that "Anthoine Seghers is residing on the estate (or Fief) conferred upon his ancestors by Guy of Elanders". The wife of Dominique Seghers

---
* The name Seghers—pronounced S-A-Y-G-A-R-E—and originally spelled with an accent on the first "e"—Séghers.

(married at the Church of the Twelve Apostles on April 19th, 1792) was daughter of of Bertrand Joseph Dotrenge, who had served as Privy Councillor to the Prince Bishop of Liege, and was Councilor of the Grand Order of Teutonic Knights, and at time of Marie Anne's birth (Dec. 11, 1765) was Ambassador to Brussels from the Principality of Liege.

Dominique Seghers was a lawyer of note (See Bench 7 Bar of New Orleans in 1823, in the "Louisiana Book" compiled by Thomas McCaleb). His five sons were all lawyers. Adolph Seghers, one of them, became District Attorney of Ascension. He died at 36, leaving three children. A brother of Mrs. Dominique Séghers the First was Théodore Dotrenge, who died in Brussels in 1836. He was a member of the States General of the United Netherlands, and was named by King William I a member of the Council of State. He was also named as one of a committee to revise the fundamental laws of the United Netherlands. For his biography, see "Biographie Universelle" in Howard Library.

The last surviving grandsons of Adolph Seghers are: Edward D. Seghers, II, of New Orleans; Theo. Seghers Landry of Willswood, La.; and W. C. Morrison of New Roads, La. Each has sons and daughters to carry on the name and traditions of the family.

The home of the de la Vergne family is of the Chateau Renaissance style, surrounded by an attractive and spacious garden and shaded by beautiful magnolia trees. It was built in the late 90's and is a veritable treasure house, filled with family heirlooms, authentic pieces of early furniture and original paintings. During the Spring Fiesta this home is one of the outstanding attractions. Many ancestral portraits of distinguished Louisianians and their forbears adorn the walls of the large rooms. There are authentic portraits of the parents of George de la Chaise and his wife Renee de Roquefort in Court costume over 200 years old. They were the father and mother of the celebrated priest, Father de la Chaise, Confessor to King Louis XIV, and direct ancestors of the de la Vergne family, who descends from them, through their great-grandfather, Governor Jacques Philippe de Villere.

Having travelled extensively, Madame Landry de Freneuse, the former Mrs. Hugues de la Vergne, has a general fund of knowledge and is a most interesting conversationalist. She is a born hostess and all of her life has been a social leader. She has done much charity work and has always carried to a successful issue any enterprise in which she was interested. As a young woman she was considered one of the prettiest Creoles of her day in this city of beautiful women. She still retains her girlish figure and is one of New Orleans' most charming personalities.

Among the heirlooms of special interest are two dinner plates, and a crystal vase that belonged originally to the Marquis de Lafayette—a Miss de la Vergne having married into the de Lafayette family. The splendid bronze "Mercury" by Jean de Bologne is one of three of the original pieces made in the same mold, one of these is in the Louvre in Paris, the other in Italy. The magnificent ormulu mounted commode, "Prince de Conde", to be seen in the Louis XIV room of the de la Vergne home, is a duplicate of the one made for the King of France in the Chateau de Chantilly. Much of this beautiful collection of objects of art was purchased in Europe during the childhood days of Mrs. de Freneuse, on her extensive and frequent trips taken by her with her parents.

(Crest of the Farwell family)

CHAPTER VI.
THE MILLIKEN AND FARWELL FAMILIES

RICHARD ALLEN MILLIKEN.

THE late Richard Allen Milliken of New Orleans was born at Waterford, Ireland, on Sept. 15th, 1817. His family, according to ancestral records, stems to one of the ancient regal families of Ireland that held sway in the 13th century, the spelling of the name originally being O'Melaghlins, the "O" having the same significance in Ireland as the "de" in France. On the distaff side of the family among his ancestors were many distinguished officers of the English army and navy. Mr. Milliken's mother came to the United States before her son and settled in Louisville, Kentucky, young Milliken joining her when he was still in his teens. She placed him in the Bardstown College where he remained until he completed his education, graduating in the fall of 1834. Soon afterwards he came to New Orleans and engaged in the sugar business in which he continued up to the time of his death, becoming one of the largest and most successful producers in the state of Louisiana.

On October 6th, 1864 he married Deborah A. Farwell of Unity, Maine, a sister of Nathan A. Farwell. Mr. Milliken and his wife enjoyed a long and happy life together, and at the death of Mr. Milliken, Mrs. Milliken donated to the State of Louisiana a hospital known as the Milliken Memorial, considered to be one of the finest children hospitals in the United States. Mr. Milliken was a most representative citizen, progressive and charita-

Crest and Coat-of-Arms of the Farwell family.
(Courtesy of Miss Nellie Farwell.)

MR. AND MRS. RICHARD ALLEN MILLIKEN

MR. AND MRS. CHARLES FARWELL, II.

Mrs. John James Blair (neé Miss Martha Couturier Ray), maternal grandmother of Miss Nellie Farwell.

John J. Blair, who married Miss Martha Couturier Ray, maternal grandfather of Miss Nellie Farwell.

Martha Shannon Blair of Camden, S. C., mother of Miss Nellie Farwell.

Chas. A. Farwell of Unity, Me., father of Miss Nellie Farwell. (A captain in the Confederacy, killed at Battle of Griswold, Ga.)

(All pictures copies of oil portraits in home of Miss Nellie Farwell.)

Mrs. Charles A. Farwell I, (neé Martha Shannon Blair. (From ivory miniature belonging to Miss Nellie Farwell.)

Miss Nellie Farwell at the time of her graduation. (From ivory miniature.)

William Blair. (From an oil portrait in home of Miss Nellie Farwell.)

Henry Dickinson Blair, husband of Mary Lou Saunders. (From an oil portrait in home of Miss Nellie Farwell.)

ble, public spirited and deeply interested in every movement for the betterment of this city and state, to which he contributed generously and frequently.

THE NAME AND FAMILY OF FARWELL.

The surname of FARWELL is thought by some writers to be derived from the place of residence of early bearers of the name in or near the Parish of Farwell in Stafford, England. Other writers, however, are of the opinion that it is a corruption of the French name **Varaville**. It is found in ancient English and early American records in the various spellings of Farwell, Fairwell, Favell, Favel, Varwell, Fauvell, Farwel, and Farwell, of which the form last mentioned is that most commonly used in America today. Families bearing this name were established in England at early dates in Yorkshire, Suffolk, Salop, Staffordshire, Somerset, Devonshire, Wiltshire, Norfolk, and Lincoln. They and their descendants were largely of the landed gentry and yeomanry. Earlier mention of the name seems to be that of Richard Farwell, who was living in Yorkshire in 1280. He married the heiress of Elias de Rillestone and brought that estate and several others into the family. A Simon Farwell removed from Yorkshire to Somerset and built the mansion house at Bishop Hill. He married Julia Clark and had issue of a son Simon. Simon married Dorothy, daughter of Sir James Dyer, Speaker of the House of Commons. He died in 1568, leaving eight children, Simon, John George, Christopher, and four daughters. Of these, John who died without issue, sold Bishop Hill to his brother George. George, born in 1532, son of Simon and Dorothy, married Philippa Parker and had issue of George, who was knighted, John, who was also knighted, and Arthur. Christopher, son of Simon and Dorothy, was ancestor of the Devonshire branch of the family. Sir George Farwell, son of George and Philippa married Lady Mary Seymour, daughter of the Duke of Somerset and a descendant of the Plantagenets. They had twenty children, among whom were Thomas, John, George, Nathaniel Edmund, and James. Of these, John married Dorothy, daughter of Sir John Routh, by whom he had issue of Henry and John. Some writers on the family history consider it possible that it was this Henry who settled in New England and who is further mentioned below. Christopher, son of Simon and Dorothy Dyer Farwell, married Mary Barker, a widow, in 1605. They had issue of Christopher, Elizabeth (who married William Searle). Christopher, son of Christopher, married Mary Southcott, by whom he had Christopher and Mary (who married Francis Drake in 1690). The son Christopher married Catherine Ayshford and had three children. Christopher, a doctor, who died unmarried; and Katherine.

Among the earliest records of the family in America are those of Henry Farwell, son of William Farwell. He was born in England in 1605 and married Olive Welby (or Welbie) in 1629. A tailor by trade, he emigrated to New England with his wife and two children, Elizabeth and Samuel. Four more children were born to them in this country, John, Joseph, Mary, and Olive. John, son of the immigrant Henry, married Sarah Wheeler. They had one daughter, Sarah, who married John Jones. Joseph, son of the Immigrant Henry, married Hannah Learned, by whom he had issue of Hannah(who married first Samuel Woods and secondly Peter Joslin), Joseph. Elizabeth (who married John Richardson), Henry, Isaac, Mary Sarah, John, William, and Oliver.

Joseph, son of Joseph and Hannah Learned Farwell, married Hannah Colburn and removed to Groton. He had issue of Joseph, Thomas, Hanna (who first married Eleazer Gibson and secondly Ephraim Sawtell), Elisabeth (who married John Stone), Edward, Mary, (who married James Stone), John, Samuel, Daniel, and Sarah.

Henry, born in 1674, son of Joseph and Hanna Learned Farwell, married Susannah Richardson. They had issue of Henry, Isaac, Sarah (who married Henry Parker), Elizabeth, who married Timothy Bancroft), and Hannah (who married first Jerahmeil Cummings and secondly Stephen Jewett). Isaac, born about 1674, son of Joseph and Hannah Learned Farwell, married Elizabeth Hyde. They had issue of Elizabeth, Mary (who married Edmund Hovey), John, William, Dorothy, Isaac, and another Isaac. William, born in 1688, son of Joseph and Hannah Learned Farwell, married Elizabeth Solendine, of Dunstable, Mass. They had six children, Elizabeth, William, John, Oliver, Henry, and Josiah.

Oliver, born in 1692, son of Joseph and Hannah Learned Farwell, married Mary Cummings. He was killed by Indians when he was thirty-three. His issue were Mary, who married first Thomas Clark and second John Russell), Oliver, Benjamin and Sarah.

Joseph, son of Joseph and Colburn Farwell, married Mary Gibson. They had issue of Anna, (who married Josiah Brown), Isaac, Joseph, Jonathan, Thomas, Oliver (who married Barnabas Davis), Mary (who married Joseph Hoar), and Susannah (who married John Cheney).

Edward, born in 1706, son of Joseph and Hannah Colburn Farwell, married Hannah Russell. They were the parents of six children, Edward, Submit (who married Jonathan Adams), Hannah (who married Archelaus Adams), David, Able, and Sarah (who married Silas Rand). John, born in 1711, son of Joseph and Hannah Colburn Farwell, married Jane Lakin and by her had two daughters. By his second marriage, to Susannah White, he had five children, Thirza, Olive, Thomas, Eunice (who married Ebenezer Pratt), and Henry. Samuel, born in 1714, son of Joseph and Hannah Colburn Farwell, married Elizabeth Moors. They were parents of ten children, Samuel Elizabeth, (who married Thomas Gary), Eunice Abraham, John, Sarah, Lydia (who married first John Ireland and secondly Deacon William Stewart), Susannah, Joseph, and Isaac.

THE MILLIKEN AND FARWELL FAMILIES   31

Daniel, son of Joseph and Hannah Colburn Farwell, married Mary Moor and removed to Towsend, Mass. He was the father of Daniel, Anna (who married Silas Snow), Isaac, Timothy, Mary, Edmund, Zaccheus, and Benjamin. Henry, born in 1696, son of Henry and Susannah Richardson Farwell, married Esther French, a widow, and by her had issue of Eleazer, Esther, Olive (who married Nathaniel Carlton), and Elizabeth (who married Benjamin Marshall). Josiah, born in 1698, son of Henry and Susannah, married Hannah Lovewell. He was killed by Indians, leaving a daughter Hannah, who married John Chamberlain. Jonathan, born in Dunstable in 1700, son of Henry and Susannah, married Susanna Blanchard. He was drowned in Amoskeag Falls leaving three children, Susanna (who married Jonathan Butterfield), Rachel), Rachel (who married Nehmiah Lovenah, married Sarah Howard and removed to Vassalboro, Maine. They had issue of Elizabeth, Josiah, Relief, Bunker, Abigail (who married first Levi Richardson and secondly Ebenezer Bacon), Isaac, Jane, Ebenezer, Susanna, Sarah, and Molly. John, born in 1711, son of Isaac and Elizabeth Hyde Farwell, married Dorothy Baldwin and by her had issue of Olive (who married Aaron Hovey), John, Isaac, Thomas, and Asa. William, born in 1712, son of Isaac and Elizabeth, removed to Walpole, N. H. He married Bethia Eldredge and by her had thirteen children, William, Elizabeth (who married Elijah Parker) Jemima, Elisha, Joseph, John, Dorothy, Isaac, David (who finally settled in Michigan, Jesse, and Eldredge.

William Farwell, son of William and Elisabeth Soldendine, was born in 1714 or 1715. He married Sarah Parker, by whom he had eight children, Eunice, Elizabeth (who married Samuel Gould), Henry, Sarah (who married John Todd), Susannah (who married John Solendine), Phineas, Sybil, and William. John, son of William and Elizabeth, married four times. By his first wife, Sarah Sawtell, he had issue . . . who married William Farwell: Sarah, who married Thomas Willard: David and John, twins; and six children who died in infancy. By his second wife, Eunice Snow, he had issue of Eunice, who married Gladwin Chaffin; Betzey, who married Phineas Holden; and Mary, who married John Con. By his third marriage, to Lydia Taylor, he had issue of a daughter Lydia, who married Timothy Stone. His fourth wife was Sarah Warren. Oliver Farwell, born in 1722, son of William and Elizabeth, married Rejoice Preston. There were ten children by this marriage, William, Isaac, Jonathan, Abigail, Benjamine, Levi, Olive, Elizabeth, Mercy, Olive, Elizabeth, and Calvin.

Henry, born in 1724, son of William and Elizabeth married Lydia Tarbell and by her had issue of Anna, Samuel, and William. By his second wife, Sarah Taylor, he had further issue of Lydia, Sarah (who married James Brazer), Lydia (who married first John White and secondly Joseph Sawtell), and Jonathan. This Henry commanded a company at the Battle of Bunker Hill and was severely wounded. Josiah, son of William and Elizabeth, married Lydia Farnsworth and removed to Charleston, N. H. They had ten children, Lydia (who married Moses Willard), Hannah Josia, Mary (who married Calvin Judevine), Anna (who married Frederick Locke), Oliver Debora (who married Nathan Allen), Hannah (who married Benjamin Larabee), Olive (who married Rufus Larabee), and Henry.

Oliver, son of Oliver and Mary Cummings Farwell, was born in 1717, he married Abagail Hubbard and by her had issue of Rebecca (who married Jonathan Blanchard), Oliver, Mary (who married Noah Lovewell), Abagail (who married Samuel Wilkins), Joseph, another Joseph, Sarah, and John.

There is record of a Thomas Farwell, who settled in Virginia in 1652, but nothing further is known about him.

The several lines of the Farwell family in America have produced a fairly numerous progeny who have established themselves in many parts of the United States. The record of the family is that of a vigorous, practical, enterprising and God-fearing race, thrifty, ostentatious, and capable on the whole, and possessed in certain instances of executive ability and intellectual talents.

Among those of the name who served in the American Cause in the Revolutionary War were Captain Francis Farwell, Lieutenant Isaac Farwell, Captain Francis Farwell, and David, Abraham, Benjamine, David, Eleazer, Ephraim, Henry, John, William, Zaccheus, and Eleazer Farwell, all privates of Massachusetts.

Richard, Simon, George, Christopher, Nathaniel, Henry, John, Joseph, Josiah, Jonathan, Isaac, Oliver, Samuel, David, and Edward are some of the masculine Christian names which have been favored by past generations of the family.

The following are a few of the members of the family who have distinguished themselves in America in comparative recent times. Arthur Farwell (born 1872), Minnesota, composer; John Villiers Farwell (born 1858), of Illinois, merchant; Charles Benjamine Farwell (1823-1903) business man and politician; Nathan Allen Farwell (1812-1893), of Maine, Senator; Earl Farwell (born 1885), of England and New York, lawyer; Arthur Burrage Farwell (born 1852), of Massachusetts, business man; Samuel Farwell (1800-1875), of Mchigan, contractor.

The coat-of-arms of the ancient English family of Farwell is described in heraldic terms as follows (Burke, Encyclopaedia of Heraldry, 1844):

ARMS:—"Sable a cheveron engrailed argent between three leopards' heads or."

Crest:—Two oak branches orleways vert, acorned or."

BIBLIOGRAPHY

Bardsley. English and Welsh Surnames. 1901.
    Burke. Encyclopaedia of Heraldry. 1844.
    Greer. Early Virginia Immigrants. 1912.
    Notes and Queries. 4th series. Vol. 8. 1871.
        5th series. Vol. 4. 1875.

Beautiful Home and Garden of Miss Nellie Farwell, St. Charles Avenue, New Orleans.

CHARLES A. FARWELL, III.

Home of Mr. and Mrs. Charles A. Farwell, III.

Miss Lynne Payton Hecht as Queen of Proteus (Mrs. F. Evans Farwell.)

F. EVANS FARWELL.

Home of Mr. and Mrs. F. Evans Farwell.

Abbott. The Farwell Family. 1929.
Holton. Farwell Ancestral Memorial. 1879.
Frost. Swan - Farwell Genealogy. 1925.
Saunderson. History of Charlestown, N. H. 1876.
Joslin. History of Poultney, Vt. 1875.
Eaton. History of Old Constable. 1846.
Chandler. Hstory of Shirley, Mass. 1883.
Butler. History of Groton, Mass.
Heitman, Officers of the Continental Army. 1914.
Massachusetts Soldiers and Sailors of the Revolutionary War.
Dictionary of American Biography. 1931.

The Media Research Bureau.

CHARLES A. FARWELL II.

Charles A. Farwell II, born in New Orleans, La., Nov. 11th, 1860; married in Gloucester, Mass., Sept. 12th, 1900, Miss Stella (Evans) French, daughter of Robert F. and Mary (Caldwell) Evans, who was born in Shelbyville, Tenn., in 1870. He died on May 17th, 1917.

Mr. Farwell was one of the substantial business men of New Orleans, and as head of the firm of Milliken and Farwell was one of the wealthiest men in the sugar industry in the South, owning several large sugar plantations. For many years Mr. Farwell was the head of a committee in Washington, D. C., charged with looking after the interests of Louisiana planters. Beginning as an employee of his uncle Richard Milliken, at the time of Mr. Milliken's death he had gained an understanding of the business that enabled him to take over the direction of the plantations and the city business. Mr. Farwell was also as prominent in the social as in the business world, being a member of the Boston Club, a stockholder of the French Opera Co., and active in many social and charitable affairs. He was chosen "REX" in the Mardi Gras of 1898, the highest and most coveted social honor that the Southern metropolis bestows. His children are Charles A. Farwell III and F. Evans Farwell.

"The FARWELL FAMILY" Vol. I. (1605-1927) published by Frederick Henry Farwell & Fanny (Barber) Farwell, 1929.

CHARLES A. FARWELL

Charles A. Farwell, born September 26th, 1902, in New Orleans, La. High school education received at the New Orleans Academy. In 1918 attended Tulane University for one year and served in the students' military training corps. Entering Virginia Military Institute, Lexington, Virginia, in June, 1919; graduated from there with a B.S. Degree in Chemical Engineering June 1923. In the fall of 1923 entered the Medical Department of Tulane University; left there in 1924 and began work with Milliken & Farwell; since that time has remained in the sugar business.

In 1925 married Edwa Stewart, daughter of Mr. and Mrs. John Nelson Stewart of New Orleans, La; have three children, Charles, 14; Edwa, 10; and Blair, one and a half. During the past 16 years has held commissions in Officers Reserve Corps, United States Army, in Infantry, Chemical Warfare, and Military Intelligence.

At present hold the following positions:
President, Milliken & Farwell, Inc.
    President, Westover Planting Co., Ltd.
    Member of Board of Directors: Whitney National Bank of New Orleans.
    Waterford Sugar Cooperative, Inc.
    Cane Products Trade Association.
    State Agricultural Credit Corp., Inc.
Chairman: Educational Committee of the American Sugar Cane League of New Orleans.
First Stockholders' Committee of Realty Operators, Inc.
Member, Board of Administrators, Charity Hospital of New Orleans, La.

F. EVANS FARWELL.

Mr. F. Evans Farwell was born in New Orleans, Louisiana, June 7th, 1906. He obtained his early schooling at the New Orleans Academy, later attending a preparatory school at Woodberry Forest, Virginia, bearing that name, where he finished in 1925. Going from there to the University of Virginia, graduating with a B.S. in Commerce in 1920.

At the University, was president of the Psi Chapter of the Sigma Chi Fraternity; Student Instructor in Spanish; and was made a member of Beta Gamma Sigma, honorary business fraternity.

Worked in the New Orleans office and sugar plantations of Milliken and Farwell, Inc., during the fall of 1929. Moved to

Detroit, Mich., in February, 1930, and started working there for the firm of W. H. Edgar & Son, Inc., sugar brokers. In July of this year was moved to Edgar's New York office early in 1935, and left this office for a job of constant traveling throughout the eastern half of the United States in the late fall of the same year. Returning to New Orleans, Louisiana, and opened a branch office for W. H. Edgar & Son, Inc., in the summer of 1933. On February 1, 1936, again started working for Milliken & Farwell, as Vice-President.

On November 11, 1936, was married to Lynne Paxton Hecht, daughter of Mr. and Mrs. R. S. Hecht (nee Lynne Watkins of New Orleans, Louisiana). On June 30, 1939, a daughter was born and she is named Stella Evans Farwell in honor of her paternal grandmother.

THE FARWELL MANOR

St. Charles Avenue Between First and Second Streets, New Orleans, La.

A replica of a beautiful old Mansard manor located in the Rue Grand Armee near the Palace of Versailles in France; Miss Nellie Farwell's beautiful home located far back in the spacious grounds that occupy half of the city block, with entire frontage on St. Charles Avenue.

The land was purchased by Mr. Richard A. Milliken, an uncle-in-law of the gracious chatelaine of this most attractive home, some fifty years ago to enlarge his own garden grounds. The original of this manor located in France was built for a French noble at the time that the Palace of Versailles was erected. Louis XIV, in order to break up the power of the immensely powerful nobles contending against the throne, erected the Palace of Versailles and concentrated the French Court and important government bureaus about this palace, making it necessary for courtiers to live in Versailles instead of in their feudal castles surrounded by their followers.

Miss Farwell, prominent in the social life of New Orleans, entertains frequently throughout the year in this spacious home which opens on to the immense garden grounds as do European homes. It is an ideal place for large gatherings. Her gardens are always included in the Fiesta Tours. The many handsome rooms are filled with rare and exquisite antiques, most of them being heirlooms. There is much fine old carved rosewood and mahogany furniture, family silver, crystal, rare china, ancestral portraits, and all of the artistic treasures that go to complete such a home—many inherited from her mother and her aunt to whom she was so devoted for so many years. Miss Farwell is a member of The Huguenot Society, and the Society of Colonial Dames, both organizations meeting at her home several times a year.

Crest and Coat-of-Arms of the de Brierre family.
(See page 37.)

Melle. de Ternant, daughter of Claude Vincent de Ternant II. (Mother of Melle. Avegno, painted by John Singer Sargent. (See page 44, Vol. II.)

Loading sugar-cane on a Louisiana sugar plantation.

Judge Charles Parlange, father of Walter Charles Parlange, Sr.

Walter Charles Parlange, Jr.

Walter Charles Parlange, Sr.

Ethlyn Humphries (Mrs. A. A. Poirson), daughter of Angele Brierre.

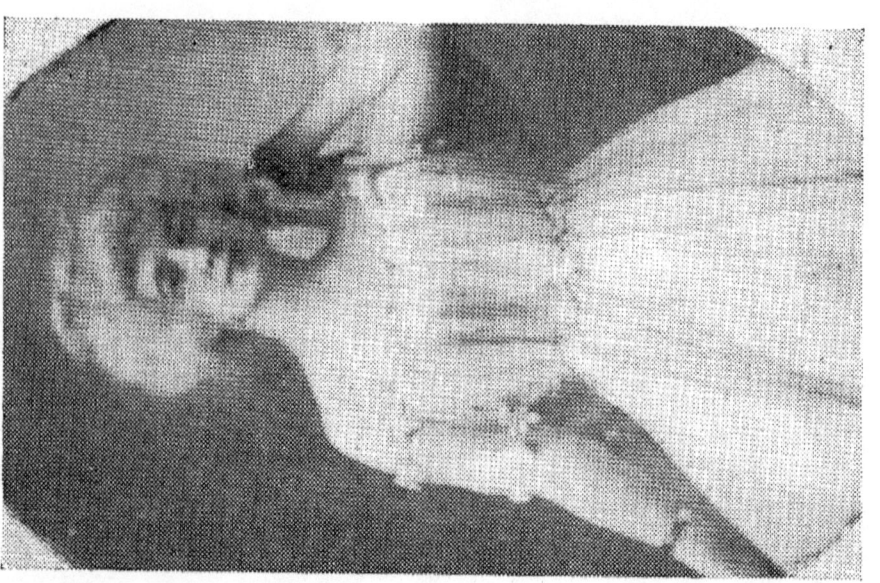

Mrs. Walter Charles Parlange (Paule Brierre) in Costume.

CHAPTER VII.

THE DE TERNANT—PARLANGE—DE BRIERRE—D'HERBIGNY—DE VEZIN FAMILIES

DE TERNANT — PARLANGE.

Marquis Claude Vincent de Ternant died in 1750. Madame la Marquise Virginie married Colonel Charles Parlange of the French Army. Their son, the Honorable Charles Parlange, United States District Judge, married Miss Louise Denis, their children are Mrs. Evelyn Parlange Allen, Mr. Walter Charles Parlange, and Mrs. Lilian Parlange Lee. (Walter Charles Parlange married Miss Paule Brierre, one son, Walter Charles Parlange, Jr.)

The Governor of the St. Louis territory, de Hault de Lassus' daughter, Felicite Odille deHault deLassus de Luzieb, married Governor Pierre D'Erbigny of Louisiana. Their daughter married Henry Denis, their son, Arthur Denis, married Mademoiselle Antoinette de Beauvais de Cuir, and their daughter Mademoiselle Louise Denis, became the wife of Honorable Charles Parlange of the U. S. District Court of Louisiana.

DE BRIERRE

Hyacinthe (de Rouen) married—————— Longer, issue three children, (1) Hyacinthe Brierre, (2) Armide Brierre, (3) Eugene Brierre. Hayacinthe Brierre married Marie Charlotte Eugenie Becus, issue three children, (1) Theodore Brierre, married Angele Wogan, daughter of Charles Wogan and Eulalie Oliver de Vezin, issue four children, (1) Georges Brierre; (2) Eugenie; (3) Maurice Brierre, who married Miss Burthe, and became the parents of three children, (1) Maurice Brierre, who married a Miss King, had one daughter, Grace Brierre; (2) Henri Brierre, married Miss Laplace and had one son named Henri. Georges Brierre, son of Theodore Brierre and Angele Wogan, married Miss Castaing, issue four children, (1) Joseph, who married Miss Lagarde, issue three children, (1) Marion Brierre; (2) Theo Brierre; (3) Theo Brierre.

Angele Brierre, daughter of Maurice Brierre and Miss Burthe, married Mr. Humphries, issue two children, Ethyln Humphries, who married; and Carlye Numa Humphries.

Paul Brierre, son of Theodore Brierre and Angele Wogan, married Ida Theresa Van Vrendenburh, daughter of William Hazard Van Vrendenburh and Valintine Oliver de Vezin, who in turn was daughter of Victor Bienvenu Oliver de Vezin and Paulinede Couzot Reynaud, who in turn was daughter of Louis Reynaud and Constance de Couzot, daughter of Le Chavalier de Couzot who married Miss de Grande Pre.

The children of Paul Numa Brierre, who married Ida Theresa Van Vrendenburh are as follows: Paule, who married Walter Charles Parlange, issue one son, Walter Charles Parlange, Jr. Olga Brierre, who married Pinkney Galbreath, her children are: Pinkney Galbreath, Marthe Brierre; Theodore Brierre married Elvina Wall, issue Elmyra Augusta; Edith Brierre married Nelson Woody, issue Nelson Stuart Woody; Eugene Brierre, married Giddre Donnaud; William Brierre; Roland Brierre, married Claire Peyronnin; Rosine Brierre; Audice Brierre; Angele Brierre.

D'HERBIGNY

Pierre Charles Auguste Bourguignon d'Herbigny was born in the town of Laon, near Lille, Department of Nord, France, in 1767. A son of Augustin Bourguignon d'Herbigny, he was one of five brothers, as follows: (1) Alphonse d'Herbigny who having completed his education, like the sons of aristocrats, became attached to the army, later becoming aide-de-camp to General Jean Marie Philippe, comte de Serrurier, a noted mar'chal de France, and was killed in active duty with comte de Serrurier during a brilliant campaign under Napoleon in Italy. (2) Francois Xavier d'Herbigny, who became secretary general de la Prefecture du Nord, Paris. (3) Casimir d'Herbigny who became an official in the department of the Marine of France. (4) Antoine Valery d'Herbigny who became a distinguished poet, and writer and Director de la enregistrement at Arras and Bordeaux.

Pierre d'Herbigny in 1792 fled from France when the French Revolution was at its height. He arrived in San Domingo only to find another upheavel in which thousands of whites were massacred by the blacks. Again fleeing he landed in Pittsburgh, where he married the only daughter of Chevalier Pierre Charles de Hault de Lassus de Luziere—Filiceté Odile de Hault de Lassus de Luziere. Her father was Knight of the Grand Cross of the royal order of Saint Michel, founder and commandant of New Bourbon, a post located two miles south of Ste. Genevieve and almost opposite Kashaskia on the Mississippi River in upper Louisiana.

Of an ancient family of Bouchaine in the town of Hainault, French Flanders, Pierre Charles de Hault de Lassus married Domitile Josephe Dumont Danzin de Beaufort. From this marriage were born four children as follows: (1) Charles de Hault de Lassus de Luziere (Don Carlos de Hault de Lassus; (2) Jacques Marcellin Ceran de Hault de Lassus de St. Vrain; (3) Camille de Hault de Lassus; (4) Felicite Odile de Hault de Lassus, who became the wife of Pierre d'Herbigny.

Chevalier Pierre de Lassus leaving France with his wife and children at the height of the French Revolution went to Spain, and later in 1794 to New Orleans about which time he was commissioned to take over Nouvelle Bourbon.

Charles de Hault de Lassus de Luziere (Don Carlos) a colonel in the service of Spain was born in Bouchaine, France, in 1764, and while in Andalusia, in the war between France and Spain, spurred his men on with such vigor that he won the victory for Spain.

At the age of thirty while in Louisiana he was made commandante of New Madrid in the Illinois District (1797-1799), when he was sent to replace Don Zenon Trudeau (last lieutenant governor of the Upper Louisiana) which post he held for the Dons until the 10th of March, 1804, until Captain Amos Stoddard took over that territory for the United States. However the Spaniards still held West Florida, the remaining Spanish possession in Louisiana and in the spring of 1807 Don Carlos de Lassus was appointed its governor. While in command at the time that the patriots from the area of the Felicianas captured the fort located at Baton Rouge (present name) tore down the banner of the dons, replacing it with the American flag (the Lone Star) where an independent government was set up. For permitting the capture of the fort and loss of West Florida, de Lassus was tried and condemned to death. He went into hiding at the home of his sister, Mrs. Pierre d'Herbigny and escaped punishment, as the sentence was never carried out.

Charles de Hault de Lassus (Don Carlos) married Adelaide Felicite Mariana di Leonardo, a daughter of Gilbert di Leonardo. He died in New Orleans on May 1st, 1842 at the age of 78, survived by a son, Auguste de Hault de Lassus. Jacques Marcelin Ce'ran de Hault de Lassus Vrain was born in Bouchaine, 1770, served in the Navy of France previous to the French Revolution, and later while in Louisiana commanded a Spanish war vessel on the upper Mississippi.

Camille de Hault de Lassus de Luziere, while in New Bourbon served as an officer of the Dons and as English interpreter gratas, and during the absence of his father commanded that post, also discharging the duties as adjutant. From his marriage he left three children—Leon, Paul, and Odile de Lassus.

Pierre d'Herbigny, whose wife became an invalid, travelled extensively with her in an effort to regain her health. After visiting a number of places in the southern part of America he came to New Orleans. In 1803 he became secretary to Etienne de Bore, during his brief term as mayor of New Orleans under the tricolor, and later when W. C. C. Claiborne became governor he appointed d'Herbigny as interpreter of languages for the new territory of Orleans.

He was notably active in all matters pertaining to obtaining the status of statehood for Louisiana in 1805. He was one of the

The Marquis Claude Vincent de Ternant, II. (From an ivory miniature at Parlange. Courtesy of the family.)

Crest, Coat-of-Arms of the de Cruzat family.

Coat-of-Arms of the deLino deChalmette family.

Antoine deCruzat, Captain in Louisiana Regiment under the Spanish Domination. (Original painting in possession of Mrs. Edwin X. deVerges.)

Madelien Victoire Heloise deLino deChalmette. (From an ivory miniature owned by Mrs. E. X. deVerges.)

commissioners who went to Washington with the memorial protesting against Louisiana being admitted as a territory.

Twice he became secretary of state, and Mr. Derbigny (as he later wrote his name) long had been recognized for his ability as a lawyer. His ability had been recognized in France, and his knowledge of the Napoleonic Code made him a valuable assistant when Edward Livingston, assisted by Moreau Lislet, revised the Civil Code. This was followed by his becoming a member of the Supreme Court with George Mathews, and Dominic A. Hall. His political career continued until 1829 when he had been elected governor of Louisiana. Within a year of his occupancy of the position on Sept. 25th, while out driving, something caused the horses to become frightened. They got beyond his control, ran away, overturned the carriage and threw him on his head. He died five days later.

Governor Derbigny left one son, Charles Zenon Derbigny, who was studying medicine in Paris at the time his father met with the accident that caused his death. On being notified, he returned to New Orleans at once. Abandoning the study of medicine he began the study of law, and completing his studies, entered politics and public life. For a number of years he was a member of the state legislature, becoming president of the state senate. He became a candidate for governor of Louisiana in 1845, but was not elected. He then devoted his energies to his sugar plantations in Jefferson Parish opposite New Orleans and on Bayou Lafourche. His home on Bayou Lafourche was a prominent one of the locality.

His wife was Josephine Eulalie LeBreton, who became the mother of his three daughters: (1) Marie Lucie Derbigny, who became the wife of Etienne Dauphin Courmes; (2) Marie Eulalie Derbigny, who became Mrs. Edmond LeBreton, and on her second marriage Mrs. Hugh D. Cochrane; (3) Felicite Odile Derbigny, who became Mrs. Pierre Glaitrais LaBarre. Charles Zenon Derbigny, the last of the line to bear the name of d'Herbigny (Derbigny) in Louisiana lived to be eighty-one years of age, dying at his plantation in Jefferson Parish, the name becoming extinct at his death. There is a street in New Orleans named after his father.

The sisters of Charles Zenon Derbigny were: Aimee, who became the wife of Henry Denis, having their plantation on False

River, Pointe Coupee Parish, and another sister married George Legendre.

OLIVER DE VEZIN.

Hugues Oliver de Vezin, Seigneur de Sionne-en Bassigny, who married Louise Leroux de Dinjolincour was the father of Pierre Francois Maeie Oliver, ecuyer, Sieur de Vezin from the Province of Champagne, who after coming to Canada in 1738 established an iron foundry that became known as Forge St. Maurice at the place known as Three Rivers. This young nobleman who had been born in the City of Nancy in 1716, and had risen to be Councillor of his King, and learning of the request made by the Governor of Canada, for an iron foundry for New France, obtained permission to go to America and establish the foundry. When his management proved that the venture was a success, he married on the 14th of June 1747, Marie Josephte Gatineau Duplessis of Three Rivers, who had been born at that place September 4th, 1720. She had been previously married and was vieuve Linier, at the time of her second nuptial. Her father was Jean Baptiste Gatineau Duplessis, her mother being Marie Celeste Le Boullanger. The young manager of Forge St. Maurice proved to be a very capable representative of his government, and was appointed by France as grand Voyer, inspecteur des ponts et chaussees et arpenteur general de la Province de la Louisiane in 1749, being transferred to New Orleans to discharge his new duties.

Here he held rank among the most prominent of the French colonial officials and when the Spaniards took over the colony, he was also honored by them, taking his seat on December, 1769, as regidor perpetuo y alguazil mayor. His children were (1) Hugues Charles Honore Oliver de Vezin de St. Maurice, born in 1748 at Three Rivers, who married Marie Madeleine Philippe de Marigny de Mandeville, daughter of Antoine Pierre Philippe de Marigny de Mandeville, and Francoise de Lile DuPart, issue three children; (2) Charlotte Constance Oliver de Vezin, who was born in New Orleans in 1750, and who died in this city on August 11, 1801— her first husband being Daniel Fagot de la Garciniere, who died in 1776, she later marrying Charles Antoine de Reggio, who was a son of Francois Marie de Reggio, and Helene Fleuriau, she leaving children by both marriages; (3) Pierre Louis Oliver d'Erneville, born in New Orleans in 1752, becoming a lieutenant colonel under Governor Galvez, later on to be promoted to a captain in the troops of Spain. He married Marie Francoise la Mollere d'Orville, on February 14th, 1777; (5) Avineent Adelaide Oliver de Vezin, born on the 20th of February, 1755, and married Etienne de la Lande d'Alcour, son of Etienne de la Lande d'Alcour and Marie Josephe Trudeau on September 15th 1770; (6) Nicolas Joseph Godfroi Oliver de Vezin, born on the 27th of May, 1757, became a grensdier under Governor Galvez, and married Eulalie Toutant de Beauregard on December 3rd, 1782, the bride being a daughter of Jacques Toutant de Beauregard, at her death later, married Marie Marianne Bienvenue, a daughter of Jean Baptiste Bienvenue, and Helene Belet (vieuve Ducret) in 1789; (7) Louise Judith Oliver de Vezin, born in 1758, and married the chevalier Augustin de Reggio after 1776; (8) Francoise Victoria Oliver de Vezin, born 1753, according to the records of the Ursuline Convent of New Orleans, entered the Ursuline Order in this city at the age of sixteen, later being known as Mere Saint Marie, becoming Mother Assistant on June 3rd, 1803, being further elevated to the office of Superioress of the Convent in New Orleans before May of 1812. A religious custom which has been kept up annually, is a solemn high mass and a Te Deum is sung annually in fulfillment of her vow made when the English General Packenham and his army were advancing against New Orleans, her vow being that this religious service would be given in gratitude for the defeat of the British. Never in all these years has this vow been broken.

The children of Gatineau Duplessis by her marriage to Hugues Charles Honore Oliver de Vezin, were Major Charles Oliver de Vezin, who married Celeste Mathilde De Blanc, daughter of Captain Charles de Blanc and Elizabeth Pouponne d'Erneville, at St. Martinville, Louisiana, in 1798. Five children were born of this union, all in St. Martinville. Another of their sons, Pierre Oliver de Closel de Vezin, whose first wife was Jeanne Aspasie Devince Bienvenu, a daughter of Alexandre Devince Bienvenu and Louise Felicite Henriette Latil de Tinecour, the marriage taking place in St. Martinville, March 2nd, 1802. Issue five children. His second wife's name was Marie Josephe Latiolais, a daughter of Joseph Latiolais and Francoise Nezat; issue of this marriage was one son.

From the marriage of Nicolas Joseph Godfroi Oliver de Vezin (6th child of Pierre Francois Oliver de Vezin) and Gatineau

Duplessis, from his marriage with Marianne Bienvenu (his second wife), were Anastasie, who became the wife of Augustin de Reggio; Eulalie, who did not marry; Jean Baptiste, who married Alix Duverje; Elmire, who married Furcy Verret; Henriette, who married Pierre Reaud; Charles Godfroi, who married Eulalie Duverje; Eulalie, who married John Wogan; Victor Bienvenu, who married Pauline Reynaud, and Cesaire, who married Henriette Lavergne.

The children of Victor Bienvenu Oliver de Vezin and Pauline Reynaud became the parents of eleven children: Emma, who married A. N. Robelot; Valentine, who married Mrs. W. H. Vrendenburg; Victor, who married Louise Marie Hebrard September 10th, 1866, survived by six children: Albert J., who married Marie Theard; Victor Wogan, who married Cecile Albert; Lucie Marie, who did not marry; Christian Louis, who married Ida Dreuschke; Pierre D., who married Marie Amelie Minor; and Berthe Marie, who married Jacques de Tarnowsky.

A FAMOUS PORTRAIT OF THE METROPOLITAN MUSEUM OF ART

New York City.

MADAME GAUTREAUX NEE MADEMOISELLE AVENGNO

(Her mother being a Mademoiselle de Ternant)

Hanging on one of the walls of a room in the permanent collection of the Metropolitan Museum of Art, there is a beautiful portrait of this member of the de Ternant family. The artist, John Sargent, considered it among the best examples of his work. Painted during an early period of his career while he was in Paris, and according to notable art critics when he had begun to outmaster his instructor, the famous Carolus Duran. While the effects of time are manifest in the deterioration of the pigments, the portrait remains one of great distinction. Here one does not find the great contrasts verging on the theatrical, which mark so many of his other masterpieces. The pose is unusual. The artist has not failed to portray to full measure her aristocratic elegance of form and feature as well as birth for from this portrait one could get no other impression but that Madame Gautreaux was an aristocrat. Her beautiful cameo-like, patrician features are shown to perfection in profile. It is a portrait that remains one of John Singer Sargent's best. Those who follow such matters recall the uproar in the Art World some years ago about this painting. Many friends and admirers of Madame Gautreaux contended at the time it was painted, that Mr. Sargent had done the lady's beauty a great injustice, and so strong was this feeling in the art circles of Paris that he became unpopular. The criticism of this portrait has been blamed for the sudden departure of Mr. Sargent from that great art center.

Chapter VIII.

THE DE VERGÈS FAMILY

COAT OF ARMS—Field of silver, a sinople tree, with crimson bank surcharged with a heart with silver roses.

THIS ancient and respected name dates back to the year 1253, when a member of this notable Bernaise house, Garsie Arnaud de Verges, (Damoiseu) is listed in the ancient chronicles as Lord of Verges and Patron of Sazos. The name is variously spelled in the records: Du Verger, de Verges, de Vergez.

The de Verges family, in Louisiana since 1720, traces in unbroken line to the Counts of Bigorre who owned and occupied the ancient feudal castle located in the parish of Sazos in the valley of Baregos. They were founders and patrons of the church and parish of St. Julien de Sazos—in the records their names appear on the Latin charts as de Viridariis and de Viridario. Chevalier Bernard de Verges, the founder of the Louisiana branch of this patrician family, comes from a branch of the tree that bore the six notable de Verges brothers. Living in the town of Bearn between the years 1560 and 1580, they bore the names and titles of captains—Guillaume, Jean, Charles, Roger, Raymond, and Joseph, each with his surname attached. Throughout that area of France they were famous and their alliances with noble houses made the name a notable one in the annals of heraldry.

The passenger list of the good ship, La Dromadaire, Capt. St. Mar in command, in the year 1720 includes the name of Chevalier Bernard de Verges. He was listed as "dissinateur" or draftsman for the colony. Later he became engineer-in-chief.

From family records in the New Orleans branch of the family, it is shown that he was born on Jan. 10th, 1693, in the City of Bayonne in Bearn, France. He was a son of Francois Artus de Verges, an officer in the regiment of the Bandes Gramontoises, and was also known in France as Bernard de Verges. He had married twice, 1661 and 1679, his second wife, Marie Lagrenade, being the mother of the Louisiana engineer. Through these marriages he became the father of six children: (1) Armand Xavier de Verges; (2) Pierre de Verges; (3) Dominic de Verges; (4) Bernard de Verges (who came to Louisiana), also two daughters.

Bernard de Verges, the young draftsman, at his own request was placed on duty at the Balise, shortly afterwards being made commandant of the post there. On July 31st, 1727 the Ship Gironde cast anchor at the mouth of the Mississippi River after a long and perilous journey, and Madeleine Hachard, a young novice, in her diary tells of the many hardships of this trip. Commandant Bernard de Verges welcomed the nuns, nine in number, of the Ursuline Order that had come at the request of the Governor to take charge of the education of the young of the colony. He turned over his home to them until they could be conveyed to the capital of the colony by pirogues.

Bernard married Marie Theresa Pinaud of La Rochelle, daughter of Pierre Pinaud, an early settler in Louisiana, and Susanne Meunier. The ceremony took place in the first church in the colony on the site of the present Cathedral of St. Louis.

After a number of eventful years in which unwarranted opposition caused no end of worry, Bernard de Verges, bearing the title of Royal Engineer, in partnership with Adrien de laPlace, a relative, acquired a plantation opposite the city of New Orleans, some seventeen arpents river frontage, on which a plantation home of the early Louisiana type was erected. Old records show that it was a structure having a frontage of fifty feet and that it contained eleven rooms, all of which were well finished, having glazed windows, and doors, all provided with bolts and keys. In fact it was one of the few plantations with a carefully finished home in that section. If we judge the Pontalba Papers, life here like that at the de Macarty plantation was very gay. As the de Verges family was of the same social class and married into the old families mentioned by Pontalba, we may be sure the de Verges home too, was a center of the social life of that era. Like most of the plantation homes at that date, it had a roof of hand-made shingles, a raised basement or lower floor, a large attic for storage room, and several brick chimneys to heat the house. Here dwelt Mrs. de Verges and her family while the Royal Engineer was occupied with his duties in various parts of the colony, coming to this rural retreat whenever his duties permitted. From his marriage to Susanne Meunier there were born seven children: (1) Bernard de Verges II, who became an infantry officer, in Louisiana, and married Mrs. (widow) Marguerite Chauvin de Lery, widow of Chevalier Dominicque de Verbois, a former officer in the colony. She was a daughter of Joseph Chauvin de Lery, Captain of Militia in Louisiana, and Francoise Laurence LeBlanc, her marriage to Bernard de Verges II, taking place on Aug. 14th, 1759; (2) Pierre de Verges, who became a notable character in military annals in the State of Louisiana. He married in the city of New Orleans on May 4th, 1759, Marie Josephe Catherine Poupart, widow of Antoine Simon Grifon d'Anneville, Royal storekeeper in the colony. Marie Josephe Catherine Poupart was a daughter of Sieur Joseph Poupart and Marie Roy. Marie Josephe Poupart was born in Fort Conde de la Mobile, and died in the City of New Orleans in 1740. From her first marriage to Antoine Simon Grifon d'Anneville, she had four children living: (1) Charles Antoine; (2) Daniel; (3) Catherine; (4) Victoria Marie Josephine Grifon d'Anneville, who became Madame Jean Marc Coulon Jumonville de Villiers. In the historical record of Pierre de Verges, the episode of Sept. 14th, 1758 appearing among the brilliant pages of Louisiana's history.

From his marriage to Madame (widow) Griffon d'Anneville, three daughters were born, Marie Josephe Modeste de Verges, born in New Orleans, who married and became the second wife of Jean Rene Huchet de Kernion an alcalde under the Spanish regime and made her home on their plantation in Gentilly where she died on June 7th, 1815; (2) Marguerite Constance de Verges, who also married in New Orleans a son of Jean Rene Huchet de Kernion named Jacques Huchet de Kernion, by his first wife who had been Melle. de Lery des Ilets; (3) Marie Prudence de Verges, died unmarried; (2) Pierre de Verges; (3) Francois Xavier Dagobert de Verges, Sieur de St. Sauveur, who married Madeline Victoire Josephine Martin de Lino de Chalmet, and of Magdeleine Broutin. Their son Pierre married Heloise Martin de Lino de

Mrs. Pierre Paul deVerges neé Mathilde Cruzat. (From an old photograph. Courtesy of Mrs. Edwin X. deVerges.)

De Poupart Coat-of-Arms.

Chateau Mont L'Evecque near Paris, France. The home of Baron de Pontalba, reproduced from a painting given to the father of Mrs. Edwin X. deVerges by Baron Edouard de Pontalba. (See article page 135, Vol. II.)

Crest and Coat-of-Arms of the Butler family. (Courtesy of the Misses Sarah and Mamie Butler.)

A wall of the living room of the home of the Misses Sarah and Mamie Butler, New Orleans.

Chalmette was born in 1788, and was the daughter of Ignace Martin de Lino de Chalmette and Madeleine Victoire de Vaugine, and became the parents of two sons: Paul de Verges, born 1812, and married Jan. 19th, 1836, Marie Stephanie Lanuse, leaving seven children at the time of his death on May 27th, 1870: (1) Pierre Henry, born 24th of March, 1837, died March 23rd, 1904; (2) Charles Ernest, born Dec. 21st, 1838, died Jan. 7th, 1920; (3) Jean Baptiste de Verges, born Feb. 14th, 1843, died July 9th, 1915; (4) Pierre Paul de Verges, born July 21st, 1840, died April 2nd, 1919, married Mathilde Cruzat on Feb. 16th, 1870, and left children; (5) Louis Edmond de Verges, born Nov. 17th, 1844, died Sept. 29th, 1906; (6) Marie Alice de Verges, born Nov. 6th, 1847; (7) Corinne de Verges, born Dec. 17th, 1844, died May 12th, 1855. (4) Louis Joseph Augustin de Verges, (Sieur de St. Luc) who died a bachelor. (5) Marguerite de Verges, who married April 26th, 1753, Henry Le Grand d'Orgon. (6) Marguerite Francoise de Verges, who married Jean Baptiste Chauvin de Lery des Islets, File de Antoine Chauvin de Lery des Islets, an officer of Militia in the colony, her mother being Charlotte Faucon du Manoir. (7) Charlotte de Verges, who became Madame Gabriel Fazende, her husband Colonial Secretary in Louisiana. He was a son of Jean Baptiste Gabriel Fazende and Charlotte Dreux of the wealthy aristocratic plantation family of that name. He also was Commissaire under Rochmore in 1762, holding important civil offices until 1776.

Pierre Francois de Verges, 2nd son of Francois Xavier Dagobert de Verges, Sieur de St. Sauveur, was born Sept. 1st, 1807, and died Feb. 19th, 1865, married Victoire Coralie Lanusse, daughter of Paul Lanusse and Marie Celeste de Macarty, of the prominent plantation family of that name. (3) Malvina de Verges, who became Madame Manuel Cruzat, and left two daughters. The year 1763 is a memorable one in the annals of Chevalier Bernard de Verges, for at this time King Louis XIV, in recognition of and as a reward for 43 years of faithful and untiring services to the colony, conferred upon Chief Engineer de Verges the great honor of the Cross of the Royal and Militray Order of St. Louis, the greatest honor that can be bestowed upon a military man of French birth.

Pierre de Verges de St. Sauveur, son of Francois Xavier Dagobert de Verges de St. Sauveur and Madeleine Josephine Martin de Lino de Chalmette, born in 1779, died Jan. 30th, 1839, married Madeleine Victoire Heloise Martin de Lino de Chalmette and Victoire de Vaugine, born in 1788, died Jan. 16th, 1856. Issue: Pierre Francois de Verges de St. Sauveur; Paul de Verges de St. Sauveur; Malvina de Verges de St. Sauveur.

Pierre Francois de Verges de St. Sauveur, son of Pierre de Verges de St. Sauveur and Madeleine Victoire Heloise de Lino de Chalmette, born Sept. 1st, 1807, died Jan. 19th, 1865, married Victoire Coralie Lanusse. Malvina de Verges de St. Sauveur married Manuel Cruzat, son of Antoine Gerthoude Cruzat and Victoire Morenciana de Lino de Chalmette. Paul de Verges de St. Sauveur, son of Pierre de Verges de St. Sauveur and Madeleine Victoire Heloise Martin de Lino de Chalmette, born June 27th, 1812, died May 27th, 1870, married Jan. 19th, 1836, Marie Stephanie Lanusse, daughter of Paul Lanusse and Marie Celeste de Macarty. Issue, Pierre Henri de Verges; Charles Ernest de Verges; Pierre Paul de Verges; Jean Baptiste Richard de Verges; Marie Alice de Verges; Corinne de Verges.

Charles Ernest de Verges, son of Paul de Verges and Marie Stephanie Lanusse, born Dec. 21st, 1838, died Jan. 7th 1920, married Feb. 16th, 1870, Mathilde Cruzat, daughter of Gustave Cruzat and Marguerite Elizabeth Vienne, born June 30th, 1844, died Jan. 16th, 1896. Issue: Marie Alice de Verges; Aloysius Gonzaga Albert de Verges. Edwin Francois Xavier de Verges married Marie Josephine Cruzat, daughter of Joseph William Cruzat and Marie Heloise Hulse. Marie Anna de Verges married Dr. Thomas William Breaux, issue two daughters, Marie Gladys Breaux, married Dr. John Robert Flowers and Marie Hazel Breaux; Agnes Alice de Verges; Marie Lydia de Verges.

Philip Cajetan de Verges, M. D., married Marie Nelville Poupart, daughter of Sidney Joseph Poupart and Marie Cecile Cagnolatti; Joseph Henry de Verges. Louis George de Verges married Mrs. Sadie Unsworth Miller; three children, Nelville, Marjorie and Leonard de Verges. Theresa Lydia de Verges. Louis Edmond de Verges, son of Paul de Verges and Marie Stephanie Lanusse, married Oliver Soniat du Fossat.

Charles Ernest de Verges born Dec. 21, 1838, married April 27, 1867 Francoise Edwidge Fortier. Issue: Joseph Edward de Verges, married Alice Helena Flotte—two children: Joseph Edward de Verges and Edwidge de Verges Stockton (Mrs. Cleveland).

Marie Corinne de Verges married Dr. L. D. Archinard—two children: L. D. Archinard and Edwidge A. Martha.

Stephanie de Verges married John Jumonville.

Original in possession of Mrs. Lucille Paule de Verges Woods, Houston, Tex.

Paul de Verges, D.D.S., married Lucille Dunbar—one child: Lucille Paule de Verges (Mrs. Merritt Thurman Woods).

Plantations

Among the de Verges Plantations in Louisiana were: Trianon, belonging to Chevalier Bernard de Verges, located opposite the City of New Orleans in Olden days; the one on the Chalmette battle grounds which burned to the ground November 13th, 1848, owned by Paul de Verges; and Elina Plantation, St. James Parish, property of Pierre Paul de Verges until 1882.

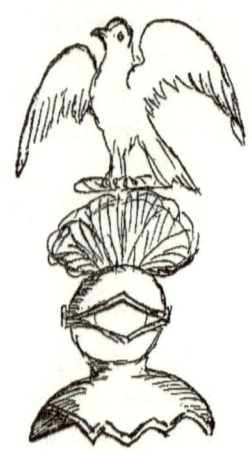

Chapter IX.

THE BUTLER DYNASTY

Crest and Coat-of-Arms of the Butler Family.
A chief (or) indented (Azure) was the coat-of-arms of Theobold Fitzwalter Butler, and is traceable on seals so far back as the twelfth century, when heraldry was first instituted. The family crest was used in early Normand days and consisted of five ostrich plumes from which issued a white falcon (argent).

Different branches of the family varied the colors, but the chief of the family always used the colors of the princes of the blood, viz:—royal blue and gold.

Descendants of Seigneur Thomas Butler, and of his brothers and their cousins the Butlers from Carlisle, Pa., all the Revolutionary stock, are entitled to use the family crest.

Prepared by Joseph Marion Butler and William David Butler. Authorities:—"Burke's Peerage" London 1906—Dictionary of Biography—Vol. 8. McMillan & Co., New York, 1886. Brady's "Episcopal Succession", England's "Life of Arthur O'Leary". Matthews' "American Armourer and Blue Book" without descent. London, 1907.

(FITZWALTER)

The name Butler obtains its derivation from the fact that in the year 1117 when Henry II went into Ireland, one Theobold Fitzwalter accompanied the King and was appointed Chief Butler of that country, hence the name. Theobold Fitzwalter, the first Butler of Ireland, acquitted himself with honor, dying in the year 1206 being succeeded by his son who also bore the name Theobold, or Theobald as some of the records have it. The second Chief Butler of Ireland, according to records of the year 1221, had attached to his name his official title, for on French records appear in conjunction with the name Theobold Fitzwalter (Butler). Up to the year 1321, the official title continued in the family, until the son of the Sixth Chief Butler, James by name, was elevated to the rank of Earl of Ormond in the Peerage of Ireland. Up until 1515 the succession of this Earldom at which time the great grandson of the Earl of Ormond, third in succession, Pierce Butler by name became the eighth Earl of Ormond, and the second son, Richard became first Viscount of Montgarret. James' wife was Joan Fitzgerald, daughter of James Fitzgerald, eleventh Earl of Desmond. His children were John, Richard, and Thomas, who became the tenth Earl of Ormond, leaving no children.

A son of John's, Walter by name, became the eleventh Earl of Ormond and was succeeded by James who became the twelfth Earl of Ormond and First Duke of Ormond. The family had distinguished members in the army and navy, as a son of the first Duke of Ormond while in command of the English army in Flanders in 1674 was killed at the Battle of Senef. The Butlers, true to the land from which came the name of Butler, developed a true fighting spirit. Known far and wide as the "Fighting Butlers", they have gained fame in Europe and America, having fine war records in every conflict form the War of Independence to and including the World War—1914-1918.

The American branch of the family stems to one Thomas Butler, who was born in the County of Kilkenny, town of Wiklow, Ireland on April 6th, 1720. He chose for his wife, Eleanor, daughter of Sir Anthony Parker, a native of Gary County, Wexford, they being married in 1741. Coming to America in 1748 with their three sons, they located in the county of Lancaster, Pa., later removing to Mount Pleasant, Cumberland County. Here, Thomas Butler invested in vast areas of land in the vicinity of which he caused to be built the first Episcopal church in that part of the country. Mount Pleasant became the cradle of his large family of twelve of which five sons became Revolutionary heroes, distinguishing themselves by the intenseness of their patriotic ardor and utter contempt for personal danger. So much was this apparent throughout the struggle for Independence, that not only did General Lafayette praise all of the family, but General George Washington at a banquet given at his home to a large number of his officers rose, and addressing them as the "Honor Band", toasted "The Butlers and their five sons". A goodly crowd of fearless warriors were these sons, General Richard Butler, Colonel William Butler, Colonel Thomas Butler, Jr., Percival (or Pierce), Adjutant General of Kentucky, and Adjutant General Edward Butler. Of the twelve Butler children four died in infancy, those reaching maturity were Mary Butler, born Nov. 5th, 1749 in West Lancaster, Pa. She married Jacob Scandrett. Rebecca Butler, also born in West Lancaster, Sept. 19th, 1751. She married Captain George McCully, a member of the Order of Cincinnati. Eleanor Butler, born at Mount Pleasant, Pa., Dec. 31st, 1763 and married James Brown.

(1) Richard (Fighting Dick) Butler, eldest and most noted of the sons of Thomas Butler, was born in the Parish of St. Bridget, Dublin, Ireland, on the 1st of April, 1745. He was killed (St. Clair's Defeat) in the battle of Miami on Nov. 4th, 1791. He had risen to be a major general. He was made second in command of the American Army and was selected to place the American flag on the English fortifications after Lord Cornwallis surrendered at Yorktown shortly before his death. General Butler's wife was Mary Smith who bore him four children. 1st William Butler, who became a lieutenant in the United States navy and died in the War of 1812. 2nd. Mary Butler who became the wife of Colonel Isaac Meason, her descendants married into the Trevor, Sower and Henry families of Philadelphia, Pa. 3rd. James, who died in infancy. 4th. Captain Richard Butler, whose wife was Anna Wilkins, daughter of General John Wilkins; their children married into the Thompson, Irvin and Biddle families of Pennsylvania.

(2) William Butler, second son of Thomas Butler, was born on Jan. 6th, 1745 in the City of London, England, and died in Pittsburgh, Pa., May 16th, 1789. He was a Captain when he entered the Revolutionary Army and was Colonel of the Fourth Pennsylvania at its close. His wife was Jane Carmichael of

Pittsburgh, who was born in New Orleans, La., in 1751 and died the 6th of March, 1834. She bore him four children. 1st Richard Butler, born in 1777 and died 5th of Oct., 1820. He entered the army and rose to the rank of Captain. Was sent by General James Wilkinson from Pittsburgh, Pa. to Natchez, Miss., to deliver important dispatches for Captain Isaac Guion—a trip of some 3,000 miles—and was gone from April 11th to June 16th. At the Battle of New Orleans, he served with the Forty-fourth Regiment. He married Miss Marguerite Farrar at the termination of the war, a native of Adams County, Mississippi, and during the epidemic of yellow fever in 1820, he, his wife and children died. 2nd. Rebecca Butler, born 20th of April, 1782, at Carlisle, Pa., died on June 23, 1844. She married Captain Samuel McCutchon, a native of Philadelphia, Pa., and became the mother of four children. 1st. Jane, who became the wife of William Frege Krumbhaar and bore him four children. 2. Eliza Ann, who was born the 22nd of January, 1811. Married Robert Rhea Montgomery and became the mother of four children. 3rd. Percival (Pierce) Butler McCutchon born 26th Sept., 1821, married Jane Butler Browder, a cousin who bore him two children. 4th. Zelia Henderson McCutchon, born 6th of April, 1828, married Geo. Carson Lawrason, and became the mother of two sons: (1) one became Judge Samuel McCutchon Lawrason of St. Francisville, La., born July 31st, 1852, who married Miss Harriet Mathews, who bore him nine children, one Anne Lawrason married Edward Butler; (2) George Bradford Lawrason, the second son, born 26th of July, 1854, married for first wife Octavia Planc, and second, Daisy Bruns who bore him three children. 4th. William Butler, was a lieutenant in the War of 1812, having a splendid record, died childless in 1815.

(3) Thomas Butler, third son of Thomas Butler and Eleanor Parker Butler, was born on May 28th, 1748 in Dublin, Ireland, and was a babe in arms when his parents came to America, and settled in Pennsylvania. Having graduated, he studied law. At the beginning of the Revolutionary War, he enlisted as a private. His great courage marked him as an outstanding figure, indifferent to danger of person, and his record shows that in the War of Independence in the area of the Middle States, he took part in almost every battle. On the battlefield of Brandy Wine, he was thanked by Washington for his great bravery and his ability to

rally about him his retreating troops. At Miami, where his brother, General Richard Butler was killed, while in command of a battalion his younger brother saved his life when he was shot off his horse. In 1805 he was a colonel in the regular army and at the age of fifty-five died of yellow fever. He was a member of the Order of Cincinnati, a membership which descends to his son, Judge Thomas Butler. His wife was Sarah Jane Semple, a daughter of Robert Semple and Lydia Steele of Pittsburgh, Pa., and their children were Thomas, Robert, Lydia and William.

Thomas Butler III, born 14th of April, 1785, and studied law in the office of his uncle, Steele Semple. Later he came South to Louisiana and opened his law office practicing law in Florida parishes, making a prominent name for himself as well as a considerable fortune. He bought the plantation now known as "The Cottage" plantation in 1811 in West Feliciana Parish where he then made his home. This property is still in the family, owned by the four children of his son, Dr. Ormond Butler. The wife of Judge Thomas Butler was Ann Madeline Ellis, whom he married August 17th, 1813, whose home was in Adams County, Mississippi, she being a daughter of Abram Ellis and Margurite Gaillard of Huguenot ancestry. The Gaillard family, fleeing from France at the time of the revocation of the Edict of Nantes, came to America and settled in the French Colony in the Southern part of Carolina which later on in the 1860's joined the Confederate Cause.

Judge Butler's death occurred on August 7th, 1847. His family consisted of twelve children, eight reaching maturity as follows: 1. Percival (or Pierce) born Feb. 21st, 1817; 2. Richard Ellis, born Dec. 31st, 1819; 3. Robert Ormond; 4. Margaret; 5. Sarah Jane Duncan; 6. Anna; 7. Mary Ellis; 8. Edward.

(1) Percival, oldest son of Judge Thomas Butler, married Mary Louise Stirling, who was a daughter of Henry Stirling and Mary Bowman. Percival died Feb. 12th, 1888. Their children were: Thomas, born Dec. 6th, 1840; (2) James Pierce, born April 6th, 1842; (3) Louise Ann, born Dec. 6, 1843. Thomas Butler, oldest son of Percival, married Mary Fort, a daughter of William and Sally Fort; they had nine children as follows: Mary Louise; Thomas; Sallie; William; Annie; Samuel; Henry Minor; James Stirling; Judge Butler (he also followed his father's profession) distinguished himself during the Civil War. (2) James

Mrs. W. J. Fort. (From a portrait by Amand, in the home of the Thomas Butler family.)

Judge Thomas Butler of the "Cottage." (From a portrait by Thomas Sully.)

James Butler, Second Duke of Ormond, who was placed in command of the army of Prince William of Orange. (From an illustration in "The Butlers in America" by David Butler.)

Adjutant General Robert Butler, General Andrew Jackson's Chief of Staff in the War of 1812.
(Courtesy of the Butler family.)

(Courtesy of Mrs. D. W. Pipes, Sr.)

Pierce Butler, second son of Judge Thomas Butler, was eighteen years of age at the beginning of the Civil War at which time he joined the Confederate Army. Later he married Mary Louise Harrison and had two children; (1) Pierce Butler, who was Dean of Newcomb College, his wife was the former Cora Waldo; they had three children, Virginia, Pierce, and Mary Frances. The second son of Pierce Butler was (2) James Pierce, who married Laura Finley and had two children, Ormonde and James Pierce, Jr. He was a prominent business man of New Orleans. (3) Louise Ann Butler, third child of Pierce Butler, married Henry Chotard Minor of Terrebonne Parish on April 28th, 1875; they had three children, Margaret, John Duncan and Mary; John Duncan married Lucille Gillis and had two children, Lucille and Joan. Margaret married Charles Krumbhaar and had two children, Charles and Margaret. Mary, third child of Ann Butler and Henry Chotard Minor, married David Pipes, Jr., and had seven children, David (died in infancy), Anna Pipes; H. Minor; John; Katherine; Mary, and Margaret.

(2) Richard Ellis Butler, second son of Judge Thomas Butler and his wife Ann Madeline Ellis, was born at "The Cottage Plantation", near St. Francisville, La., on Dec. 31st, 1819. He married Sarah Evelyn Ker of Natchez, Miss., daughter of Dr. John Ker of "Linden" plantation on October 18th, 1849. They had one son, Thomas William, born Jan. 12th, 1851. He married Sallie Fort, on October 26th, 1881, and had three children, Sarah Duncan, Richard Ellis, and Mary Fort.

Thomas William Butler died at his home in West Feliciana, La., on Dec. 15th, 1913, a man greatly beloved and respected by all who knew him. He was Junior Warden of Grace Episcopal Church, St. Francisville, until the time of his death, and served his native Parish of West Feliciana in many capacities. Sallie Fort, his wife, died in New Orleans, La., at the home of her daughters, on January 7th, 1936.

Miss Sarah Duncan Butler and Miss Mary Fort Butler reside in New Orleans. Miss Sarah Duncan Butler is Vice-Regent for Louisiana for "The Mount Vernon Ladies Association of the Union". This Association owns and cares for the home of George Washington.

Miss Mary Fort Butler has one of the outstanding collections of Early American Lighting Devices which she has used as an educational exhibit. Richard Ellis Butler married Jessie Norris Simon of Norristown, New Jersey, on April 17th, 1918, and lives in Pittsburgh, Pa., and has two children, Richard Ellis, Jr., and Jessie Norris.

(3) Robert Ormond Butler, third son of Judge Thomas Butler and his wife Ann Madelyn Ellis, born May 8, 1832, became a physician, having studied medicine in Paris, France. He practiced both in New York City and later in New Orleans, La., where he enjoyed a lucrative practice until his death on April 2nd, 1874. His wife was Margaret Burthe, daughter of Judge Victor Burthe and Estelle Millaudon, and their four children are as follows: (1) Louise, not married; (2) Robert Ormond, unmarried; (3) Edward, who married Anne Mathews Lawrason, they have four children as follows: Edward Lawrason, Harriet Mathews, now Mrs. Henry Bruns; (3) Charles Mathews; (4) Robert Ormond. Marguerite Butler, third child of Robert Ormond Butler and his wife Margaret Burthe, married Eugene Ellis, son of William Conner Ellis and Eugenie Richardson; they have four children as follows: Marguerite Butler Ellis; Eugene Ellis, Jr.; Amelia de Lesseps Ellis; and Eleanor Parker Ellis. Marguerite Butler Ellis married Richard Murrell and has two children; Amelia de Lesseps Ellis married Ross Murrell and has three children, Ross, Jr., Marguerite, and Frances.

Robert Butler, second son of Col. Thomas Butler and his wife Eleanor Parker Butler, born Dec. 25th, 1786, married Rachel Hays, daughter of Col. Robert Hays and Jane Doneldson, who was a niece of Mrs. Andrew Jackson. Robert Butler was chief of staff to Gen. Andrew Jackson throughout the War of 1812, and at the Battle of New Orleans; in 1821 he resigned from the U. S. Army and for many years was surveyor-general of Florida. Lydia Butler, daughter of Col. Thomas Butler and Eleanor Parker Butler, born March, 1788, died 1852, married Stokely Hays, a nephew of Mrs. Andrew Jackson, and had two children, Jane who became the wife of John Rawlins, had issue living in Tennessee.

William Edward, son of Col. Thomas and Eleanor Parker Butler, married Martha Thompson Hays. He was a surgeon of the 2nd Tennnessee Regiment under Andrew Jackson.

STEWART

Deo Juvante Vinco

Chapter X.

PIPES FAMILY.

JOHN PIPES was the father of four sons, born in Philadelphia, Pa. The family dating to Colonial Days in America. The sons were Windsor, John, Philip and Abner. Windsor and Abner left Philadelphia, going to what is now Illinois, and about 1780 removed to Adams County, Miss., at that time territory under the Spanish rule. According to family records, from these two brothers all of the families bearing the name Pipes living in Louisiana, Mississippi, and Texas descend. John went to Georgia where he settled, and Philip to Missouri in 1811 where he located.

Windsor Pipes, son of John Pipes, was married twice, his wife by his second marriage was Miss Jane McAfee, born on March 1st, 1745, and she became the mother of five sons and three daughters, and died Sept. 12, 1811. Her children were named as follows: Abner Pipes, John Pipes, Joseph Pipes, David Pipes, Charles Pipes, Jane Pipes, Polly Pipes, Lettie Pipes.

David Pipes was born in what is now Adams County, Miss., on May 14th, 1790. He spent his early life in the Natchez country, and at the Battle of New Orleans served with the Adams County cavalry troops, a memento of that day being a saber still in the family, that was worn by David Pipes at this battle. When grown to manhood he removed to East Feliciana Parish, La., and became a planter. His success was such that by the time the Civil War was declared in 1861, he was considered one of the wealthiest planters in the section. He studied his land, his slaves, and all the things that pertained to the plantation, and kept up with the latest improvements, etc. He did not participate very actively in public affairs, although he was a member of the Whig party, but devoted his energies to his plantation, Beech Grove. From this place in true Christian manner he dispensed many a worthy charity, and there church festivals were held in order to aid the Church fund.

His first wife was Martha Worthington, five children from this marriage bear the following names: Alexander, Mary Hill, Henrietta, Amanda, and Emily. His second wife, Mrs. Amanda Collins, nee Dunn, was born in South Carolina on July 30th, 1800, a daughter of Captain Henry Dunn, a prosperous planter of South Carolina. While quite young the family moved to Mississippi where Amanda married Dr. Collins. Their children were Zaterina and Ophelia. David Pipes and Amanda Dunn (Collins) became the parents of two sons, William H. Pipes and David W. Pipes. The oldest son, William H. Pipes, was a student at the University of Virginia at the time that the War Between the States was declared. He immediately left college and entered the army of the Confederate States of America. His army record shows he served with gallantry and distinction; he was adjutant-general on the staff of General Bates in the Army of Tennessee. In politics later he served as representative in the legislature in 1879, and during the administration of Governor Francis T. Nicholls was Treasurer of the State of Louisiana. He was greatly respected and admired throughout the state for his noble character. His wife was Sarah McKeowen, their children being David M. Pipes, Amanda Pipes, Elisabeth Pipes, William H. Pipes, and Ruth Pipes. David Pipes husband of Amanda Collins, died July 1st, 1892.

David Washington Pipes was reared in East Feliciana Parish and attended Oakland College in Mississippi. After the outbreak of the Civil War, he returned from college to assist in the management of his father's plantation and business. He begged his family to let him go to war until finally in 1862 when he was 17

David W. Pipes in Confederate uniform (right). (From an old daguerreotype.)

Mrs. D. W. Pipes (Anna Key Fort) at the time of her marriage.

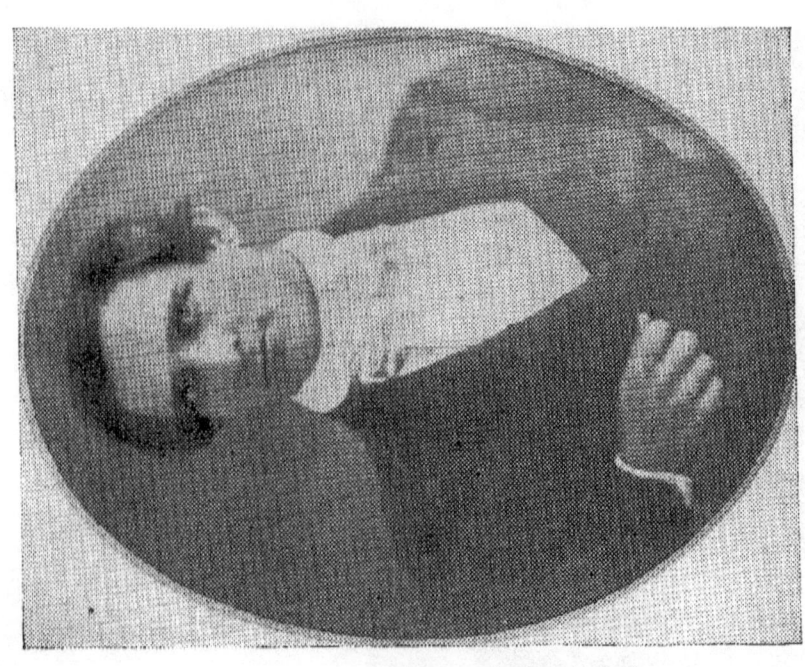

DAVID W. PIPES 1.

WILLIAM JOHNSON FORT of Catalpa.

MRS. DAVID W. PIPES neé MISS ANNA KEY FORT

Beech Grove, old plantation home of the David W. Pipes family, East Feliciana, (now Swing Along Plantation.)

years of age, he left for Virginia with his body servant, Henry Richardson. Reaching Richmond he met his nephew, John Stone, and many of his friends. He at once enlisted in the 4th Company, Battalion, Washington Artillery, from New Orleans, at that time with General Robert E. Lee in the Army of Northern Virginia. David W. Pipes remained with that famous organization until the close of hostilties, taking part in all the actions in which that battalion was engaged, leaving an honorable record to be added to those already attached to this distinguished family.

Like many of his friends, after hostilities Mr. Pipes resumed the life of a planter on the large plantation, this time on his own account. By his energy, keen judgment and thrift, he became successful in every enterprise he undertook ,and when he retired as a planter he was considered one of the large land-owners of Feliciana Parish, the greater part of his holdings being highly cultivated. In 1888 he was elected as an anti-lottery member to represent the Feliciana Parish in the State Legislature and his constituents were thoroughly satisfied with his activities. He fought the Lottery Company bitterly and was one of its most intelligent and persistent opponents. When the proposition to re-charter the company was finally defeated, no one was happier than he. He was elected to the State Senate in 1892, and also served in the Constitutional Convention of 1898.

David W. Pipes married Miss Anna Key Fort, daughter of Mr. William J. Fort, a wealthy planter of West Feliciana Parish, La. Their children are: David W. Pipes, William Fort Pipes, Sarah Randolph Pipes, Randolph Windsor Pipes.

Sarah and Randolph were named for their grandmother, Sarah Randolph, daughter of Judge Peter Randolph of Virginia and Mississippi, and wife of Colonel Tignal Jones Stewart of Mississippi, the grandmother that Mrs. Pipes lived with during most of her childhood. The three Pipes boys were educated at Washington and Lee University, and the daughter at Newcomb College of Tulane University. During his lifetime while a resident of Clinton, La., Mr. David Pipes was a member and elder of the Presbyterian Church of Clinton. He was a staunch Presbyterian, firm in his religious beliefs and faithful in the discharge of the duties and responsibilities that this implies.

Mrs. David Pipes, always a social leader, continues her social activities, living again in her grandchildren her social triumphs of her younger years. Stately, gracious, distinctly patrician looking, she has inherited from her illustrious ancestors all of those traits of character that come only through generations of good breeding. Her handsome home in the beautiful "Garden District", like her former lovely old plantation home, is forever gay with the friends of the family who make of it a joyous meeting place. She is now the recognized head of the family or clan which comprises the following families: Fort, Stewart, Pipes, Randolph, and Butler.

TOWN HOUSE OF THE DAVID W. PIPES FAMILY.

The handsome city home of the David W. Pipes family is one of the most attractive in the city. Built when the beautiful "Garden District" was in the making and splendid mansions of the Greek-Revival and similar architectural styles were being constructed then as with many that have remained, it is as attractive as when originally built. This home, among the finest, is in every way typical of the home of the cultured patricians that chose this area for their residences.

Set in great gardens, surrounded by splendid oaks, magnolias and other beautiful trees that form leafy bowers at every turn, for years this lovely old mansion has been the home of the David Pipes family—one of the most distinguished plantation families in the entire Southland. This old home is quite similar to the plantation houses, having large rooms and high ceilings, wide hallways and roomy porches, making it an ideal home for entertaining on a large scale. Most of the splendid examples of massive rosewood and mahogany furniture from the ateliers of Signorette and Prudence Mallard feel quite at home in these large rooms, for much of it was made to order for the Fort and the Pipes families, ancestors of those who enjoy these beautiful things today. Fortunately the Pipes family had removed to this fine old home before their old family plantation home burned. On entering the hallway one notes at once the fine collection of silhouettes, picturing the celebrities of a vanished day. In the drawing-rooms and other rooms of the house one finds some of the finest crystal chandeliers in the South, and the other furnishings of this fine old home are in keeping. Since occupied by the Pipes family it has been a scene of constant entertaining, a number of debutantes, granddaughters of Mrs. David Pipes have made their debut here.

The latest debutante to make her bow to society being a lovely granddaughter, Miss Sarah Pipes, pictured in her ante-bellum costume worn at the "Gone with the Wind" dance given some time ago.

FORT FAMILY OF CATALPA PLANTATION
West Feliciana Parish, La.

Originally le Fort family came from France to England at the time of the "Revocation of the Edict of Nantes" when their religious privileges were taken from them. Later they came to America.

Mrs. William Fort, a widow with three sons, came from the Carolinas and settled in the Felicianas in the early part of the 18th Century. Their first home, built on Magnolia Plantation near the river, was a large roomy two-story house built of brick, with all of the comforts to be found in plantation homes of that period.

Shortly after settling in Feliciana, one of Mrs. Fort's sons died. He had returned to Carolina with his cousins the Barrows, for more slaves, and on the way he contracted a fever from which he never recovered. Her second son William married the beautiful Mary Johnson, also a cousin of the Barrows, who had been sent to Philadelphia for her education. They had but one child, William Johnson Fort of "Catalpa Plantation". He married Sally Jones Stewart, whose mother was Sarah Randolph, daughter of Judge Peter Randolph of Virginia and Mississippi, and her father was Tignal Jones Stewart, son of Duncan Stewart of Scotland. Duncan Stewart was the first Lieutenant Governor of Mississippi. The old Stewart plantation manor, "Holly Grove", was a massive Colonial building with large brick pillars, and galleries on both upper and lower floors. Its many rooms were filled with choice pieces of mahogany and rosewood furniture, (today considered antiques fit for a museum), family portraits, old silver and rare books, which enhanced its beauty—certainly a home of real charm.

From the marks on one of the bricks, authorities state the house was erected one hundred and fifty years ago. All of its beauty is now gone, except the old wide galleried house and the cemetery near by where rest the remains of the original owners.

This little cemetery, overgrown by flowering trees and vines which climb over the handsome monuments, in olden days was as beautiful with flowers as was the immense garden filled with rare flowers and fruits. The Forts had three very large plantations, one of the sugar plantation had the largest sugar-house in the state in ante-bellum days. The ruins of this old brick building can still be traced by the brick foundations, not far from the main dwelling on Catalpa Plantation.

Mary Johnson, mother of Mrs. W. J. Fort. From a miniature loaned by Mrs. David W. Pipes.

Grace Episcopal Church, St. Francisville. (See page 254, Vol. I.)

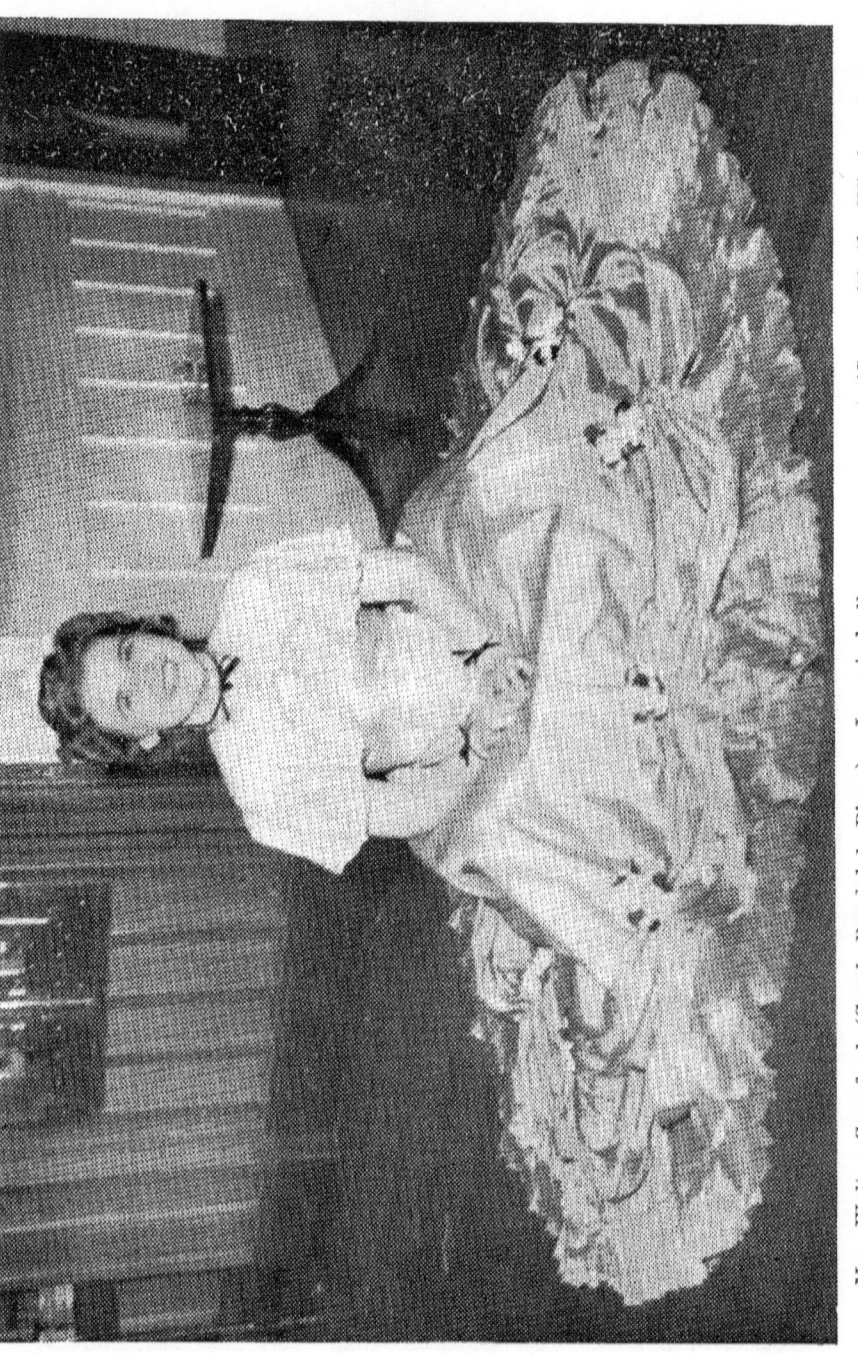

Mrs. Walter Crawford (Sarah Randolph Pipes). In ante-bellum gown worn at "Gone with the Wind party."

Chapter XI

THE ELLIS FAMILY

AMONG the families of distinction that left Virginia about the year 1776, coming South and settling in Adams County, were Richard Ellis and Mary Cocke Ellis, who purchased land near Natchez and in the vicinity of what is now Baton Rouge. Abram Ellis and Marguerite Gaillard Ellis, purchased plantation lands in Terrebonne Parish, La., and their son Richard Ellis moved there and lived on Evergreen Plantation, and later built Magnolia Plantation Manor still standing, and described in the plantation home article of that name, identified by its ancient slave call bells, as a number of plantations in Louisiana bear the name "Magnolia".

The Ellis family, cultured and wealthy from Virginia, stemming to a noble house of the British Isles owned many splendid plantations in ante-bellum days. According to members of the family old records showing how extensive and valuable these holdings were, manned by thousands of slaves, are still in the family. The name is connected by marriage ties to the leading patrician families of the South, well represented in all of the professions, and numbered among the princely planters of olden days.

Earlier Family Record

John Ellis, of Tuckahoe, Va., a member of the House of Burgesses, married Elizabeth Ware, of Varina Plantation, Va. Their son John of Nottaway, Virginia, married Elizabeth Smith. Their son Richard, married Mary Cocke, of Amelia County, Va. His son Abram, married Marguerite Gaillard of Adams County, Miss., and Terrebonne Parish, La. His son Richard, married Mary Jane Towson, and his (Richard's) daughter Anne, married Thomas

Butler (of the Cottage Plantation). Eliza married General Braxton Bragg, of Rosemount Plantation, Mobile, Ala. Thomas, married Kate Donelson, Towson, unmarried, Mary, married Thomas A. Adams of Boston, Mass., and lived to be a hundred years of age. William Conners, married Eugenie Richardson.

Their children are 1st, William, who married Isabella de Ayala, who had two children—Richard, and Gaillard. 2nd, Amelie; 3rd, Robert R., who married Rose Allen; 4th, Anna B.; 5th, Eugene, who married Marguerite Butler; 6th, Odette, who married John Moore; 7th, Sydney, who married Odile Kilpatrick; 8th, Edward; 9th, Towson, who married Ruth Denis. The children of Robert R., who married Rose Allen, are Robert R., who married Isabel Duning, whose children are Robert R., and John A. The children of Allen W., who married Dorothy Hill are Carroll Allen, and Cynthia. The children of Eugene Ellis, who married Marguerite Butler, are 1, Marguerite, who married Richard Murrell. Their children, Marguerite Gaillard, and Mary Conners. 2, Eugene. 3, Amalie, who married George Ross Murrell, their children are 1st, George R., Jr.; 2nd, Margaret Ellis; 3rd, Francis Gwin; 4th, Eleanor Parker Ellis. The children of Odette who married John Moore, are John and Ewing; John married Maude Butterworth, their two children are Catherine and John. Ewing married Janette Bloodworth. 7, Children of Sidney, who married Odile Kilpatrick, are Sydney and Barbara. 8, The children of Edward, who married 1st, Gladys Hardin, are Hardin, Virginia, and William. 9, Children of Towsen, who married Ruth Denis, are Ruth, Towsen, and Joan.

Another home of the Ellis family containing much that is artistic and interesting is that of the Eugene Ellis family on Third Street, New Orleans. Here we find paintings by noted artists, among them a portrait of an ancestor in full military uniform which hangs above a mantel. Flemish and Highland landscapes and others equally interesting fill the walls. Antiques of great charm and much fine old French oak magnificently carved fill drawing-rooms, dining-room, and hallway. Rare books and unusually attractive bric-a-brac all add to complete this most interesting home which has about it the same restful air of the plantation homes of the Ellis and Butler families.

Chapter XII.

THE PERCY FAMILY

NO family of the large number of aristocrats locating in the area that later became known as the Felicianas is more thought of or have been more representative citizens than that which bears the name of Percy. A combination of English, Scottish and Irish blood—no better combination could be found—produced the men and women that have retained the high standards of the European Percys in their American way of life.

In 1776 Charles Percy, an English army officer, came to America and located in Wilkinson county near Fort Adams in Mississippi. Robert Percy, his son, who was born in Kilkenny, Ireland, became a midshipman while quite young and obtained his commission a short time before his twenty-first birthday. He served on a number of vessels, beginning on April 26th, 1783, on the armed galley Delaware, and later saw service on the Resolution, Robust, Africa, Ville-de-Paris, Victory, Powerful, Gorgon and Lord Nelson, on which he served as commander, accomplishing the great feat of convoying forty-six sailing boats from Elsineur. For this he was commended by the Right Honorable Lord Commissioner of the Admiralty. He remained commander on the Lord Nelson until December 8th, 1801, and then was granted leave of absence on half pay until September, 1804, at which time he came to America. While still a lieutenant on H. M. S. Africa, he married Miss Jane Middlemist, the ceremony being performed on Sept. 15, 1796 at St. George Church, London. Miss Middlemist was born in Edinburg, Scotland, July 16, 1772, her parents,

Thomas Middlemist and Jane Proudfoot. Of this marriage their first three children, Jane, Edward, and Margaret, were born in London. In 1794 Lieutenant Percy's father was accidently drowned, and left a large estate. His son, visiting America in 1795 to take possession of his part of the estate, was greatly impressed by the country and decided to settle in Feliciana. Under the date of 28th of September, 1802, Lieutenant Percy made application and was granted leave of absence from the Royal Navy. Chartering the Bilboa, a ship commanded by John Ruggles Soper, he made the trip to America. The record showing that the two daughters born in London accompanied their parents (the first born son supposedly not surviving infancy). On the trip also was a nephew of Mrs. Percy, an adopted daughter, and another young lady. When the vessel arrived and matters settled, Lieutenant Percy sold the vessel and left for the Felicianas where his father had located some twenty-six years previously.

Charles Percy, British Army officer and descendant of the Earl of Northumberland, held large tracts of land in the Felicianas that first had been English posssions, but shortly afterwards in 1779, the Spanish governor Don Bernado Galvez of Louisiana, defeated the English and replaced the English Jack with the Castellated banner of Spain. Charles Percy at that time was appointed an alcalde representing his district, having become a Spanish subject. At the time he left England he was a widower, but shortly after his arrival in the Feliciana country he married Susanna Collins by whom he had a number of children. However, only three of them married; they being: Sarah Percy, who became the wife of John Ellis, a native of Ellis County, Miss., who was a son of Richard Ellis, the ceremony taking place on Dec. 31, 1799, and became the parents of two children: (1) Thomas George Percy Ellis, and (2) Mary Ellis, who became Mrs. Rene de la Rcohe, wife of a Philadelphia doctor whom she met while she attended a boarding school in that city. Dr. Roche died in 1808, and she again married, this time Nathaniel A. Ware of Kentucky, on Sept. 1, 1814; issue, Eleanor Ware, and Catherine Ware.

(B) Thomas Percy, who married Maria * * * * of Huntsville, Alabama, and died in 1888. W. A. Percy, a son residing in Washington County, Miss., while being among those that opposed secession, when war was declared led his company into the thickest part of the fray, and one of his sons later became United States Senator Leroy Percy of Mississippi.

(C) Catherine Percy, who became the wife of Dr. Samuel Brown of Kentucky, Sept. 27th, 1808. Deciding to make his home in Beech Wood, Lieutenant Robert Percy soon became an important personage of the locality. Beech-Wood was a plantation of great extent and when fully cultivated was magnificent. The names of the children were as follows: Robert, Catherine, Thomas, Anna, and Charles. Like his father before him he became an alcalde under the Spanish rule—a local judge appointed by Don Carlos de Grand Pré. Soon, however, the settlers became dissatisfied with the severity of what they considered unjust rule of Governor Carlos de Hault de Lassus, who had succeeded Governor Grand Pré. Finally deciding to become a part of the United States then practically in its infancy, determined to throw off the Spanish yoke. At this time Robert Percy performed what has been termed a brilliant service in the "West Florida Rebellion". Fulwer Skipwith, Shepherd Brown, and Robert Percy were members of the First West Florida high Judiciary At the time that the English-speaking residents learned that the Spanish Governor was acting in an unjust manner with the people of West Florida, and that they too, were likely to share the same fate, Judge Percy, with the other patriots controlling responsible positions ordered the taking of the fort at Baton Rouge. General Philemon Thomas in command of the forces accomplished this order. A spirited night battle ensued in which a number of the Spanish garrison lost their lives. The emblem of West Florida, the Lone Star flag was flown from the fort, the Spanish emblem disappearing from that section of the United States forever.

Robert Percy lived nine years longer, dying on November 19, 1819, and was laid to rest in the land he had grown to love so well. His devoted wife survived him many years, dying March 12, 1831, being buried by his side.

The vivacious Eliza Pirrie of Oakley having eloped with her handsome wealthy cousin Robert H. Barrow of Greenwood plantation, Audubon and his faithful wife were without their pupil. It was then 1823 that the widow of Robert Percy, who had continued with the plantation after her husband's death, having an immense plantation, mostly cotton, welcomed to Beech Wood Lucy Blakewell Audubon, the faithful wife of the naturalist where this charming lady became the tutor of the Percy girls, as well as to other daughters of the planters of the vicinity. Her school on this plantation became a celebrated one, and grand children of today refer with pride to the old school their grandmothers attended so long ago. Audubon sketched here as at Oakley, making his plates for "Birds of America". It is told that in the vicinity of "Sleepy Hollow Woods" this area that the artist with the aid of Robert Dow Percy, then in his twentieth year caught the monster wild turkey cock that is known as his most noted painting of birds.

Lieutenant Robert Percy's children were (Jane Middlemist issue): (1) Jane Letitia Cowan Percy, born in London, August 19, 1797, and died in New Orleans, Jan. 5, 1877. She became the wife of James C. Williams of Natchez, Miss., stepson of Winthrop Sargent, on Feb. 5, 1814. Winthrop Sargent was the first governor of the Mississippi Territory A daughter, Mary Jane Williams, married Seargent S. Prentiss, noted Mississippi statesman, and a grand son of George Kennedy Prentiss of New Orleans. (2) Edward Powell Percy, born in London, Aug. 19, 1797, died in infancy. (3) Margaret Jessie Isabella Percy, born in London, July 5th, 1799, died in Paris, France, July 10th, 1865, was married on Dec. 7, 1824, to Geo. Washington Sargent, son of Gov. Sargent and half brother of James C. Williams. (4) Robert Dow Percy, born Aug. 28th in Louisiana, married July 19, 1831 Ellen H. Davis of Wilkinson County, Miss; his home was on Weyanoke plantation, West Feliciana. Three of his sons, Dr. Robert Percy, Dr. Harry Percy and Thomas Percy, served with honor in the Confederate Army during the Civil War. (5) Thomas Butler Percy, born Sept. 29th, ——, married 4th of June, 1833, Mrs. Elizabeth Leatherbury Randolph, widow of Judge Peter Randolph.

Dr. Thos. B. Percy and Mrs. Percy resided at Beech Wood plantation. Their five sons fought in the Confederate Army. Thomas B. Percy, Jr., Clarence Percy, Dr. James Rowan Percy, William Chaille Percy, and Robert Sargent Percy. Thomas B. Percy, Jr., died of typhoid fever, Clarence Percy served the entire four years, first two in the Army of Virginia, and took part in two battles of Manassas. (7) Anna Christiana Percy, born in in Louisiana, Nov. 16, 1812, married Sept. 13, 1832, Dr. Addison Dashiell of Maryland. She died October 20, 1877. (8) Charles Evans Percy, born Oct. 20, 1815, married three times, first on 5th of January, 1843, to Mary E. Rowan, issue a son; second on 18th of November, 1847, to Mary H. Doherty of West Feliciana, issue four children; third, to his second wife's sister, Catherine B. Doherty, issue nine children. His oldest son, Charles E. Percy, Jr., by Mary Rowan, was killed in the battle of Atlanta.

Accompanying Lieutenant Percy and his family to America was Charles J. H. Middlemist, a nephew of Mrs. Percy, who married Ann Tuell, a daughter of Samuel Tuell, March 20, 1817. C. J. H. Middlemist died in 1827, and left two children, Jane and John Byron Middlemist, the daughter died in childhood. Ann Tuell Middlemist, a widow married Albert F. McCall of Rapides Parish. At the time that John Byron Middlemist reached manhood in 1848, family records show that his father's estate was turned over to him by Charles Evans Percy, his tutor.

* * * * *

Clarence Percy, born Feb. 1st, 1836, died Feb. 22nd, 1909, married Anne Mathilde Hereford, born Feb. 3rd, 1836, died July 2nd, 1909; issue: (1) Catherine Sarah Percy, who was born in Pointe Coupee Parish on North-Bend plantation, Nov. 21st, 1866. (2) Clarence Percy, born in West Feliciana Parish, on Retreat plantation, Feb. 25th, 1868. (3) John Bronaugh Hereford Percy, born in West Feliciana Parish on Stirling Plantation, Feb. 2nd, 1870. The next two children, twins: (4) William Richard Percy, (5) Robert Ryland Percy—born in West Feliciana Parish on Bush Hill plantation, Aug. 8th, 1874. (a) Catherine Sarah Percy was married on the 28th of August, 1895, to Mathew Gilmore, of West Feliciana Parish. (b) Clarence Percy, married Mathilde D'Armond of Clinton, La., Dec. 27th, 1906, issue one son, Rhea D'Armond Percy. (c) John Bronaugh Hereford Percy, married Christina Dashiel Howell, daughter of Charles Johnson Howell and Jane Percy Dashiell on the 14th of August, 1893. (d) William Richard Percy, married Mary Maud Stirling, who died 21st of November, 1918, in Minden, La.; issue, Nanine Stirling Percy and John Hereford Percy. (e) Robert Ryland Percy—1st wife was Frances Eugenia McGhee of West Feliciana Parish—two children by this marriage: John Edward Percy and Eugenia Corinne Percy. His second wife was Katherin Roark of West Feliciana Parish, Louisiana. Their sons are Robert Ryland Percy, Jr., and William Conner Percy.

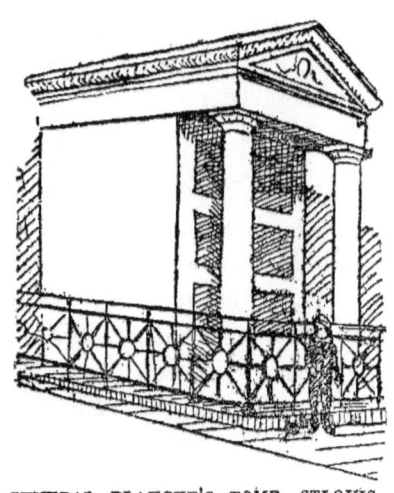

GENERAL PLAUCHE'S TOMB. STLOUIS. CEMETERY.

CHAPTER XIII.

THE PLAUCHÉ FAMILY

PLAUCHE' (PLOCHE') (PLAU) (PLO), ETC.

THE Plauché family of patrician origin has been one that has carried on the name with credit since coming to America. It is a tree with many branches, stemming to France, England, Germany, and many other parts of the globe—with a goodly number among the representative citizens of Louisiana.

The notes which have been furnished me by a prominent member of the family are as follows:

(Exact copy of page 274, paragraph 5, the second edition):
"So You're Going to Germany", Clara E. Laughin, author, says; . . . . . take the main road to Ulm via Esslingen, and south to Kirchheim-unter-Teck. Crowned with the ruins of the ancient castle of the Dukes of Teck. The Dukedom had for a long time been swallowed up in Wuttemberg, when King William of Wuttemberg conferred the title upon his grandson, Francis, who was married to a daughter of the Duke of Cambridge, George III's seventh son. Queen Mary, consort of George V, is a child of this union. (Coburg is where King George's grandfather came from . . .)"This location in Germany of the town or village of

General Jean Baptiste Plauché in full dress uniform, U. S. Army, 1812. (From a drawing given the author by Hon Chas. Gayarré and presented by him to the Louisiana Historical Society.)

Portrait of Mary Barrow, painted by Thomas Sully. (Courtesy of Mrs. Mary Barrow Collins.)

Portrait of Robert Hilliard Barrow II, by Thomas Sully. (Companion picture.)

Plochingen, is between the Rhine and the Black Forest, beyond the Vosge Mts. (see map, same book and literary page). Facts listed in Hof Kalendar Gotha 1907: resident in Prussia is a family of Plau, Graffin (Count and Countess).

> The data following is fact gathered from Personal Memoirs of the late Henry Plauche Dart, prominent lawyer and historian: From the diary of his father, Henry Dart of England, a naturalized American; from his father-in-law's own entry in the Family Bible, Jacques Urbain Plauche (Ploche); from the statements of the aforesaid Henry P. Dart's maternal great-great grandparents, namely: Etienne Henry Plauche (Ploche) and Marguerite Zelam (Selamme) (Selam) in their last wills and testaments, sworn to before a notary public; from the White Registry of the Archives of Baptism, Marriage, and Death records of the St. Louis Cathedral, previously the Church of St. Louis of New Orleans, La., and an exact copy thereof sworn to and attested by the Seal of the Roman Catholic Church of New Orleans, La.; and the White Registry of the Birth, Marriage, and Death Records of the Roman Catholic Church of St. Patrick, of New Orleans, La., with an exact copy thereof sworn to and attested by the Seal of the Roman Catholic Church of St. Patrick, of New Orleans, La., all testamentary evidences not to be contraverted.

From the aforesaid last wills and testaments, I include herewith further family data, of the Sieur Etienne Henry Plauché (Ploché and Dame Margueritte Zélam (Sélamme-Selam), his wife, concerning their children of their lawful marriage:

Joseph Alexandre Plauché, died 1823; married Eugénie Bougéat, Pointe Coupeé, La.; issue: children; domiciled Avoyelles Parish, La.

Jean Baptiste Plauché, died 1858, married Miss Mathilde St. Amant of St. Charles Parish, issue six sons, one daughter; domicile, New Orleans.

Jacques Urbain Plauché, born May 25, 1787, New Orleans, married July 9, 1809, Miss Molly Brown of Red River Parish, daughter of William Brown and Daisy White, of Kentucky, domicile first in Rapides Parish, then in New Orleans; issue, six children, three sons, three daughters, namely: Stephen; William; Zelam;

Euphémie; Mary; Marguerite; (Mary married Henry Dart of Devonshire, England, June 22, 1841, issue: ten children, namely: four sons, six daughters, of these living to maturity were one son, Henry P. Dart, and three of the daughters, namely: Agnes Martha, Frances Isabella, and Mary Emily. All married and have children).

Marie Magdelaine Plauché, married Jean Jacques Chessé; domicile in New Orleans, La.

Margueritte Melanie Plauché, married Jean Vital Michel, domicile in New Orleans; descendants.

Louisa Margueritte Plauché, married François Chessé, domicile, New Orleans.

André Plauché, married, domicile, Pointe Coupeé Parish. A descendant (Male) of the Plauché men went to New York City to live.

Marie Victoire Plauché, domicile, New Orleans.

The residence, where Etienne Plauché died and where his lawful wife, Margueritte Sélam (Zélam) (Selaume) made her last will and testament before a notary public is in existence (in 1941); it is located at No. 619 Bourbon Street, New Orleans, an attractive two-story and attic brick building. Their children were people of wealth and social prominence during their lifetime. Then came the Civil War, with its devastation and destruction.

General Jean Baptiste Plauché ranks high in the military annals of the State of Louisiana. It was he who commanded that famous contingent of valiant Creoles known as the "Famous Battalion d'Orleans" at the Battle of New Orleans, when Jean Baptiste Plauché held the rank of major. This body of brave Creoles, learning of the arrival of the English, ran all of the way from the Fort (Spanish Fort) at the head of Bayou St. John to New Orleans, fighting many encounters with the Red Coats and acquitting themselves with honor. After the cessation of hostilities Jean Baptiste rose to be colonel of the famous Louisiana Legion, later becoming its first brigadier general. He was lieutenant-governor of the State of Louisiana in 1850. After an honorable career as distinguished soldier, officer of the state and prominent citizen— at the age of seventy-five years he died. He was mourned by a large circle of friends and was buried with full military honors.

Barrow Coat-of-Arms.

Chapter XIV.

THE BARROW DYNASTY IN LOUISIANA

WILLIAM BARROW, SR.

THE main trunk from which a great number of the Louisiana Barrows' stem is centered in the one from which William Barrow, Sr., descends. William Barrow, Sr., however, is the starting point of most of the Louisiana trees.

We learn that he was a cultured gentleman who lived in Edgecomb County in the Northern part of Carolina, where he had been a prominent citizen, taking an active interest in the affairs of the community. He had been high sheriff, an appointee of the governor of the state, more of an honorary position than a monetary one. It was a position of quite some importance, in early colonial days. Family records of the Barrows show that he was physically disabled, which accounts for the lack of a military record of that period. However, he did his part in other ways, as he was an ardent patriot. In July, 1760, he was married to Olivia Ruffin, daughter of Robert Ruffin and Ann Bennett. They became the parents of nine children, six sons and three daughters. William Barrow, Sr., died at his homestead near Enfield in the Northern part of Carolina, in Halifax County, on Jan. 27th, 1787, and is supposed to have been buried there.

The children of William Barrow, Sr. and Olivia Ruffin were: 1st, William Barrow, Jr., born Nov. 29th, 1761, died Nov. 27th, 1762; 2nd, Robert Barrow, born Feb. 18th, 1763, died May 29th, 1815. He married Mary Haynes, and was probably buried on Highlands plantation. 3rd, William Barrow, Jr. (second of that name), born Feb. 26th, 1765, died Nov. 9th, 1823. He married Pheraby Hilliard in North Carolina on June 26th, 1792. She was born Feb. 11th, 1775, died Oct. 10th, 1827. Both are buried in the cemetery of Highland plantation. William Barrow, Jr., died in Washington, D. C., where he had gone to place his youngest son in school, his body was later brought back to Highland plantation by his son, and interred in the family plot. 4th, Bartholomew Barrow, born Oct. 16th, 1766, died Feb. 15th, 1852. His first wife was Elizabeth Slatter, who died in North Carolina; his second wife was Beththier Brantly, born 1777, and died in 1843. Bartholomew was one of the sons that remained in Carolina, and later came to Feliciana in 1820. He settled on the plantation that was to be renamed Afton Villa, where both he and his second wife are buried in the family plot of that plantation. 5th, Ann Barrow, born Sept. 11th, 1768. 6th, Mary Barrow, born May 16th, —. She became the wife of William or David Lane. 7th, Sarah Barrow, born April 14th, 1773. She married John Dawson and became the parents of General Bennet Dawson, born in Nashville, Tenn. 8th, Ruffin Barrow, born April 9th, 1775, died Dec. 16th, 1799. 9th, Bennett Barrow, born June 22nd, 1777, died July 22nd, 1833. He married Martha Hill. He evidently was a banker in Halifax, North Carolina, for in the record of the sale of a lot there is a clause excepting "a large vault to the bank". It was he who remained in North Carolina with his brother, coming to Feliciana in 1816 where he located on Rosebank plantation across Little Bayou Sara from his brother's home (William Barrow, Jr.). He is buried with Martha Hill, and many of his decendants on Rosebank plantation, but no tombstone mark their resting places, the wooden headboards disappearing long ago.

Rosebank manor is of the Spanish type of architecture, having brick paved floors, and large pillars surrounding the wide gallery enclosed by iron railings. It is a quaintly beautiful old place surrounded by a garden planted by the girl wife of one of the sons of Bennett Barrow. In olden days according to the history of the place it was the gathering spot, as well as scene of many great social events of that era. The children of William Barrow, Jr. and Pheraby Hilliard, the owners of beautiful Greenwood plantation manor: 1st, Robert Hilliard Barrow, born Feb. 7th, 1795, died July 21st, 1823. He was buried on Highland plantation. He married Eliza Pirrie, born Oct. 6th, 1805, died April 20th, 1851. She was a daughter of James Pirrie and Lucretia Alston.

Robert Hilliard Barrow's plantation home was on Prospect plantation. He represented the County of Feliciana in the Louisiana Legislature during the years 1820-1822. He died of pneumonia resulting from the wetting he got when crossing the Homochito Bayou while eloping with the beautiful Eliza Pirrie. He died before the birth of his son, Robert Hilliard Barrow, Jr., who was born March 27th, 1824, who also was in the legislature representing West Feliciana in 1856. It was he who organized and equipped the Rosale Guards and was elected the first captain of that company. Later when the company was mustered into the 11th Louisiana Regiment he was made lieutenant-colonel of the regiment and afterwards promoted to colonel, succeeding Col. I. N. Marks of New Orleans. 2nd, Ann (Nancy) Ruffin Barrow, born Sept. 17th, 1795, died 1856. She became the wife of John Benoist, and they had one child, Rosina E. Benoist, who became the wife of Herman Groesbeck. 3rd, William Ruffin Barrow. 4th, Bennett Barrow, born Dec. 23rd, 1803. 5th, Martha Hilliard Barrow, born Sept. 11th, 1809, died Sept., 1899. She married Daniel Turnbull, born June 5th, 1796, died Oct. 30th, 1861.

They had three children: Sarah Turnbull, who married Lieutenant James Pirrie Bowman, son of David Bowman, born Sept. 15th, 1805, died Feb. 9th, 1874. He married first in 1823 Sarah Hatch, of North Carolina, born Feb. 27th, 1808, and died Jan. 9th, 1846. She was a daughter of Charles Hatch and Mary (Polly) Mosely. They were the parents of Bartholomew Barrow, who married Martha Semple; Mary Eliza Barrow, born in 1825, died 1920, who married Col. Robert Hilliard Barrow II, and six other children, who died young.

David Barrow, born Sept. 15th, 1805, died Feb. 9th, 1874, had remained behind in the old homestead in North Carolina, came to Louisiana in 1830 with his wife and young children, purchasing a plantation on the Pinkneyville Road, in West Feliciana Parish, where they remained for a period of two years, when selling this place he returned to his old North Carolina home where he remained until 1836, when he moved to the large cotton plantation which he bought near Tallahassee, Florida. Not liking the Florida climate which was affecting his wife's health, sold the place, and in a few years returning again to Louisiana. On Jan. 9th, 1839, he bought from his father the plantation with the six-room house which later on was to be enlarged into the present French Gothic Villa now known as Afton Villa.

After the death of his first wife, and the marriage of his daughter Mary, he had the present Gothic structure built, retaining the original six-room house in the plan, as a home for his second wife. David Barrow's second wife was Mrs. Susan Ann Woolfolk, born 1820, widow of a Mr. Rowan, and daughter of Col. Joseph Harris Woolfolk and Martha Mitchum. The original smaller Afton house was given its name because David's beautiful daughter Mary sang the Scotch ballad so sweetly, and so often her throng of admirers named her home "Afton Villa" after the refrain "Flow Gently Sweet Afton". David Barrow is buried beside his first wife in the little cemetery of Afton Villa plantation.

The children of David Barrow by his second wife, were three sons and one daughter, two of the sons dying young. The daughter, Florence Roberta Barrow, born Florence, Mass., July 24th, 1856, married Maximillian Fisher, born 1844, died 1906, son of Frederick Fisher and Catherine Clauss, their home first was at Bayou Sara and later they removed to Kenmore plantation. Their other son, David Barrow, born at Afton Villa, Aug. 31st, 1858, died Aug. 1932, located in Lexington, Ky., in 1887, where he became an eminent physician, and distinguished surgeon. He had the distinction of being the only surgeon in Kentucky that was a senior fellow of the American Surgical Association. He married Mary Blount Parham and they became the parents of six children.

The six children of Mary Barrow and William or David Lane, are as follows: (a) William Lane, Jr., died without issue. (b) Ann Lane, married Frank Routh, issue two children. (c) Olivia Ruffin Lane, married first time to William Ratliff, and had two children. Her second husband was William Wade, and they became the parents of four children. Jointly Olivia Ruffin Lane and William Wade built "handsome Ellerslie" plantation manor, now owned by Mr. and Mrs. Edward Percy, who purchased it from Joseph J. Wade, a descendant of the builders.

The seven children of Sarah Barrow and John Dawson are as follows: 1st, John Bennett Dawson, born 1800, died 1845, married Margaret Johnson. A large portrait of him in uniform hangs in the courthouse of St. Francisville, La. Children of Bennett Barrow and Martha Hill: Olivia Ruffin Barrow, who married William Ruffin Barrow, son of William Barrow, Jr., and Pheraby Hilliard. William Hill Barrow married Eliza Eleanor Barrow, daughter of William Barrow, Jr., and Pheraby Hilliard, issue nine children. Margaret Barrow died young. Bennett James Barrow, born 1811, died 1878. He married Caroline Hall and they became the parents of nine children. Robert James Barrow, born Oct. 5th, 1817, died Dec. 16th, 1887, married Mary Eleanor Crabb, daughter of Judge Henry Crabb and Jane Ann Barrow of Tenn., on July 11th, 1839; issue eight children. She was born March 23rd, 1822, died Feb. 20th, 1897. Robert James Barrow was a general in the Confederate Army.

United States Senator Alexander Barrow.

His birth being on March 27th, 1801, near Nashville, Tenn. He was the son of Wylie Macajah Barrow, often spelled Willie Barrow, and his first wife's name was Jane Grier, often seen written Jane Green.

Wylie Macajah Barrow, father of Alexander Barrow, came to Tennessee from Carolina, having emigrated when a young man 25 years of age, from the Northern part of Carolina. He became a successful and prominent planter, and an influential citizen of his adopted state. He was born on July 24th, 1770, and his death occurred on June 7th, 1825. His first wife, Jane Grier of Kentucky, who it is said had relatives in Covington, Kentucky. A daughter was born in Virginia, where Jane Grier died at the time of her child's birth. Later Wylie Macajah Barrow married Anna H. Beck, whose birth was July 27th, 1789, and death occurred Aug. 8th, 1831. Both Wylie Macajah Barrow and his second wife are buried near Nashville, Tenn., in adjoining graves. The children of Wylie Macajah Barrow and Jane Grier are three in number. Alexander Barrow, David Barrow, and Jane Ann Barrow. By his second marriage Wylie Macajah Barrow and Ann H. Beck became the parents of four children. George Washington Barrow; Wylie Macajah Barrow; Albert G. Barrow; and John E. Barrow. Alexander Barrow chose for his wife Mary Ann Barrow, a sister of David Barrow (of Afton Villa) who was a daughter of Bartholomew Barrow, who was born in 1766, and died in 1852, and his second wife Berthier Brantly (1777-1843), who came to Louisiana in 1820 from the Northern part of Carolina.

Alexander Barrow by his marriage to Mary Ann Barrow became the father of three children: Alexander Barrow II; Wylie Macajah Barrow, and Jane Barrow. Alexander Barrow II married Effie Cockerell, and they became the parents of one son, Alexander Barrow III. Wylie Macajah Barrow married Martha Pitcher; issue three children. Merritt Barrow, Nanine Barrow, and Ratliff Barrow. Jane Barrow married Thomas G. Sparks, and they became the parents of the following children: Wylie Sparks; Isabelle Sparks; Thomas Sparks; Mary Eleanor Sparks; Effie Sparks; Jane Sparks; Lise Sparks, and Lou Gale Sparks. Alexander also had many great grand children.

A brother of Alexander Barrow, David Barrow by name, married and became the father of a son named David Barrow, and a grandson David N. Barrow II, whose home is in Plaquemines, La. A sister of Alexander Barrow became the wife of Henry Crabb, a Judge of the Supreme Court of Tennessee. (Jane Ann Barrow) and Judge Crabb were the parents of three children: Henry Alexander Crabb, Jane Ann Crabb, and Mary Eleanor Crabb. Mary Eleanor Crabb became the wife of Robert James Barrow I, of Rosebank plantation, West Feliciana Parish, Louisiana. Their son Robert James Barrow II became the husband of Sarah Louise Barrow, who was a daughter of Col. Robert Hilliard Barrow, and Mary Eliza Barrow, who was a daughter of David Barrow of Afton Villa, whose sister, Mary Ann Barrow was the wife of Honorable Alexander Barrow. Honorable Alexander Barrow had four half-brothers, whose names are as follows: George Washington Barrow, born 1817, died 1866, who became U. S. Minister to Portugal 1841-1844.

Wylie Micajah Barrow, born 1810, died 1853, married Cordelia Johnson Barrow, born 1845, died 1924, who married for the second time Maratha Robertson; from this marriage was born Honorable Micajah Barrow (1874-1934) of Baton Rouge, La. John E. Barrow, Indian Agent at St. Joseph, Mo., between there and Salt Lake City, and who later went to New York City and

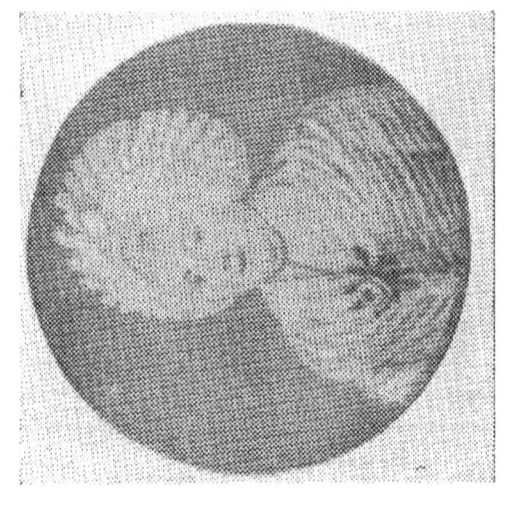

Marie Francoise Durand, daughter of Jean Baptiste Durand and Catherine Arnoux; married Marius Pons Bringier; died at White Hall Plantation in 1803. (Pictures courtesy of Trist Wood.)

Marius Pons Bringier, builder of White Hall (Maison Blanche). The first Bringier to settle in Louisiana.

became quite wealthy. Albert G. Barrow, who married a Miss Marie J. Swift, the ceremony performed by the Rev. J. L. Mullon of St. Patrick's Church of New Orleans on Jan. 11th, 1833, Albert Barrow dying on Jan. 25th, 1842, leaving a wife and son, Bennett H. Barrow, who later in life settled in Southern Louisiana where he married and raised a family.

ANCESTORS OF CORDILIUS JOHNSON BARROW.

Wylie Micajah Barrow, married Ann Eliza Beck, 2nd wife; children: Albert Gallitin, Wylie Micajah, George Washington, John E., Jane Douglas.

Wylie Micajah Barrow married Cordelia Johnson. Issue: (1) Alexander Douglas Barrow; (2) Wylie Micajah Barrow; (3) Ann Eliza Barrow; (4) Cordelius Johnson Barrow.

Cordelius Johnson Barrow married Martha Johnson Robertson, daughter of Edward White Robertson and Mary Jane Pope. Issue: Leita Mattie Barrow, Wylie Micajah Barrow, Mary Jane Barrow, Edward Robertson Barrow, Martha Johnson Barrow, Cordelius Johnson Barrow, (died in infancy).

Leila Mattie Barrow married John Robert Mays. Children: John Robert Barrow, Daisy Lavina Barrow.

John Robert Barrow married Kate Carothers Perkins. Children: Kate Perkins Barrow, Caroline Barrow, John Robert Barrow III.

Daisy Lavina Barrow married William Prentis Obier. Children: Leila May Obier, William Prentis Obier II. Mr. J. R. Mays is the son of Samuel Mays and Caroline Hill, his birthplace being Warpeth, Tenn.—Mr. Mays coming to Louisiana in 1890 and engaging in the cotton business in which he continued for eighteen years.

This branch of the Barrow family were a part of the Colony of Nashville, Tenn.—instrumental in its founding.

Bartholomew Barrow married Elizabeth Slatter, and became the parents of Volumnia Roberta Barrow, and Robert Ruffin Barrow, who married Jennie Lodiska Tennent. Their children are: 1st, Volumnia Hunley Barrow, who died early. 2nd, Irene Felicite Barrow, not married. 3rd, Robert Ruffin Barrow, died. 4th, Zoe Gayoso Barrow, who married Dr. Robert Samuel Topping. 5th, Jennie Tennent Barrow, who married Dr. H. P. Dawson of Montgomery, Ala. 6th, Hallette Mary Barrow, wife of Christian

Greene Cole. Jennie Lodiska Tennent, who married Robert Ruffin Barrow, is the daughter of Charles Tennent, and Felicité de Beauregard Gayoso, Felicité de Beauregard Gayoso was the daughter of Lodoviska Victoria, (Cecelia) Perez, who was a daughter of Jacques Toutant de Beauregard, and wife of Emanuel Zirill Perez.

GREENWOOD

West Feliciana.

The charm of Greenwood Plantation Manor consisting of its magnificent setting, its immense size, which dwarfs one when standing close by, and the beauty of its architecture and splendid interior. The interior plan is similar to most of the finer mansions of the South, with a grand stairway with easy sweep. There are two immense rooms on each side with a similar planning on the floor above. The furnishings, like those of the original owners, are very fine and in splendid taste. Above the fine woodwork of the windows are handsome cornices crowning the splendid draperies. The gold leaf ornamentation above the Irish Point lace-curtains of the immense drawing-rooms add greatly to the furnishings of the rooms.

In these rooms the oyster-white walls and fine door frames form an ideal setting for the rosewood furniture of solid wood with handsome fire gilt mounts, all of the Louis XV period, and Aubusson tapestry covering with Watteau designs of medallions, cupids and festoons, and wreaths of flowers, all in soft tones on a delicate greenish background. All of the other furnishings of the rooms in keeping with the elegance of these articles.

In the dining-room are other priceless curtains of finest Belgian lace over a century old, and of beautiful design. This banquet room, and as such is the record of this stately chamber, contains elegant hand-carved antique furniture of English make with gorgeous designs of fruit and birds, with a full set of chairs of matched ornamentation, all high backed, making indeed an imposing ensemble. Among the treasures of this home is an unusual as well as immense silver venison dish from Scotland, taken to America by the Fisher family, a Scotch branch of the English family of that name. This venison dish is two centuries old. This Fisher family also brought over much of the other furnishings of Greenwood Manor.

BRINGIER ARMS

The above was copied in 1884 from an engraving. Arms in possession of Marius Ste. Colombe Bringier, "Houmas" and New Orleans, who had the arms from his great uncle in France, the Canon J. B. Hippolyte Bringier (born 1757). It is interesting to note that similar arms are borne by the English families of Beringer, Berenger and Boranger—offshoots in earlier times of the parent stock in France. (Arms and data courtesy of Trist Wood).

CHAPTER XV.

THE BRINGIER—KENNER—DU BOURG—BRENT
TRIST—WOOD—STAUFFER FAMILIES

BRINGIER

IGNACE BRINGIER, a judge in the district of Limagne, Department Puy-de-Dôme, France, was the father of Jean Bringier, related to the Count de Rochebriant. Jean was the father of Pierre Bringier, whose wife was Marie Doradou, a member of the family of Baron Doradou d'Auvergne. This Pierre Bringier had his home at Lacadière near Aubagne, and became the father of Emanuel Marius Pons Bringier, born Oct. 27th, 1752, who moved to Louisiana, and owned White Hall Plantation in St. James Parish. He died April 21st, 1820. His wife was Marie Francoise Durand.

Their children were: 1st, Louis Bringier, born Aug. 25th, 1784, in the Tchoupitoulas District, La., and known as Don Louis; he was Surveyor-General of Louisiana; died in New Orleans, La., Oct. 29th, 1860. 2nd, Françoise (Fanny), the eldest daughter, was born at White Hall Plantation, March 9th, 1786, died May 10, 1827; in 1811 she married Christophe Colomb, a native of Corbeille, near Paris, France. 3rd, Louise Elizabeth, born at White Hall Plantation, April 21st, 1788, died Nov. 23rd, 1863; she married Judge Augustin Dominique Tureaud. 4th, Michel Doradou Bringier, born at sea Dec. 6th, 1789, of whom later. 5th, François Laure, born at White Hall Plantation, July 23rd, 1792, married Noël Auguste Baron, a native of Caen, Normandy, France. 6th, Elizabeth Mélanie, born August 16th, 1793, married first, William Simpson, and second, James Fisher Wilson.

The 4th child, mentioned above, Michel Doradou Bringier, born at sea Dec. 6th, 1789, died March 13th, 1847. He married in Baltimore, Md., June 17th, 1812, Louise Elizabeth Aglaé Du Bourg de Ste. Colombe, a daughter of the Chevalier Pierre François Du Bourg, Sieur de Ste. Colombe, and Elizabeth Etiennette Bonne Charest, daughter of François Charest de Lauzon, and granddaughter of Etienne Charest, last Seigneur de Lauzon.

Madame Michel Doradou Bringier, died at her New Orleans home, a plantation type of residence, called Melpomène, thirty-one years after the death of her husband, on June 8th, 1878. Their children were as follows:

(1st) Marius St. Colombe Bringier, known as "M S", born at White Hall Plantation, Oct. 17th, 1814, died in New Orleans, Aug. 22nd, 1884. He married his cousin, Augustine Tureaud, daughter of Augustin D. Tureaud, and Elizabeth (Betzy) Bringier, and they were the parents of five children:

(I) Louise Bringier, who became the second wife of Dr. James de Berty Trudeau; (II), Augustine Bringier, who died in childhood; (III), Félicie Bringier, died unmarried; (IV), Marius Ste. Colombe Bringier, also died unmarried; (V), Eda Bringier, who became Mrs. Holmes Thomas, of Baltimore.

(2nd) Marie Elizabeth Rosella Bringier, who was born at the Hermitage Plantation on June 24th, 1818, died on the same plantation July 20th, 1849, married General Hore Browse Trist of Bowden Plantation, Ascension Parish, La., who was born in Washington, D. C. on March 19th, 1802. (Both General Trist and his elder brother, Nicholas Philip Trist, were the wards of Thomas Jefferson, and were reared at Monticello; later Nicholas Trist became the husband of Miss Virginia Randolph, a daughter of Governor Mann Randolph of Virginia, and a granddaughter of Thomas Jefferson.) Hore Browse Trist was Commander-in-chief of the State troops of Louisiana. He died Nov. 16th, 1856.

Their children were: (I), Nicholas Browse Trist of Totness Plantation, located on the Atchafalaya River, who married his cousin, Augustine Gordon; (II), Julien Bringier Trist, like his brother, N. Browse, was educated at Stuttgart, Germany (at that time considered one of the finest universities in the world); was killed in the Battle of Murfreesboro; (III), Wilhelmine Trist, married Colonel Robert C. Wood, son of Brigadier General R. C. Wood, assistant surgeon general U.S.A., and Ann Taylor, daughter of President Zachary Taylor. Colonel Robert C. Wood commanded Wood's Cavalry of the Confederate Army in the Civil War. (IV), Rosella Trist, died in childhood. (V), Nicolas Philip Trist, who was a lieutenant in the Confederate Army. He was married twice, his first wife being a cousin, Marie Tureaud, his second wife being her sister, Alice Tureaud.

(3rd) Louise Françoise Bringier, who was born in New Orleans on Oct. 6th, 1820, and who became the wife of Martin Gordon, she dying on Nov. 13th, 1889. Their children being as follows: (I), Aglaé Gordon, who was the wife of Guichard Bienvenu; (II), Anna Gordon, who did not marry; (III), Augustine Gordon, who married her cousin, Nicholas Browse Trist; (IV), Martin Gordon, Jr.; (V), Bianca Gordon, who died in early womanhood; (VI), Loutie Gordon, who became the wife of Dr. P. S. O'Reilly of St. Louis, Mo.; (VII), Wilhelmine Gordon, unmarried.

(4th) Anne Guillelmine Nanine Bringier, who was born at the Hermitage on Aug. 24th, 1823, and died in New Orleans on Nov. 6th, 1911, married Duncan Farrar Kenner, of Ashland Plantation, their children being: (I), Duncan Farrar Kenner, who died in childhood; (II), Blanche Kenner, who married Samuel Simpson; (III), Rosella Kenner, who married General Joseph Lancaster Brent; (IV), George Kenner, who died unmarried.

(5th) Louis Amédée Bringier, born Feb. 4th, 1828, died in Florida, where he later had become a sugar planter, Jan. 9th, 1897. Before going to Florida he resided at the Hermitage Plantation in Ascension Parish, La.; a colonel of Cavalry in the Confederate Army. His wife was a cousin, Stella Tureaud, their children being: (I), Louis Amédée Bringier, Jr., whose wife was Ella Threlkeld (Veuve Hobbs); (II), Alice Bringier, who married Thomas McCormick; (III), Louise Bringier, who became Mrs. William C. Bateman; (IV), Julien Trist Bringier, M.D., whose wife was Mary Cuthbert Jones; their Plantation Tezcuco in Ascension Parish, La. (Their children are: Suzanne Bringier, who married Logan McConnell and Miss Trista Bringier.) (V), Stella Bringier, who married Robert Thach of Birmingham, Ala. (VI), Nicholas Browse Trist Bringier, unmarried; (VII), Mather Du Bourg Bringier, his first wife being Jennie E. McGalliard, his second wife, Helen Jane Mills.

(6th) Marie Elizabeth Aglaé Bringier, born Jan. 17, 1830, married her cousin Benjamin Louis Michel Tureaud, of Tezcuco Plantation. Their children being: (I), Aglaé Tureaud, who married first, William Brooks, and secondly, George Parks; (II), Benjamin Tureaud; (III), Henri Tureaud—both of whom remained bachelors.

(7th) Louise Marie Myrthé Bringier, born Jan. 28, 1834, died at the Bringier home Melpomène, New Orleans, La., on March 16th, 1875, was the wife of Lieutenant-General Richard (Dick) Taylor of Fashion Plantation, in St. Charles Parish, La. Their children: (I), Louise Margaret Taylor, who did not marry. (II), Betty M. Taylor, who became Mrs. Walter R. Stauffer. (III), Zachary Taylor, who died in childhood. (IV), Richard Taylor, who also died in childhood. (V), Myrthé Bianca Taylor, who married Isaac Hull Stauffer.

(8th) Ann Octavie Marie Bringier, born at the Hermitage Plantation, Jan. 1st, 1839, died in New Orleans on Nov 20th, 1917, was the wife of General Allen Thomas of New Dalton and New Hope Plantations, a brigadier-general in the Confederate Army, and U. S. Minister to Venezuela. Their children: (I), Allen Thomas, who married a cousin, Marie Sauvé, (II), Julien Bringier Trist Thomas, who married Mary Agnes Saal; (III), John Ridgeley Thomas, unmarried; (IV), Dall Thomas, whose first wife was Elma Bergeron, his second wife being Louise Moret.

(9) Martin Doradou Bringier, born August 3rd, 1842; a lieutenant and aide-de-camp in the army of the Confederacy, who did not marry.

HONORABLE DUNCAN FARRAR KENNER

Honorable Duncan Farrar Kenner, youngest son of William Butler Kenner and Mary Minor Kenner, was born in New Orleans at the family home in Bienville Street near Exchange Alley on the 11th of February, 1813. He was tutored privately and later attended the schools of New Orleans. He then attended Miami College at Oxford, Ohio, graduating in 1831 at the age of eighteen years, with the degree of Bachelor of Arts. He went to Europe to finish his education. He remained in England and in France for four years where he learned to speak French fluently, a necessity in New Orleans at that time. John Slidell, an able Louisiana attorney and friend of young Kenner's father, took the young man into his office that he might learn enough law to enable him to assume the responsibilities of any political office that he might seek or be appointed to. Later this experience was to be of great help to him as he became one of the most brilliant men of his day —statesman, planter, lawyer and diplomat. His interest in the Ashland Plantation which he owned with his brother in Ascension Parish demanded his attention, so after being in Mr. Slidell's office for some time, he reluctantly left the office to live upon the plantation.

Later he bought his brother's share in Ashland which gave him a free hand in its management. His knowledge of the sugar industry and his ability as an administrator soon made Ashland an outstanding plantation, and when he purchased other plantations adjoining his land, such as the Bringier holdings, Ashland soon was ranked among the great sugar plantations of Louisiana.

Duncan Kenner from the age of twenty-five years represented Ascension Parish in the Legislature, being one of its youngest members. His keenness and abilty as an administrator was at once recognized. His ability as a convincing speaker combined with his unquestioned good judgment won listeners to his way of thinking. On many occasions he had the opportunity to display his skill in diplomatic matters. From the time he settled on the plantation until 1861, when one no longer doubted that the South would secede, Duncan Kenner ardently supported the Southern cause. He devoted his time and wealth to it, and when the State Assembly adopted the Secession resolutions, he became one of the seven Louisiana delegates to the Provisional Congress at Montgomery which met on Feb. 4th, 1861.

Kenner was a strong supporter of President Jefferson Davis and throughout the duration of the Confederate Congress was one of its most active and prominent members. When the capital was removed to Richmond, Duncan Kenner continued to represent Louisiana. Judah P. Benjamin and Duncan Kenner "messed" together as they called it, and when Benjamin saw the crisis in the Confederacy approaching he used his influence to have Kenner sent to England and France in a last attempt to obtain recognition of the Confederate government.

According to his grand-daughter, Mrs. Thomas Sloo of New Orleans, by sheer ability and perseverence, Duncan Kenner regained almost all of his property after having started life over again at the age of fifty-two. New methods in the sugar industry had been developed and he installed improved machinery and adopted new agricultural procedures. Realizing the labor saving advantage of a railroad for hauling cane, he was among the earliest to institute that innovation. In many other ways he improved the Ashland plantation. Realizing the benefits to be derived from co-operation, he was active in organizing the Sugar Planters' Association in 1877, and became its first president, an office he held until his death. He was also president of the Sugar Experimental Station of which he was the earliest founder, another position he held until his passing.

When Duncan Kenner came to his New Orleans home to spend his last days, he continued to occupy himself with many enterprises, still possessing a keen mentality and a strong constitution. He arose on most mornings at about 7:30, had breakfast, arrived at his office about 9 A. M., remaining there until 1 P. M., and usually lunched at the Boston Club, after which he returned to his office, once more visiting the club before going home for supper about 5 P. M. His evenings he spent with his family, often remaining at work in his library until early morning.

Mr. Kenner passed away at the age of seventy-four, dying suddenly on the morning of July 3rd, 1887, at the family residence, number 237 Carondelet Street, New Orleans. The body lay in state that his many New Orleans friends might pay their final tribute before the body was put in the handsome family tomb at Donaldsonville.

Unusually brilliant, he was naturally a very entertaining person, well informed on a great number of important subjects, with

Madame Michel Doradou Bringier, neé Louise Elizabeth Aglaé duBourg de St. Colombe. (From a life-sized portrait in the home of Mr. and Mrs. Thomas Sloo, New Orleans.)

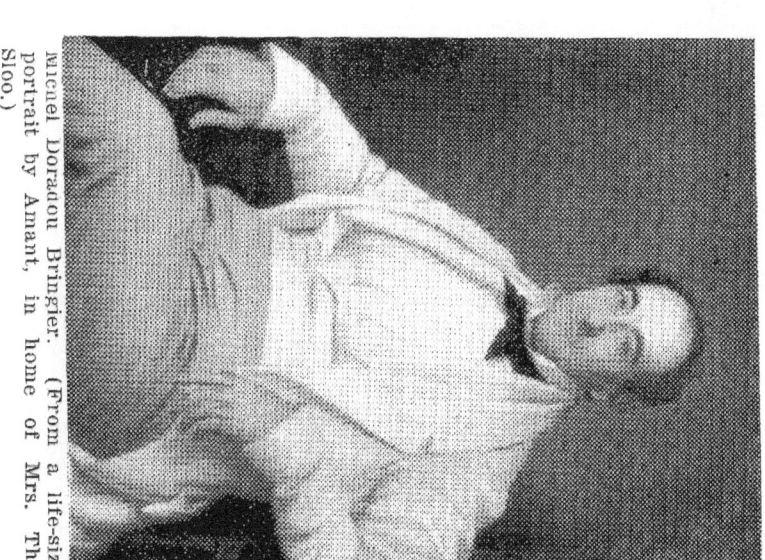

Michel Doradou Bringier. (From a life-sized portrait by Amant, in home of Mrs. Thos. Sloo.)

MADAME DUNCAN F. KENNER
Neé Guillemine Nanine Bringier. Born at the Hermitage, Aug. 24th, 1823. Died in New Orleans Nov. 6th, 1911. (From a portrait in home of Mrs. Thos. Sloo.)

HONORABLE DUNCAN F. KENNER

Louise Elizabeth Aglaé DuBourg de St. Colomb. (From a miniature owned by Mrs. Thos. Sloo.)

Augustin Dominique Tureaud, husband of Elizabeth Bringier. (Courtesy of Mrs. Thos. Sloo.)

Mrs. Joseph Lancaster Brent neé Rosella Kenner.

General Joseph Lancaster Brent. (From ivory miniatures belonging to Mrs. Thos. Sloo.)

Miss Mary Minor, daughter of Don Estavan Minor, who married William Kenner. (Courtesy of Mrs. Thos. Sloo..)

DON ESTAVAN MINOR

Concord—the splendid Colonial Plantation Home built for the Spanish Governor de Lemos. It later became the residence of Don Estavan Minor, and the Minor receptions were on a scale of magnificence befitting the representative of His Majesty, the King of Spain.

"Ma Grande", faithful negro mammy in the Bringier family.

Colonel Amedee Bringier, by Amans. At the age of 18 years. (From Bringier Collection, Tezcuco Plantation.)

The Old Family Home of the du Bourg—de Lauzon families, Dumaine Street, near Royal Street.

Marguerite Armand de Vogluzan, married Pierre Du Bourg, Chevalier, Sieur de Rochemont.
(Courtesy of Trist Wood.)

Perrine Therese Elizabeth de Gournay, married Francois Charest de Lauzon.

Pierre Francois Du Bourg, Sieur de Ste. Colomb. (Courtesy of Trist Wood.)

Elisabeth Etiennette Charest de Lauzon, who married Pierre Francois Du Bourg de Ste. Colombe.
(Courtesy of Mrs. Thos. Sloo.)

Ancestral portraits of the family of Thomas Sloo, II.

Richard Henry Lee, Belmont, Leesburg, Va.

Mrs. Ludwell Lee neé Eliza d'Armstadt, (pronounced Armstat).

Ludwell Lee of Belmont, Leesburg, Va.

Mary Ann Lee of Belmont Leesburg, Va., wife of Robert Blair Campbell.

Robert Blair Campbell of South Carolina.

Maria Frances Campbell, wife of Thomas Sloo I, and mother of Thomas Sloo II.

Thomas Sloo, I.

Nanine Maria Brent, wife of Thomas Sloo, II.

Thomas Sloo, II.

Thomas Sloo, III.

(Courtesy of Mrs. Thomas Sloo.)

Louis Guillaume Valentine Du Bourg, Bishop of New Orleans, Archbishop of Besacon, France. (Courtesy of Mrs. Thos. Sloo.)

"Tristford", Devonshire, England. Ancestral seat of the Trist family. (Courtesy of Trist Wood.)

"Birdwood", Trist Place, Albemarle County, Virginia. (Courtesy of Trist Wood.)

Hore Browse Trist of Birdwood, Albermarle County, Va.

Gen. Hore Browse Trist of Bowden Plantation, Louisiana.

Marie Elizabeth Rosella Bringier

Mary Wilhelmine Trist

a deep knowledge of scientific subjects. He was an unusually well-informed, cultured gentleman of the old school, uniting the virtues one instinctively associates with one to whom the term is applied. Duncan Farrar Kenner was a peer among peers, and his life full of honor.

Du Bourg Crest and Coat-of-Arms

ARMES: *D'azur trois branches d'epines d'argent pesecs 2 et 1. Supports: Seux sauvages armes de massues, Cimier; Une fleur de lys d'or accostec de 2 demi—vols de-mene.*
Devise. Lilium inter spinas.

ARMS: *Az. three thorn branches 2 and 1. Supporters: two savages armed with clubs. Crest: A fleur de Lys or between two wings of the same.*
Lilium inter spinas.

DU BOURG

In the Bibliothèque Nationale in Paris can be found among the genealogical records, a "Maintenance de Noblesse", dating back to 1623, which was deposited there in the eighteenth century by a young nobleman of France by the name of Pierre Du Bourg, as he was about to start on an extended trip, or as is stated "on the point of undertaking a long journey".The Louisiana branch of this patrician family begins with "M. Pierre DuBourg, écuyer et Capitaine de Navire", who in 1623 filed his "maintenance de noblesse" in the City of Paris. He married Margurite Vogluzan. They went to St. Domingo, where he became the owner of the immense plantation estate of Rochemont.

In 1766 a son was born to Monsieur and Madame Pierre Du Bourg who was later to become the great Archbishop Du Bourg, and the first American Bishop of New Orleans. Louis Guillaume Valentin, as he had been christened, when he reached the age of two years was sent to France to be educated for the Catholic Church. He finished his seminary studies, and about 1798 became head of a Sulpician school at Issy near Paris. Because of the French Revolution he was forced to leave and by disguising himself he was able to reach Paris where he made his way to Rue Cassette in which was located the superior branch of the Sulpician. The revolutionists had invaded that place, capturing the head of the institution and executing him. Rev. DuBourg, hiding at a friend's home, escaped with his life when the terrible September massacres took place. He again disguised himself and fled from Paris, reaching Bordeaux where his family was located. Here he found his life doubly in danger, for the revolutionists were slaughtering churchmen as well as aristocrats. Knowing that he would not be safe in any part of France, he went into Spain and a little later sailed from there to America, reaching Baltimore, Md. in 1794. So capable did Rev. DuBourg prove to be, that he became President of Georgetown College two years after he arrived in Baltimore. Under his able management it became one of the leading universities of the United States, George Washington honoring it with a visit while still under the management of Rev. DuBourg. Abbé DuBourg also founded St. Mary's College, and had the Legislature of Maryland raise it to the rank of University.

Another son Pierre Francois DuBourg, who became known as Sieur de Ste. Colombe, was born a year after the Abbé DuBourg. He eventually succeeded his father as the owner of the estate of Rochemont, he too being educated in France and later in England. During the slave revolt in 1793 in San Domingo, he escaped to Jamaica and in 1797 married Demoiselle Elizabeth Charest de Lauzon, daughter of M. Francois Charest de Lauzon and Demoiselle Perrine Thérèse de Gournay, the marriage contract in which all are shown as Residents of "Quartier de la Marmelade, Island of Ste. Domingo, now by reason of the misfortunes of the colony, refugees in the town of Kingston, Jamaica". Then

Pierre Francois DuBourg and his family came to the United States, and remained for a short stay in New Orleans, continuing on to Baltimore taking with them their little daughter Aglaé. There she was left to be educated at Mrs. Seton's whom Abbé

de Lauzon

DuBourg had assisted in founding of the Order of Sisters of St. Joseph, popularly known as the Sisters of Charity. Leaving Baltimore the DuBourgs came south to New Orleans about 1800, and made their home with his wife's parents, who lived in Dumaine Street, New Orleans, a bustling business place at that date. Offered great opportunities, DuBourg became a merchant and succeeded beyond his greatest hopes, repairing his heavy financial losses, and occupying again a prominent position in both the social and business world. After three years residence in the United States, he became an American citizen. He was a Major in the Louisiana Volunteer, an aristocratic organization. Among the other notable positions he held was that of Collector of the Port of the City of New Orleans, and Consul of the Kingdom of Sardinia. He was likewise broker for Michel Doradou Bringier and a number of the other immensely wealthy Louisiana planters. Pierre Francois DuBourg owned a large plantation called "Plaisance", which was located near where that street is today, and situated as most of them were at that date, a short distance back from the river-road, Louisiana Avenue being about the center of the plantation.

His daughter, Aglaé, who had become Madame Michel Doradou Bringier, for many years was one of the most prominent social leaders in the deep South. Pierre Francois DuBourg died in New Orleans in 1830, leaving five daughters, all but Aglaé residing in New Orleans where they were educated. Noémie became the wife of General Horatio Davis, whose father was Colonel Samuel Boyer Davis noted for his gallant defense of Lewes during the War of 1812. Gen. Davis' country home, La Corderie, occupied the space between the canal for which Canal Street is named and the river-road. The Davis family originally came from Delaware.

Eliza DuBourg became the wife of Seaman Field, their daughter marrying Bailly-Blanchard of New Orleans, whose son Col. Arthur Bailly-Blanchard was attached to the American Legation in Paris, became a Chevalier of the Legion of Honor, and whose daughter was the Vicomtesse Henri Chazelle of France. The Seaman Field plantation home later became the property of Madame Michel Doradou Bringier at which time it became known as Melpoméne. The house faced Apollo Street, now changed to Carondelet Street, and at the time of the Bringier's occupancy was between Carondelet and Baronne Streets with the Melpomene canal as a downtown boundary. In later years Melpoméne was sold to Hon. Duncan Kenner who had the place demolished, selling the land for building lots as land values had increased.

Victoire, another daughter of Pierre Francois DuBourg, became the wife of James Harvey Field, a nephew of Seaman Field. The descendants of her sister Adèle, who married John Thibaut are many and scattered about the state. Joseph DuBourg, third son of Pierre Du Bourg and Margurite Vogluzan, is remembered as "le beau DuBourg". He made a trip to America, visiting his family in Baltimore and New Orleans, but returned to France. Thomas Patrice DuBourg, fourth son, had two daughters who married in Jamaica, and a son who was educated under the supervision of his uncle in Baltimore, Md., and who later made his home in New Orleans. He was a judge in Plaquemines Parish, La. in 1815, and later a Judge in New Orleans. This son, Arnould DuBourg, never married and died in New Orleans in 1829.

Brent Coat-of-Arms

Odo de Brent, Lord of Cossington
Cire 1066 - 1037.

ARMS:—Gu a Wivern passant arg.
Motto Silentis et Diligentia.
It is said that their ancestors in their arms, recommended to their posterity by the serpent, Prudence—by his color, Innocence in a red field, a bloody and troublous world.

BRIGADIER-GENERAL JOSEPH LANCASTER BRENT

Brigadier-General Joseph Lancaster Brent was born on the 30th of November, 1826 at Pomony, Charles County, Maryland; and educated at Georgetown College, Georgetown, D. C. He studied law in Washington, D. C. and in Louisiana and practiced law with his father, William Leigh Brent, and later with his brother, Edward C. Brent in St. Martinsville, La., until 1850 when he went to California, where he became a leading lawyer in Los Angeles. General Brent was a son of William Leigh Brent and Maria Fenwick. He left California in 1861 to join the Confederate army and was arrested on the high seas. The ship on which he was making the trip between California and New York was stopped and Brent along with Dr. William Gwin, who was an ex-United States senator and Calhoun Benham, who was United States district-attorney in California were arrested by General E. V. Sumner of the U. S. Army. They were imprisoned at Fort Lafayette, and held there for nearly three weeks, when finally they were paroled and permitted to proceed to Washington, D. C. While in Washington the United States authorities were unable to prove the charge of treason against them. They sought to be released and eventually through the influence of Hon. George D. Prentice, who was a brother-in-law of Mr. Benham, J. L. Brent was freed from restraint without being forced to take the oath of allegiance which he had refused to do. He proceeded to Richmond, Va. in the winter of 1861-1862, and enlisted at once in the Confederate service with the rank of Captain on the staff of General J. B. Magruder in command of the Yorktown district. He ran the blockade into Virginia and after the Yorktown campaign was advanced to the rank of Major of Artillery and ordered to Alexandria, Va., as ordnance officer of the right wing of the Army of Northern Virginia commanded by General Magruder. He held this position until the Peninsula campaign of 1862 and the Seven-Day Battle around Richmond. He was then assigned to the staff of General (Fighting Dick) Richard Taylor in command of the Western district of Louisiana. Here in July 1862 promoted to the rank of Colonel, he participated in the military operations of the district—as chief of artillery and ordnance and commander of the First Louisiana brigade cavalry. He remained in this position until October 2nd, 1864 when he was promoted to brigadier-general of cavalry in which rank he served until the end of the war. When the war ended he was in command of the front line forces in the West, which extended from Arkansas to the Gulf of Mexico, being the last line to be held by the Confederate Army at the time of the surrender.

Once when failing to obtain paper for the making of cartridges, he used wall paper. Another notable achievement was the capture of the "Indianola", a powerful Federal boat heavily iron clad with only one armed towboat called the "Webb" and a river steamer named "Queen of the West". The capture of this iron clad Indianola in the early part of the spring of 1863 was one of the most exciting exploits of Brigadier-General Brent's work in Louisiana. The Indianola, after running the batteries at Vicksburg, Miss., had passed on to the mouth of the Red River, and encouraged by its success, started back towards Vicksburg. General Taylor assigned Brigadier-General Brent the command of two boats to engage the Indianola, the boats available were a side-wheeler, the steamer "Webb", which had been used as a towboat previous to hostilities and was devoid of protection, save a tier of bales of cotton placed about the boiler. This and the "Queen of the West", a gunboat captured from the Federals at Fort De Russy on the Red River, the gunboat being a modern boat with bow reinforced and strengthened for ramming, but also unprotected, tiers of bales of cotton being the only defense of her machinery. General Brent started in pursuit of the Indianola with this flotilla, overtaking her twenty miles south of Vicksburg. He immediately engaged her in battle, notwithstanding the Indianola carried 11-inch guns, a shot from one of them properly directed would have put out of commission either of the Confederate boats. However, each time the Indianola raised her iron shutters to fire a gun, the men of the Queen of the West or the Webb would open on them with rifles. The Federal gunmen became demoralized and only one ball from the Indianola struck the Queen of the West, that shot doing no further damage than to scatter a lot of dirt, and the cotton bales torn asunder sent flakes of cotton flying like leaves in a gust of wind. In the meantime, the Indianola was being rammed again and again until her commander surrendered, but her crew showed their humiliation after they realized how easily they had been taken by the unprotected boats that had given them battle. General Brent lost only eight men killed in the encounter.

In May 1865 after the surrender, General Brent was paroled at the town of Alexandria. He returned to Baltimore, Md. and resumed the practice of law in which he had been engaged at the outbreak of the war. Later he came to Louisiana (1870) and married Rosella Kenner, youngest daughter of the Hon. Duncan Kenner and Nanine Bringier, becoming a plantation owner. He remained in Louisiana until 1899. While a resident he served twice in the legislature of the state. In 1899 he again returned to Baltimore, Md., but came back each winter with his family to Louisiana where they spent the winter season visiting their many relatives.

In Baltimore as in Louisiana Gen. Brent was held in highest regard by the legal profession and his Confederate comrades of army days. He was a member of the Society of the Army and Navy. General Brent died in the City of Baltimore, Md., Nov. 27, 1905.

Az. a quatrefoil pierced of its field within an orle of estoiles or, a canton ermine.

Crest: On a mount vert an osprey ppr. holding in the beak a fish arg.

Motto: Nec triste nec trepide.

THE TRIST FAMILY

(Authorities: Trist pedigree at the Heralds College, London, 1799 with the American branch. Pendarves Chart of Trist family completed at the Heralds College. Trist pedigree in Burke's "Royal Descents".)

According to the Heralds Visitations and Burke's monumental work on Northhamptonshire, England, its Trists held Maidford Manor in that county from early times. John Trist married Jean Pulesdon, daughter and co-heir of Edmond Pulesdon, whose mother Joan de Kyme, was second daughter and co-heir of John de Kyme, Lord of Maidford Manor, and this John de Kyme's great-grandson, William de Kyme, released the manor of Maidford, in the 30th year of Henry VI (1452) to William Trist, son of the above John Trist and Joan Pulesdon. The manor remained in the Trist family for many generations (by primogeniture to the oldest son).

A branch of the Trist family established themselves in County Devon, England, becoming owners of "Hernaford". Of this

Major John Wood, born 1770.

Gen. Robert Crooke Wood, born 1799.

Ann M. Taylor, wife of General R. C. Wood.

Col. Robert Crooke Wood, C.S.A.

RECORD OF THE SEAL RING OF THE TAYLOR FAMILY.

This seal ring bearing the crest of the Taylor family is now in the possession of Frances Bell Evans, the great-great-great-great granddaughter of James Taylor of Carlisle, England. It has descended through all these generations to her, and with it a legend has been transmitted from father to son, from mother to daughter.

This legend evidently had its origin in the same event which is said to have added the fourth Boar's head to the "Arms", and related that, when the chase was at its height, a wild boar driven, turned upon the royal huntsman, whereat there sprang to his defense one of the attending knights, who thrust the animal through with his lance. The King, in gratitude, told him to prefer any request whatsover and that it would be granted. From this time on the "crest" and distinguishing mark of this knight and his descendants was the uplifted arm with lance in hand, accompanied by the motto "Consequitor quodcunquepetit. He strikes what he aims at," or "He gains what he seeks".

(Courtesy of Trist Wood.)

branch was Nicholas Trist, born about 1668, died 29th, 1741. Patrimony, he inherited from his bachelor uncle, Nicholas Browse, the estate of Dorseley and Manor of Aptor. He bought Bowden, which anciently had been in the Browse family, and also acquired the borough and lordship of Modbury, all in County Devon. His tomb is in the Trist aisle of St. Mary's Church, Totnes, garvested with the Trist arms, quartered with various ancestral shields. He married Elizabeth Rooke, a daughter of George Rooke, and cousin of Sir George Rooke, who captured Gibraltar. They had a number of sons and daughters, the younger sons died unmarried. The eldest son and heir was Hon. Browse Trist, born 1698, died May, 1777. He inherited the family properties, being described in its Pendanus chart of the Trist family as "of Heraford, Dorsely and Bowden, Lord of its Manors of Lambside, Aptor, Noss Mayo and of its Manor and Borough of Modbury". He served as a Member of Parliament, 1761-1763. He married Agnes Hore, daughter and heiress of Thomas Hore, of "Nymph", County Devon. They had a number of sons and daughters.

Their only son who left male issue was Nicholas Trist, born 24th of May, 1743, died 24th of Feb., 1784. He was a lieutenant in the regiment of his oldest brother, Col. Hore Browse Trist. Their commissions as officers, signed by George III, are preserved in the American branch. They were sent to America when revolt was threatening and their regiment participated in the storming and taking of Bunker Hill.

When Lord Howe occupied Philadelphia, the British officers were billeted in various American homes. Lieutenant Nicholas Trist found quarters in the home of the House family, where he met Miss Elizabeth House. Despite the fact that she was a patriotic American girl, and her family on intimate terms of friendship with the leaders of the American cause, Washington, Madison, and Madison family friends of her family, she and the British officer fell in love with each other, and were married, the ceremony taking place on the 10th of June, 1774.

Their only child was Hore Browse Trist, of "Birdwood", Albemarle County, Va., born in Philadelphia, Penn., 22nd of Feb., 1775, and who died in New Orleans, La., 29th of Aug., 1804. He was named after his uncle Col. Hore Browse Trist, who as mentioned above, took part in the affair of Bunker Hill. This uncle on hearing of the death of his father, Hon. Browse Trist in 1777, returned to England to take possession of the Trist estates. He died unmarried in 1786, whereupon the estates went to his brother, Rev. Browse Trist, who in turn, died in 1791, leaving three daughters, Elisabeth Ayshford Trist, Susanna Hore Trist and Tryphana Trist. Hore Browse Trist, born 22nd of Feb., 1775, being the only male heir left in the family, to attend to the succession proceeded to England and treated his three cousins, the daughters of Rev. Browse Trist with great generosity in settling the estate. To be near his friend, Thomas Jefferson, he acquired "Birdwood" near "Monticello" in Virginia. When Jefferson acquired Louisiana from Napoleon, he appointed him his Collector of the Port of New Orleans, he then being 28 years old.

He married Mary Louisa Brown, born in Dublin, Ireland, daughter of Clement Colquhoun Brown and Catherine Byrne. She married second, Philip Livingston Jones and thirdly, Philip St. Julien de Tournillon, they had issue, two sons. 1st, Nicholas Philip Trist, born in Charlottesville, Va., 2nd of June, 1800; died in Alexander, Va., 1st of Feb., 1874. He and his younger brother were wards of Thomas Jefferson and brought up at Monticello.

Nicholas Philip Trist negotiated the Treaty of Guadalupe Hidalgo at the close of the Mexican War, and married at Monticello, Miss Virginia Randolph, granddaughter of Thomas Jefferson. Their children constitute what is known as the Virginia branch of the Trist family. Issue 1st, Martha Jefferson Trist, who married John Wolfork Burke; 2nd, Thomas Jefferson Trist, who married first, Ellen Dorotea Strong Lyman, and secondly, Sophia Knabe. 3rd, Hore Browse Trist, M.D., who married Ann Mary Waring. When a young man went to England as the adopted heir of Mrs. Tryphana Trist Wynne Pondarves, of "Tristford" —the Tryphana that is mentioned above.

General Hore Borwse Trist of Bowden plantation, Ascension Parish, La., was born in Washington, D. C., on the 10th day of Mar., 1802; died at "Bowden" on the 16th of Nov., 1856. He married Rosella Bringier, daughter of Michel Doradou Bringier and Aglaé Du Bourg de Ste. Colombe, their children and descendants constitute the Louisiana branch of the Trist family; issue: 1st, Nicholas Browse Trist; married his cousin Augustine Gordon. 2nd, Julien Bringier Trist—Lieutenant in C.S.A., killed at the Battle of Murfreesboro. 3rd, Mary Wilhelmine Trist; married Col. Robert C. Wood, son of Brig.-Gen. Robert C. Wood, Asst. Surgeon,

U. S. Army, by Ann, eldest daughter of Gen. Zachary Taylor. 4th, Louise Rosella Trist; died young. 5th, Nicholas Philip Trist; married first, Marie Tureaud, and second, Alice Tureaud, sister of his first wife.

Wood Coat-of-Arms and Family Crest

ARMS: Per pale or and sable two eagles displayed counter-charged.

Crest: Issuing from a ducal coronet or demi eagles with wings spread per pale or and sable.

THE WOOD FAMILY

The Wood family from early Colonial days was established in Newport, Rhode Island. The immigrant founder of the family was Thomas Wood, of Essex, England. His great grandson: Peleg Wood, of Newport, R. I., was born 1711, died May 1, 1759; married Mary Coggeshall, widow of Joseph Fry. They had two daughters, and an only son.

Capt. Peleg Wood, of Newport, R. I., born March, 1741, Commander of the sloop "Florida" in the Revolutionary War; died on the 15th of Jan., 1806. He married, first, Jan., 1763, Elizabeth Godfrey, daughter of Caleb Godfrey and Abigail Prince, and second, on the 17th of August, 1786, Mary Wickham, daughter of Col. Benjamin Wickham and Mary Gardner, and thirdly, on the

2nd of April, 1797, Margaret Suget. He had five sons and one daughter by his first marriage, and one daughter and one son by the second marriage. The five sons were: 1st, Capt. William Wood of Newport, R. I., born 6th of April, 1764, died in Batavia, East India, 22nd of May, 1807. Married Sarah Wickham. 2nd, Capt. Peleg Wood of Newport, R. I., born 21st of April, 1766, died 26th of Dec., 1809; married Elizabeth Read Warner. 3rd, Capt. John Wood, of whom hereafter. 4th, Capt. Joseph Wood of Newport, R. I., born Sept., 1772; died in Rio de Janeiro, South America, 10th of Sept., 1819; married Amey, daughter of Lt. Gen. Simeon Martin, Governor of Rhode Island. 5th, Capt. Godfrey Wood of Newport, R. I., born 1775, never married, and died at sea on way home from Havana, on the 30th of June, 1803.

All of the above five sons were in the merchant marine service, and were "sea captains". The only daughter, 6th, Elizabeth Wood, born 28th of Nov., 1779, died unmarried. The daughter and son by the second marriage (with Mary Wickam) were: 7th, Mary Wood, born 18th of July, 1787; died at a very advanced age in 1865; and, 8th, Wickam Wood, who died unmarried on Jan. 1813. The 5th son was: Capt. and Major John Wood of Newport, R. I., born Newport, R. I., on 6th of April, 1770; in command of the forces defending Newport Harbor in the War of 1812; he died in Cape Coast, Africa, 31st of Jan., 1826; married Rebecca Wickham Crooke, daughter of Robert Crooke of New York and Ann Wickham. They had eight children, as follows: 1, Ann Elizabeth Wood, born 13th of March, 1796, died young. 2, Bt. Brigadier General Robert Crooke Wood, of whom hereafter. 3, John Wood, born 22nd of May, 1802, died young. 4, Ann Wood, born 7th of Nov., 1803, died young. 5, John Wood of Rome, N. Y., born Feb. 23rd, 1806; died at sea on his way from New York to Newport, Oct., 1846. 6, Mary Ann Dudley Wood, of Le Roy, N. Y., born 8th of Sept., 1808, died unmarried, 1890. 7, Rebecca Wickham Crooke Wood, born June 7th, 1810, died July 14th, 1880; married Rev. Henry Stanley of Le Roy, N. Y. 8, Charles Edward Dudley Wood, of New York, born 13th of May, 1814, married Susan Jane Thomas. 9, William Wood, born 12th of Mar., 1815, died unmarried. The second child (as above noted) was Bt. Brig. Gen. Robert Crooke Wood; he was born 23rd of Sept., 1799. Grad Columbia Medical College, N. Y., became a surgeon serving in the Black Hawk War, Florida War, Mexican War, Civil War; in Civil

War, assisting (and sometimes acting) Surgeon General U.S.A. with headquarters at Washington, D. C., later with headquarters at St. Louis, Mo., in charge of all armies of the West until the close of the war: died in New York City 28th of March, 1869. Married Ann Mackall Taylor, eldest child of General Zachary Taylor, they had issue.

I. Col. John Taylor Wood, U.S.N. and C.S.N., born at Fort Snelling, Mississippi Territory, 13th of Aug., 1830; Annapolis Naval Academy; Mexican War; Commander of the Confederate cruiser "Tallahassee"; died at Halifax, Nova Scotia, 19th of July, 1904; married Lola Mackubin, daughter of George (Maccubin) Mackubin of "Strawberry Hill", Md., and his cousin Eleanor Maccubin, issue: 1st, Ann Mackall Wood, died young. 2nd, Lieut. Col. Zachary Taylor Wood; Gov. of the Yukon District, Canada. By George V of England, made a Companion of the Order of St. Michael; married Francis Augusta Daly. 3rd, Elizabeth Simms Wood, died young. 4, Lola Mackubin Wood, living unmarried. 5, Robert Crooke Wood, died in infancy. 6, Eleanor Mackubin Wood, married Duncan John D'Urban Campbell. 7, John Taylor Wood. 8, George Mackabin Wood, who married Mary Muriel Buss. 9, Blandina V. Grabow Wood. 10, Mary Catherine Hammond Wood, died early. II. Charles Carroll Mackubin Wood, British Army; killed (then a Lieutenant in the Boer War). His portrait at Queen Victoria's request was sent to her. 2, Col. Robert Crooke Wood, born at Fort Snelling, M.T., 4th of April, 1832; West Point Military Academy; served in Texas as Lieutenant in 2nd U. S. Cavalry, in Civil War Colonel of Wood's Cavalry, C.S.A., died in New Orleans 4th of Dec., 1900; married Wilhelmine Trist, daughter of Hore Browse Trist of "Bowden", Ascension Parish, La., and Rosella Bringier, issue: 1, Bringier Trist Wood; 2, Minette Trist Wood; 3, Richard Taylor Wood; (twin died in infancy); 4, Nina Sarah Wood, died young. 5th, Marie Rosella Wood, married William Edwin Brickell, Jr. 6, Zachary Taylor Wood, Lieut. U. S. A.; married first Helen McGloin; second, Beatrice Thomas.

3. Blandina Dudley Wood, born Prairie du Chien, Wisconsin. Born Jan., 1834; married first, Edward Boyce; second, Baron Guido von Grabow, Prussian Minister to Venezuela. By first marriage a son, William Boyce von Grabow, married Caro Bolles. By

second marriage, a son, Ernst Romanus Guido Roudolph von Grabow.

4. Sarah Knox Wood, born in Prairie du Chien, 21st of Nov., 1835, died unmarried.

MR. ISAAC STAUFFER—A NOTED CITIZEN.

Of Swiss and French ancestry Mr. Stauffer combined the best of both nations, becoming one of the most representative citizens of New Orleans during his life in this city. His father was of Swiss descent, his mother's family, French (Huguenots). His early life was spent on his father's farm in Lancaster County, Penn., where he learned from the frugality of his parents the lessons of thrift and conservation which was to make him an outstanding character, and bring wealth and position to himself and family. His charities were manifold when once he knew the object was a deserving one.

After leaving his father's farm he was employed by the city of Lancaster and later accepted a position with the firm of John Steinman, one of long standing, the founder receiving young Stauffer into the family circle, at once recognizing his worth. He stayed in the city of Lancaster for many months, all of the time building up a reputation of a sterling character, and so much was this the case Mr. Steinman with whom he was employed realized that if given the opportunity, his protegé would rise to great heights. With this in mind Mr. Steinman sought a position for young Stauffer and discovered that Courtland Palmer of New York City, had decided to establish a branch of his business in New Orleans, and was in quest of capable men to carry his ideas to fulfillment. The letter that Mr. Steinman gave to Mr. Stauffer as his recommendation, reads in part as follows: "I recommend a man who has ever sustained a character, nobility, integrity and general moral worth and unblemished."

As he rose in this city he became a clerk of the Canal Bank for fifty years, a subscriber to the American Sugar Refining Co. Association. One who in a great measure financed James B. Eads when he constructed Eads' Jetties at South Pass, La., and at the time told him "if you succeed we shall be paid, if not we shall accept the loss. And further from this I will subscribe to carry on your work. I believe if you open the passes of the Mississippi River, sufficient to admit the largest sea-going vessels, a wonderful future for the South is assured. You will make a permanent port of New Orleans and subsequent developments will make us one of the greatest sea ports in the United States".

Two daughters of Myrthe Bringier and General Richard (Fighting Dick) Taylor married sons of I. H. Stauffer—Betty Taylor married Walter R. Stauffer and Myrthe Taylor married Isaac H. Stauffer.

CHAPTER XVI.

THE KNOX—SEMMES—WALMSLEY—RANLETT FAMILIES

HONORABLE THOMAS JENKINS SEMMES

JUDGE Thos. J. Semmes, one of the most distinguished lawyers the South has ever known, comes from an aristocratic line that stems back to the ancient nobles of Normandy, where many of the name still can be found. With the historic family of Talliaferro, the Semmes family are also connected, the descendants of that Talliaferro (Talliafeuro) the sword-bearer of William the Conqueror, who opened the ever memorable Battle of Hastings, and whom Bulwer so graphically describes in his "Harold".

Thomas Jenkins Semmes was born on Dec. 16th, 1824, at Georgetown, D. C. He was a son of Raphael Semmes, a prominent merchant of that place who married in 1818 Miss Matilda Jenkins and died in the year 1846. His wife who survive him was a woman of great intellect, remarkable strength of mind, and with a wonderful fund of information. She was a born leader in social affairs and her salon in Washington was like that of Madame de Stall's for over half a century. During that time she entertained every president of the United States from President Monroe to President Lincoln, and in these gatherings all of the distinguished men and their wives participated, including Calhoun, Clay, Webster, Berrien, Silas, Wright, Dickinson, Bayard, Horace, Binney, Sargent, Watkins, Lee, Wirth, Pinkney, The Tazwells, Taney, Marshall, etc.

One can readily understand why it was that T. J. Semmes was such an unusually brilliant man, when his early life was

MOVEO ET PROFICIO

Crest and Coat-of-Arms of the Knox family.

Semmes, Knox, Walmsley and
Ranlett Families.

HON. THOS. J. SEMMES

ROBERT MILLER WALMSLEY

spent in such surroundings and whose mother was such a representative woman and so capable. In speaking of his home life before moving to the South, he always stated that his mother was largely responsible in the formation of the character of her large family of children. Judge Thomas J. Semmes received his early education in Georgetown at the private primary school of a Scotch-named McLeod, and so bright did young Semmes prove to be, that at the age of 11 years we find him entering Georgetown College, from which he was graduated in 1842 at the age of seventeen and one half years of age. He then read law for one year in the law office of Clement Cox of Georgetown, before enrolling at the Harvard Law School from which he graduated in January 1845. Associate Justice Story of the United States Supreme Bench was the dean of the Harvard Law School. Among J. T. Semmes' contemporaries at Harvard were Rutherford B. Hays, Henry C. Semple of Montgomery, Ala., nephew of the then president, and Anson Burlingame, afterwards minister to China. T. J. Semmes was admitted to the bar of Washington, D. C. in 1845, six months before he was twenty-one years of age, passing his examinations before Chief Justice Cranch and Associate Justices Mossell and Dunlap. He began his practice of law in the City of Washington with Walter D. Davidge as a law partner, and at once became a successful attorney.

Thomas Semmes married the brilliant and beautiful daughter of Mr. William Knox, Miss Myra Eulalie Knox, in January 1850, her father being one of the wealthiest and most prominent bankers in the South with a magnificent home in Montgomery, Ala. Her mother was Anna C. Lewis, a member of the distinguished Lewis and Fairfax families, who were relatives of the Washingtons of Virginia. In December 1850, the Semmes moved to New Orleans where they built a beautiful home on Annunciation Street, which joined another beautiful mansion with lovely garden belonging to the Slark family. This neighborhood was at that date the most aristocratic of the American section of New Orleans. The "Garden District" while quite lovely, was not the beautiful area we find it today. When the Federals took the city because Judge Semmes and Mr. Knox had been such staunch supporters of the Confederate Cause, the magnificent Semmes home was seized and confiscated with its entire contents, and only long afterwards was the house returned. Untold damage was done to the place and the furnishings were never recovered. The site of many of those splendid old homes is now occupied by the depot of the Texas and Pacific Railroad Co.

The brothers and sisters of Thomas J. Semmes were: Virginia the eldest daughter, married Major Rice W. Payne, of Warrenton, Va., who was an officer in the Confederate army; B. J. Semmes became a merchant in Washington, D. C., was in the Confederate Army and was wounded at the battle of Shilo; Thomas Jenkins Semmes was the second son; Dr. Alex J. Semmes, the third son, was a graduate of Georgetown College, studied medicine in Paris, and located in New Orleans previous to the Civil War. He was surgeon of the Eighth Louisiana Regiment, and married a daughter of Senator Barrien of Georgia. The Southern Historical Publishing Society of Richmond, Virginia, has the following to say of Dr. Semmes: "Alexander Jenkens Semmes, surgeon, cousin of Admiral Semmes, brother of Thomas J. Semmes—born in Georgetown, D. C. Dec. 17, 1828. Studying in hospitals of London and Paris he went to New Orleans where he made a reputation as a surgeon. During the war of Secession he had much to do with the organization and supervision of the hospitals in Virginia in 1866-1867 was connected with Charity Hospital of New Orleans. He then removed to Savannah from 1870-76 was professor in Savannah Medical College. Upon the death of his wife he became so disconsolate that he abandoned his profession and studied for the priesthood, was ordained and became president of the Catholic School at Macon, Ga., later transferred to New Orleans dying in this city about 1897. He also wrote numerous medical and surgical treatises of great interest, among them the following: "Medical Sketches of Paris, 1852", "Notes from a surgical diary 1866", Surgical Notes of the late war 1867", The Fluid Extracts, 1869", "Evolution of the Origin of Life, 1873", "Influence of Yellow Fever on Pregnancy and Parturition, 1875".

The fourth son, Raphael Semmes, at the age of 16 years while on a voyage from San Francisco, California to New York City was lost at sea. The youngest son, P. Warfield Semmes, was also a graduate of Georgetown University and became a captain in the First Louisiana Regiment in the Confederate Army. The second daughter, America Semmes, became the first wife of Major Rice W. Payne, and died during the Civil War. Clara

Semmes another sister like the other ladies of the family had been educated at the Convent of the Visitation, Georgetown, D. C., before the outbreak of the Civil War, she married Lieutenant Fitzgerald of the U. S. Navy, who joined the Confederate Navy and died in 1863 at Greenville, S. C., while in service. Another daughter, Cora Semmes, became the wife of Lieutenant J. C. Ives, U. S. Engineer Corps, who was a member of the personal staff of President Jefferson Davis during the Civil War, and died shortly after cessation of histilities. Sabina Semmes, next to the youngest daughter, married a distant cousin, Dr. Alphonse Semmes of Canton, Miss., a prominent planter. Ada Semmes, youngest daughter, became the wife of Richard H. Clark, a Washington lawyer, who later removed to New York City.

In later years Judge Semmes in reminiscing, enjoyed talking about his early days in Louisiana, of the bar as he found it at that date. His brilliancy soon gained for him the intimate personal admiration and close friendship of this distinguished galaxy of cultured legal lights, most of whom helped to furnish the male quotas at the yearly series of banquets for which the first Semmes home became famous, and which continued in the later homes in Iberville and Rampart Streets. The second home was on Customhouse Street, now called Iberville Street, one door from North Rampart Street, a large three-storied brick structure, quite like many of the fine old homes in the French Quarter. It overlooked the beautiful and spacious garden of the Letchford's mansion, for this neighborhood too had become a very fashionable one. Business encroachments caused the Semmes to again remove to their last residence in this city, located on South Rampart Street. Here in this splendid old mansion the Semmes family continued to entertain on a lavish scale where one was sure to meet some of the most distinguished personages of our country. The Semmes annually gave a banquet for the distinguished Catholic churchmen. James Cardinal Gibbons, who visited the city yearly attended by the Archbishop from the St. Louis Cathedral, and prominent people of New Orleans. It was a social event of the season. Among the notables who frequented the first beautiful home of the Semmes family were such distinguished ones as that of Alfred Hennen, John R. Grimes, Judah P. Benjamin, Christian Roselius, John Slidell, Judge Charles Gayarre, Judge Martin, Judge Alexander Walker, S. S. Prentis, Dr. Newton Mercer, Dr. Warren

Stone, Dr. Augustus Cenas, The Eustises, Elliotts, Parkers, Hutchersons, Stauffers, Whitneys, Sloos, Buckners, Farwells, Millikens, Hendersons, and so on.

MRS. THOMAS J. SEMMES.

From "Belles, Beaux and Brains of the Sixties": Mrs. Semmes was queen among ante-bellum hostesses. As Miss Myra Eulalie Knox of Montgomery, she was the belle of her own and other cities. When she married the rising and brilliant lawyer she continued her conquests in New Orleans, the watering places and in the capitals of the old and new federations. Gracious, quick-witted and tactful, she had been educated in the more solid as well as the showier accomplishments. She was a born actress and an admirable musician, playing the harp with especial grace and excellence. These gifts quickly carried her to social leadership in Richmond, and there met at the house the most distinguished of the men of the hour, as well as the young set whom she entertained to their hearts' content. The Semmes practically kept open house.

Another habitue of the Semmes household and almost a member of it was the Hon. Pierre Soulé of their state, former Senator and Minister to Spain. This statesman, advocate and orator, had a handsome face, introspective and rather priestly, that suggested little of the hot blood that would have spitted the Marquis de Tourgot, French Ambassador to Spain, because the young Duke Alva let too glib a a tongue suggest an unpleasant likeness to Madame Soulé. The cause celebre of that challenge and the resulting and harmless duel of young Neville Soulé with the Duke of Alva was laughed out of becoming an international complication. He was a widower in the Richmond days, "the gentle, motherly woman I recall so well in Washington having passed away.

"Full freighted with friendships and pleasant memories of Richmond, Mrs. Semmes returned to New Orleans after the war, her husband returning to the bar and rising to the head before his death."

Until Judge Semmes' passing, the old family mansion on South Rampart Street continued to be the scene of many brilliant entertainments, banquets, suppers and other forms of social activity, among which numbered the one given when President Cleveland became a house guest of the family during his stay in this city. Other affairs were given for distinguished U. S. Senators, Congressmen, scientists, business leaders, artists and writers. Musicals were given where celebrated singers and musicians attended. The greatest dignitaries of the church, James Cardinal Gibbons, Cardinal Satolli, Msgr. Martinelli, Chapelle and Elder, as well as an endless list of distinguished members of the hierarchy, all have enjoyed the lavish hospitality of this cultured home. With the death of Judge Semmes, Mrs. Semmes no longer felt the desire to keep up the social life as in the past, so she gave up her large mansion in South Rampart Street, taking a suite in one of the leading hotels of the city. Later she removed to the spacious handsome home of her daughter, Mrs. Sylvester Walmsley, located in the beautiful aristocratic "Garden District". Here for many years surrounded by her daughter, her grand children and great-grandchildren, sharing their social triumphs, she lived to a splendid old age, intently religious, busied herself with good works and charities, all the while her life a continuous quiet triumph. Apparently she never grew old, remaining the "grand dame", in full possession of stately dignity, looks (a patrician way of growing old gracefully) and faculties until the very end. Her beautiful life-size portrait by Healy hangs on a wall of the drawing-room of this old home that, too, has been a leading social center during the married life of her daughter, Mrs. Sylvester Walmsley, Sr. The passing of Mrs. Semmes, like that of her honored husband, was marked by universal sorrow, the service and floral tributes magnificent and impressive mute testimony of the high regard in which she was held by this community in which she had played so prominent a part, and had done so much for, and in which she had been such a leader.

Mrs. Semmes' children are: Mrs. Sylvester P. Walmsley, Sr. Mrs. A. S. Ranlett; Thomas Jenkins Semmes; Hubert Semmes; Francis Joseph Semmes; Charles Louis Semmes. Mrs. Semmes' daughters have many children. On one occasion a waggish old friend visited her city and the proud grandmother told him that one of them had eleven and the other seven. He replied promptly: "The youngest of each set should be named: "Craps, of course", and when asked what he meant, replied: they "come seven" and "come eleven". The children of Mrs. Sylvester P. Walmsley, Sr., are: S. P. Walmsley, Jr.; Mrs. D. C. Loker; T. Semmes Walmsley; Mrs. Leon Irwin; R. M. Walmsley; Mrs. Ennals W. Ives; Carroll B. Walmsley; William K. Walmsley; Lucille Walmsley; Hughes P. Walmsley.

The children of Mrs. A. S. Ranlett (Miss Cora Semmes) are: Mrs. Carroll Curtis; Mrs. Alex. T. Thomson; A. S. Ranlett, Jr.; David L. Ranlett; Mrs. George Kantzler.

ROBERT MILLER WALMSLEY

Robert Miller Walmsley, who became one of New Orleans' leading citizens, public-spirited and active for the advancement and betterment of both City and State, was born at Elkton, Maryland, on March 5th, 1833. The son of Robert M. and Margaret (Beard) Walmsley was educated at the Elkton Academy, and at an early age displayed marked ability as a realtor. Upon completing his education, he began his real estate career in the City of Philadelphia. Keen as a whip and abreast of opportunities, upon learning that Dubuque, Iowa, was booming, he disposed of his holdings and removed to Dubuque. His advanced ideas and sense of fair dealing won the confidence of the people of the city and he became the leading real estate man there. He became financially independent, but his health was impaired so he moved to the South where the climate was milder. Natchitoches and Grand Encore, thriving settlements in the heart of the rich plantation country, attracted him. Here he was able to speculate in land which he liked to do.

The Civil War came on and with the defeat of the South, Mr. Walmsley suffered heavy losses as with the others of the Confederacy. After hostilities had ceased Mr. Walmsley realizing that land investments would be at a standstill for many years abandoned the idea of continuing as a realtor, and came to New Orleans where he engaged in the cotton business with his cousin under the firm name of C. L. Walmsley & Co. Later as R. M. Walmsley & Co., business increased by leaps and bounds, the firm ranking high in financial circles. In the early part of the eighties, Mr. R. M. Walmsley was elected president of the New Orleans Cotton Exchange, which honor he held for three successive years. He was a director of the Louisiana National Bank and at the death of Mr. Joseph Oglesby in 1889 he was elected to fill the vacancy. At the time of his death, Dec. 26th, 1919, he was president of the Clearing House Association, and of the Board of Liquidation and had been President of the Canal Louisiana Bank for years and was chairman of the Board up to the time of his death.

SYLVESTER PIERCE WALMSLEY, I.

Sylvester Pierce Walmsley, son of Robert Miller Walmsley and Caroline Gratia Williams, was born in Dubuque, Iowa, where his father was a leading realtor and financier. When the family moved to the Natchitoches area young Sylvester Walmsley was sent to New Orleans to be educated. By the time young Walmsley had completed his education, his father moved to New Orleans where he went into the cotton business with a cousin, the firm being known as C. L. Walmsley & Co., later as R. M. Walmsley & Co. Entering his father's cotton business, Sylvester P. Walmsley was soon recognized as a wide-awake addition to the firm. Later he founded the firm of S. P. Walmsley & Co., which for many years was one of the leading cotton firms of the nation. Following closely in his honored father's footsteps, his firm too enjoyed the same enviable name for high class dealing that had made his father's business recognized throughout the country.

Mr. Sylvester P. Walmsley served as President of the New Orleans Cotton Exchange, and at the time of his retirement in 1920 was an honorary member of the Cotton Exchange. He became vice-president of the Louisiana National Bank of which his father was president. He was also at one time vice-president of the Canal Bank, and for half a century was associated with every movement that tended to the betterment of the social and civic life of New Orleans. His courteous, tactful manner of handling difficult situations made him an outstanding as well as well as one of the most representative citizens of his day. Like his father before him he was esteemed and greatly respected throughout the South. Like the Semmes family into which he had married, Mr. Walmsley performed in an unnoticed way a multitude of charities, never letting his left hand know what his right one was giving.

He married the daughter of Honorable Thomas J. Semmes and Myra Eulalie Knox of Montgomery, Ala., who was one of the most famous hostesses the South has ever known. Named for her brilliant mother, Myra, Mrs. Sylvester P. Walmsley, became the social helpmate of this gentleman who was equally prominent as a social leader and as a business man. He directed the destinies of many of the most exclusive carnival organizations in the city. In 1900 he was King of the Carnival, and for twenty-seven years was Captain of Comus, one of the most exclusive carnival organizations in the City of New Orleans.

The spacious old Walmsley home during Mr. Walmsley's lifetime was a continuous scene of social activitiy for Mrs. Walmsley, like her mother, is a born hostess and their home on Second and Prytania Streets was forever the center of some notable gathering. A home full of sons and daughters always furnished an excuse for a frolic of some sort, and with a brilliant season such as this city offers yearly, life in the old home was gay indeed.

In 1928 at a time when Mr. Walmsley had grown too old to stand the tedious exertion of riding horse-back, the Comus Carnival Organization in order to honor their captain for the first time in the history of Carnival, headed the parade with a gilded coach. In this Cinderella coach sat this aged social leader who had been King of the Carnival years before. All cheered as he passed realizing no doubt that he was making an effort to do his bit for the organization to the very end.

Mr. Walmsley comes from a long line of distinguished ancestors, his family tree numbering among its branches a great uncle, Charles Carroll of Carrollton, a signer of the Declaration of Independence. In the 1880's he was an outstanding military man— one that had many responsibilities, with the carpet-bag rule not completely eliminated. A member of the famous Crescent Rifles of New Orleans, one of the greatest military companies in the United States for many years, he later became Major of the Southern Athletic Battalion, one of the crack units of the old Louisiana National Guard. His brother-in-law, Harry Allen, was a captain in the famous Crescent Rifles.

Mr. Walmsley was a life member of the Boston Club, the most exclusive club in the city, first president of the Southern

MRS. THOMAS JENKINS SEMMES, neé MISS MYRA EULALIE KNOX. (From a portrait by Healy in drawing room of Mrs. S. P. Walmsley.) Below: Miss Margaret Carroll Loker, daughter of Mr. and Mrs. David Cartan Loker, who became Mrs. David Cattrell, Jr. (Courtesy of Mrs. S. P. Walmsley, Sr.)

SYLVESTER PIERCE WALMSLEY, I.

MRS. SYLVESTER PIERCE WALMSLEY, SR.,
neé MISS MYRA SEMMES.

MRS. SYLVESTER PIERCE WALMSLEY, II

Always the grand dame to the very end—MRS. THOMAS JENKINS SEMMES, neé Myra Eulalie Knox.

Athletic Club, and held office in several social and civic organizations.

The family finding Mr. Walmsley's health failing, planned with him a trip to California hoping that the sunshine and change of climate would prolong his life. Making the trip in April of 1930, he seemed improved when in an unaccountable manner he contracted pneumonia. He died after a week's illness, surrounded by his family. Mr. and Mrs. Sylvester P. Walmsley's children are: Thomas Semmes Walmsley, former Mayor of New Orleans; Sylvester P. Walmsley, Jr.; Mrs. David Loker; Mrs. Leon Irwin; Robert Miller Walmsley; Mrs. Ennals Ives; Carroll B. Walmsley; and Hughes Walmsley.

A. SIDNEY RANLETT.

A. Sidney Ranlett, born in New Orleans, was the son of David Low Ranlett and Eleanor Stone Ranlett. David Low Ranlett, his father, was from Holyoke, Mass., coming to New Orleans, where he married. A. Sidney Ranlett attended Hanover University in Virginia, and was well known in the business and social world of New Orleans and New York where he moved with his famly to live in 1908. He was a member of the Boston Club of New Orleans, and the New York Club of New York City, also several Carnival organizations in New Orleans. He continued in the stock and bond business in New York City with the firm of Shearson, Hammill & Co. at the time of his death in 1918. His son David Low Ranlett was a member of the A. E. F. with the 107th Regiment of New York, during the World War. Cora Semmes (Mrs. A. Sidney Ranlett,) daughter of Honorable Thomas J. Semmes, and Miss Myra Eulalie Knox, was born in Warrenton, Va., attended school at the Convent of Holy Child, Sharon Hill, Penn., and at Georgetown Convent, Georgetown, D. C. She was Queen of Momus in 1887 and Maid of several balls later. She is honorary president of the Louisiana Society in New York, and Member of American Legion Auxiliary in Paris, France, also Honorary member of Raphael Semmes Society in New York. She maintained during the World War a bureau and Canteen for Louisiana Soldiers in New York.

Chapter XVII.

THE SMYTH—SULLY FAMILIES
JOHN SMYTH.
1869 - 1935.
By Rudolph Matas, M. D.

Dr. John Smyth, the subject of this sketch was born on November 16th, 1869, at Wavertree Plantation, Tensas Parish, La. He came from a long line of distinguished Scotch-Irish ancestry. His father was a civil engineer of the Louisiana State Levee Board. His grandfathr was John Smyth, country gentleman of Darten's Castlederg, County Tyrone, Ireland. His great-grandfather was Lord Mayor of Londonderry. His mother was Rebbecca M. McMurtrie, born at Andalusia Plantation, Isaquena County, Mississippi. She was of Scotch ancestry, a direct descendant of Sir Christopher Wren, the famous architect of St. Paul's Cathedral, London, England, who was also a Physiologist of note and one of the first scientists of the 16th century to experiment with blood transfusion.

Dr. Smyth's father's mother was Annie Woods Smyth, of Ardcane County, Tyrone, Ireland. His uncle, Dr. Andrew Woods Smyth, for many years a celebrity as house surgeon of the Charity Hospital, New Orleans, became world famous in 1864 by performing the first successful ligation of the Innominate Artery, an operation which, up to his day, had proved invariably fatal. Another uncle, Dr. William Woods Smyth, who died recently at Maidstone, Kent, England, was a distinguishd Oculist and personal physician to King Edward VII, of England.

Doctor Smyth's early education was by tutor at his father's plantation. Thence he went to Centenary College, Jackson, La. He wanted to be a doctor, but his father persuaded him to be, like himself, a civil engineer. He was graduated from the Academic and Engineering department of Tulane, with distinction, and in 1886 entered the service of the United States Corps of Engineers with the

Mississippi River Commission, working in Louisiana under Colonel Kingman, Colonel Derby and Captain Millis. Excelling in this field, he won three promotions in one year. He built the large levee at Kemp's Bend and another at the head of Lake St. John, a notable responsibility for a youth.

In 1896 following his own bent, he determined to change his career, and, 27 years old, was matriculated at the Medical School of Tulane University. His mathematical education, innate taste for mechanics and his engineering experience served an admirable preparation for the Scientific study of Medicine and Surgery, an ambition in which he was much stimulated by the example of his distinguished uncle, Dr. Andrew W. Smyth. In 1889-1890, he was an interne at the Touro Infirmary and in 1900 was graduated with his M. D., at Tulane.

Soon after his graduation, he was invited by Dr. Matas, his friend and preceptor, to share his office and for nine years thereafter—until 1909, he remained in close contact and affiliation with him. During these years he was one of the first physicians in the city to utilize the x-rays for diagnostic and therapeutic purposes. His knowledge of physics and mechanics then served him a good purpose in transforming old and obsolete electrical generators into efficient x-ray machines, with which he obtained results that were amazing when his rudimentary equipment is considered. Several diagnostic feats in locating foreign bodies and in curing a number of seemingly hopeless cases of malignant disease, and of toxic goitre, gave him a reputation as an x-ray expert that soon brought him an appreciative clientele.

His absorbing interest in Roentgenology is well attested by early papers in the Transactions of the Orleans Parish, the Louisiana, Mississippi and other Regional Medical Societies during the period 1902-1907. In these contributions, he extended the indications and the applications of x-ray therapy and obtained unusual results which were undoubtedly due to his technical skill and discriminating knowledge of the potentialities and limitations of the rays, far in advance of the experience of his time.

His ability as a teacher and conscientious worker was soon recognized by his appointment as Instructor and Chief of the Laboratory of Minor Surgery for the manual training of junior students in the elementary technics of Surgery and first aid in emergencies, which Dr. Matas had established at the Medical School in 1902.

From this on, he rose rapidly in successive steps to the title of Assistant Professor of Clinical Surgery. He was holding this title with distinction when, on April 17, 1917, with America's entry into the World War, hospital units were organized to serve with the American Expeditionary Forces in France, Doctor Smyth immediately volunteered and was appointed to the Surgical Staff of Base Hospital No. 24, organized by Dr. Matas, Major and Director of the Unit in

New Orleans, under Red Cross Auspices, from the Tulane Medical Faculty and student body. Dr. Smyth by distinguished service at Limoges, France, rose from Captain to Major (chief of the Surgical Staff July 16, 1918—March 28, 1919) and was honorably discharged after the Armistice as Lieutenant Colonel, with the United States Military Cross. In 1919, on the return of Tulane Unit from overseas, the Faculty decided to recognize the patriotic and distinguished service of the Junior officers of the Unit by promoting them to a higher rank in the Faculty. Dr. Smyth was one of those elected to a full professorship of Clinical Surgery, a title which he held until 1927, when he resigned to meet the demands of private practice.

During the twenty-five years, 1902-1927, that Dr. Smyth was connected with the Tulane Medical Faculty, he was also visiting surgeon to the Charity Hospital on Dr. Matas' staff. During these years he worked assiduously and successfully as a teacher and operator in the clinic and in the laboratory. Besides his pioneer work in the development of the x-ray technic and therapy previously referred to, Dr. Smyth's training as an engineer and his innate mechanical genius and inventiveness were never more strikingly displayed than in an experimental research on the physiologic and pathologic effects of positive and negative atmospheric pressure on the lungs and the respiratory function in states of pulmonary collapse induced by acute surgical pneumothorax. In 1900 and 1901 when this research was undertaken, the surgery of the chest was still in the cradle and the fear of pulmonary collapse following the free opening of the thorax in intrathoracic operations, held back the boldest surgeons. As early as 1897 his chief, Dr. Matas, had demonstrated the protective value of rythmic intralaryngeal insufflation with the aid of a modified Fell-O'Dwyer apparatus used for artificial respiration in opium narcosis and other non-surgical state of respiratory failure. Though the practical value of this simple contrivance in maintaining the respiration in surgical pneumothrax had been experimentally and clinically demonstrated by Dr. Matas, it was evident that the practice of insufflation with a bellows would not do for this investigation and that a pneumatic pump accurately graded and capable of delivering definite quantities of air into the trachea under manometric control was indispensable. It was at this juncture that Dr. Matas availed himself of Dr. Smyth's expert collaboration for the construction of a pump that would meet the scientific requirements of the investigation.

Dr. Smyth went to work with enthusiasm and promptly designed and constructed several pumps, the last of which was fitted with connections for the administration of oxygen, ether and other anesthetic mixtures. With the aid of this perfected machine, a large series of experiments were performed on dogs and human cadavera which furnished the basic data for an accurate and rational application of intralaryngeal insufflation in intrathoratic operations which involved the pleurae. This was all pioneer work done long before the discussions of the relative merit of positive (plus) and negative (minus) pressure began to excite controversies among thoraric surgeons.

A full report of this inquiry with working models of Dr. Smyth's ingenious pump was presented by Dr. Matas with full acknowledgment of Dr. Smyth's invaluable collaboration, to the American Surical Association and published in the Transactions of May 1901.

This contribution of Dr. Smyth is especially mentioned as it is a most characteristic of his type of mind which found its greatest expression in problems which demanded mathematical precision and exactness for their solution. This tendency was displayed more in his works than in his writings which were relatively few and did not do justice to his best accomplishments. The practice of medicine and surgery did not adjust itself readily to his mathematical and mechanistic ideals but in striving for these he obtained the best results. He was not a prolific writer or inclined to erudite bibliographic search and display, but his papers all had a point which gave them originality and instructiveness. Apart from his early papers on Roentgen Technic and therapy and his contribution to the mechanics of artificial respiration in thoracic surgery.

He collaborated with Dr. Matas in an experimental study of the effects on the Heart and Circulation of Momburg's method of Aortic compression by circular Abdominal Constriction. The experiments were conducted on volunteer medical students and are summarized in the Transactions of the American Surgical Association for 1910 (vol. 28, pp. 622-623). He also wrote to Bone Transplantation to close defects in the cranial vault, on hernia, on gastric and duodenal ulcers, on vicious circle after gastroenterostomy, on oral anesthesia and analgesia, on abdominal pain and its interpretations on the lessons learned in the World War which were applicable to civilian practice, and following in the lead of his chief, he was among the first to perform endoaneurismorrhaphy. All these papers are scattered in the proceedings of the many local and regional societies of which he was a member. But some of his work in fractures and arthroplasty, in which he excelled, still remain dormant in unpublished manuscripts.

Early in his surgical career Dr. Smyth became associated with the Hotel Dieu where he centered the bulk of his practice from 1902 until his death. In these years countless patients gratefully remember his skill, charity and devotion and that memory is probably his most enduring monument.

Though not gregarious in his tendencies and always retiring, unpretentious and reserved, he was a strong believer in organized medicine and was early a member of his local and state organizations and of the American Medical Association. He was a Fellow of the Southern Surgical from 1920 to his death, of the American College of Surgeons, of the Association of Military Surgeons, of the Association for Thoracic Surgery, Endocrinology, and correspondent of the Edinburgh Research Society and still others, including the social clubs of the city and of the student Greek letter fraternities, too numerous to mention in this connection.

In 1911, he married Miss Jeanne Sully, daughter of Mr. Thomas Sully, a distinguished architect of New Orleans, and Eugenia Rocchi Sully, daughter of Giovanni Rocchi, one of New Orleans' most cultured and loved citizens of Italian birth. He was survived by his widow and two sisters, Mrs. Dwight Stone and Mrs. Fannie Le Sassier Young, both of Pecano Plantation, Tensas Parish, La.

The fatal illness which put an end to Dr. Smyth's earthly career, was foreshadowed on October 15, 1934, when at the end of a hard day's work and in apparently the best of health, he was seized suddenly with a profuse hematemesis which practically exsanguinated him. His medical friends promptly rallied to his side. The hemorrhage stopped and by means of transfusion and other means he revived and was apparently on the way to recovery when ascites and other signs indicating a progressive and complete portal obstruction appeared as an ominous forerunner of the inevitable end, which occurred on February 25, 1935. At the post-mortem a hypernephroma of the right kidney which had developed silently and without symptoms, was revealed as the probable source of his strange and unaccountable pathology.

As a friend of 37 years, the writer can do no better in expression of his sentiments than by repeating his own words in a tribute of personal appreciation that was published at the time of Dr. Smyth's death.

"Our early personal and professional relations, ripened into a warm friendship, based on mutual regard, trust and affection which never faltered or suffered an instant of doubt or hesitation. As a student he drew me by his earnestness, studiousness, sincerety and high sense of duty. Later, as an assistant and colleague, I found him true as steel, the incarnation of honesty, the soul of honor and unswerving loyalty. Very discriminate in his friendships, his affection and fidelity to those to whom he was attached was indeed a prized privilege and a great compliment.

"As a surgeon he was conscientious and cautious to an extreme degree, fastidiously meticulous in every detail for the patient's safety, anxious to do no harm if he could do no good. All conscientious surgeons share in the same anxieties, but his sense of responsibility so worried him before and after any serious operation, that it imposed great hardship upon his energy and his sensibilities by his sleepless vigilance. This made him extra cautious and deliberate, where others of far less knowledge did not hesitate. His solicitude and care for his patients, poor or rich, won their confidence and rewarded him by their grateful affection and friendship. Many who shed tears at his funeral mourned his loss as a veritable calamity.

"In his professional relations with his colleagues, Dr. Smyth was always courteous and punctilious in observing the Golden Rule, treating others as he wished them to treat him.

"He met death like a true doctor. Conscious almost to the last, he bore his trials with a calm and stoic fortitude, an equanimity of spirit characteristic of his courage, and becoming a physician who had met Death and stayed his hand too often to be fearful of his presence when he came, not as a foe, but as a friend to ease him of the pangs of disease which he knew was beyond all power of human help to conquer. He passed away painlessly and in peaceful slumber, attended by the loving hands of those dearest and closest to him."

—RUDOLPH MATAS.

SULLY GENEALOGY.

Matthew Sully married Sarah Chester. Their son, Chester Sully married Harriet Jane Green from Topsham, Maine, U.S.A. Her father was Ballard Green, a son of Jacob Green whose family traces back to five Sir Thomas Greens, one having a daughter Maude, whose daughter, Katherine Parr became the last wife of King Henry VIII of England and out-lived that much-married monarch.

Thomas Sully, the noted Southern architect, was a direct descendant of Chester Sully, who was a son of Matthew Sully, father of the famous portrait painter Thomas Sully for whom the architect was named. George Washington Sully, the father of the architect, a son of Chester Sully sat for the first miniature ever painted by his brother Thomas Sully the famous portrait painter. George Washington Sully was a resident of Mississippi City, Mississippi in 1855 when his son Thomas was born. The young man completed his education under the difficulties that faced every Southerner, following the devastating effects of the Civil War and carpet-bagger period that followed. Young Sully had shown marked ability in drawing as well as brilliancy in his classes. His family realizing that the impoverished South could not offer the advantages of an architectural education, young Tom was sent to New York City, after he had spent some time in the office of Lamour & Wheelock of Austin, Texas, where his architectural studies began. Always a keen observer, he had been a great admirer of the work of the Galliers, father and son, but he fully realized that the Civil War had been the death knell of the Greek Revival. On all sides he could see mongrel types of homes and buildings, that were to be eye-sores for half a century or more, replacing the quiet restful lines of the places that were vanishing. In New York City young Sully accustomed to the classic lines of the Southern structures could not abide the great piles of brown-stone and tile-inlaid stuccoed structures with towers, turrets and battlements stuck at every available angle. Nor could he abide the Queen-Ann fronts and Mary-Ann backs and all of the other jig-saw, so-called Gothic manors and villas that flooded the countryside during the middle and latter Victorian era. Mr. Sully was determined to crusade against these atrocities, but he found it a difficult task, so thoroughly had the craze for these types taken hold of the country.

The years spent with H. R. Marshall in New York City as well with J. Morgan Slade gave Sully the knowledge needed to make sky-scrapers spring from the soil where a few years before, one struck water at a depth of two feet. He had become an engineer as well as an architect. Sully was a close friend of my father's and was unusually considerate to me. He often took me on his drives when in quest of new motives for city and rural homes. He would stop and admire the work of architects of a century before, and ask, "Why do people want to fill Louisiana with buildings and homes that belong in Florida or California?" He was a great reader and liked to talk when he found an appreciative listener, and I tried to be a good listener for it is an accomplishment that well repays the effort.

Often I have had him tell me, "Never pass our City Hall without studying its perfection of line and detail. Not that we want a city filled with City Halls, but such a poem of architecture cannot but be an inspiration to better things be it architecture or clothing."

The day for the classic had passed, but on none of the buildings connected with Sully's name, be they early or late, do we find over ornamentation or senseless decoration. He would often say to my father in bringing in some sketch he had made, "The Sully will out."

Through the many years of his career in this city which covered the stuffy years of the nineties, Sully's work always showed simplicity of line, particularly when compared with others of the same era.

After studying in New York City, the lure of the South that he loved caused him to establish himself in New Orleans in 1881,

Mrs. Albert Sidney Ranlett, neé Miss Cora Semmes. (Courtesy of Mrs. S. P. Ranlett, Sr.)

Albert Sidney Ranlett, II

Thomas J. Semmes Ranlett.

Mrs. Myra Semmes Curtis
(Myra Semmes Ranlett)

David Low Ranlett

Mrs. Cora Ranlett Thomson
(Cora Ranlett)

Mrs. Eleanor Ranlett Kantzler
(Eleanor Ranlett)

Adele Ranlett

Thomas J. Semmes Ranlett, II

Cora Ranlett Blankenship

Albert Sidney Ranlett, III

Cora Semmes Curtis,
neé Cora Semmes Ranlett

Theodora Ranlett

Marie Ranlett

Eleanor Torrence Thomson

where his firm continued for nearly thirty-eight years. During this long period it was considered the leading one in the city and of the entire South. Among the buildings that he designed, are the St. Charles Hotel, the Milliken Hospital, the Tulane and Crescent Theatres, the Cosmopolitan Hotel, the old Hennen Building, which was the first sky-scraper in the city, the old Whitney Bank Building, the old Liverpool, London and Globe Building, as well as many fine residences in the uptown section of this city, besides the many buildings, hotels, and residences built elsewhere.

Mr. Sully retired from business about twenty years ago, after a long life crowned with success. His gracious daughter, one of the most popular members of the social set, is a talented artist, and has gained for herself quite a reputation as a moving-picture entertainer for the beauty and charm of the subjects she selects on her tours make her showings unusually entertaining travelogues.

Thomas Sully was an ardent yachtsman and designed a number of unusually fine yachts. He was a former commadore of the Southern Yacht Club. His last years were spent quietly at his attractive home in Richmond Place, this city, where he died at the age of eighty-three.

The Sully family came from England to live in the City of Charleston, South Carolina in the year 1792. Charleston at that date was one of the five cities of importance in the United States, but none of the five New York, Philadelphia, Boston, Baltimore and Charleston could boast of a population of 50,000.

The South through the invention of the cotton gin by Eli Whitney, made rapid strides from 1793 when his invention appeared thus enabling the planters to fill the immense orders for cotton from Europe especially from England.

Matthew Sully and his affectionate wife, the lovely and charming young Sarah Chester, braved parental anger when they were married. Sully's father had planned to make a Catholic priest of his son. He had obediently complied with his father's wishes and entered a Catholic seminary, but he soon discovered that the life of a priest was not for him, especially having met the lovely Sarah. At that time the family home was in the quaint old village of Long Credon in England, where in the ancient Anglican church can be seen on the walls many memorials to the family. This village had been the childhood home of Matthew

Sully's father, where he married and lived with his wife, a son and daughter, until in middle life he moved with his family to London. Upon learning that his son had married, Sully's father vowed he would disinherit him. Realizing that his father was in earnest and that their only wealth lay in each other's love, Matthew decided to use his ability as an orator for the stage instead of for the church. The fact that both he and his wife were musical greatly helped their mutual admiration and understanding. It is not known how long they remained in London after their marriage, but it is positively known that Thomas, their youngest son who became the famous portrait painter, was born in Horncastle, England, and that they lived there for some nine years before coming to Charleston, South Carolina.

Histrionic talent undoubtedly was a family accomplishment, for a sister of Matthew joined them in their stage venture, although she knew how opposed her religiously inclined father would be. She joined the young troupers, and shortly afterward married Thomas West, a supervisor and Actor-Manager. At that date supervising the building of theatres was very profitable. It was the contract to build the Charleston Theatre (lately restored by that city), that induced this branch of the Sully family to come to Charleston and join their relatives.

After their arrival in America Matthew Sully, Jr., who had reached manhood became an actor, appearing in Charleston in Pantomine. Lawrence Sully, eldest son of Matthew Sully I, did not become an actor, but studied art and became a miniature painter. In 1799 he married Sarah Annis of Maryland, and his brother Matthew Sully II, married Elizabeth Robertson of Virginia. Their son, Robert Matthew Sully, in whose veins also flowed the blood of artists, studied with his uncle Thomas (the famous portrait painter), in Philadelphia and in 1824 went to England where he continued his studies. Returning in 1828 he settled in Richmond, Virginia. In 1855 he was commissioned to paint for the Historical Society of Madison, Wisconsin, portraits as well as scenes of the battlefields of the Indian Wars of that section. Starting for Madison in 1855 he was taken ill at Buffalo, N. Y., and died after an illness of a few days. His son Robert Matthew Sully was Superintendent of the Atlantic Coast Line Railroad. He married Elisabeth Rucker Williams, their only child is Miss Julia Sully of Richmond, Virginia.

The five daughters of Matthew Sully were married in the city of Charleston, S. C., the announcement appearing in the "City Gazette" on May 30th, 1793, of his daughter Charlotte: "Married on Thursday evening, by Rev. Dr. Purcell." On the day following another announcement stating in the same paper, "Mr. Chambers, Comedian, to Miss Charlotte Sully". The Mr. Chambers referred to was a distinguished English actor who had made his first appearance in America at the Southwark Theatre in Philadelphia in 1792, and had made a reputation at the Theatre Royal and the Haymarket in England before coming to America. A daughter, Julia Sully, became the wife of a miniature painter of Charleston, S. C., by the name of Belzons, in 1794. Another daughter, Jane, married J. B. Leroy, a prominent resident of Charleston. Harriet, who had only acted in child parts, was the fourth daughter to be married, became the wife of Dr. Porcher. Elisabeth, romantically inclined, eloped with Middleton Smith, a son of the Landgrave. The family was a handsome one. Elizabeth in her early twenties enjoyed the reputation of being a radiantly beautiful young woman with all of the town at her feet.

THOMAS SULLY

Noted Portrait Painter.

Thomas Sully's real talent began to manifest itself when he reached the age of fourteen. As a small child he was forever making pictures, and his teachers chided him about his everlasting drawing to the neglect of his studies. The family being one theatrically inclined, young Sully thought to follow in the footsteps of his family, but soon abandoned the idea and interested himself in his art with greater enthusiasm. He worked in a broker's office before finally deciding to make art his life work. From then on for more than forty years we find him incessantly at work. The record that he has kept of his work confirms this. In the shaping of his career he was encouraged by Benjamin West and Gilbert Stuart who told him to keep what he had and get all he could get. West's advice to Sully was "study portraiture, and above all study it in England", for in West's opinion the English School offered the greatest opportunities. He encouraged the young man in every way possible, and pointed out details of his various pictures, explaining the value of poses and lighting, etc. Benjamin West realized that Sully had in him the making of a great painter. This is confirmed by a letter that he wrote to a friend of his in Philadelphia on Nevember 3rd, 1809. In the letter he deplores the fact that the finances of young Sully may prevent his continuing his studies. He points out what a tragedy it would be to the art world for one with the talent young Sully possessed to have to abandon his career owing to his curtailed finances. He ended by stating, "When the success of Mr. Sully in his profession as a painter is so much to be desired."

In glancing over the register of his work, we find that on May 10th, 1801, Thomas Sully painted a miniature of his brother Chester Sully from life, the first item of his work to be entered in the register. As we glance through it, we find he carefully details each entry with name of sitter, color of complexion, eyes, hair, the price of the picture, etc. His brother Lawrence also painted miniatures, but never became the great artist that his younger brother did. Lawrence was some years older than Thomas Sully, and after the misunderstanding Thomas had with his brother-in-law, he bent his steps towards the home of his older brother who also painted various devices along with miniatures to earn a living. Thomas Sully had been apprenticed to Mr. Belzons who had married his sister Julia in 1794, and during a painting lesson his hot-tempered brother-in-law quarreled, whereon young Thomas departed for Richmond, Va. Downhearted and discouraged he determined not to go back to his sister's home. Only sixteen years old, his father and mother dead, and he without finances, wondered how he was going to reach Richmond. When almost in dispair he met a friend, who permitted him to share his home and food until Sully met a naval officer by the name of Reed. Reed used his influence in obtaining a midshipman's birth for Sully, which gave the young artist an opportunity to reach Richmond. The tradition has it that young Thomas was on the point of continuing as a marine, when his brother wrote him and advised him to come to his home in Richmond, thus turning into a good artist one who no doubt would have made an indifferent sailor. The suggestion that he become a pupil of his older brother of whom he was very fond, save the world a noted portrait painter while if Lawrence had been indifferent, young Sully's life would have been entirely altered.

At Lawrence's home he was warmly welcomed by his sister-

Crest and Coat-of-Arms of the McMURTRIE family

"WAVERTREE MANOR", built in 1834 for Mr. Elam Bowman, birthplace of Dr. John Smyth.

THOMAS SULLY,
Noted Architect.

Mrs. John Smyth (Jean Sully), in Spring Fiesta Costume.
(Pictures courtesy of Mrs. John Smyth.)

in-law, who had been a Miss Sarah Annis of Annapolis, and their two children who made much of the new arrival. Lawrence at the time was thirty years of age, and before the year had passed another daughter was born. Lawrence and his family with young Thomas moved to Norfolk, and here it was that Thomas painted his first miniature from life, a portrait of his brother Chester.

In 1803 we find Thomas Sully and the family back in Richmond. Thomas had made some headway with his art, but the death of his brother, Lawrence, that year threw great reponsibilities on the shoulders of the young artist, for we learn that he assumed all of the household expenses which heretofore had been paid by Lawrence. This seemed to develop further his great talent. Naturally the constant contact with a charming young widow only four years his senior, one who had shown her devotion when he needed encouragement most, soon gained his affections. They were married two years after Lawrence's death. Their marriage proved to be a most happy one and was blessed with nine children, forming a large and affectionate family. Notwithstanding that his art duties kept him constantly occupied he never neglected his family. He realized his responsibilities and his duties to the communities in which he resided, and left an unblemished name crowned with honor.

Thomas Sully visited England on two occasions, his work showing strongly the influence of these visits. On his second visit to England at that time at the height of his powers, twenty-seven years after his first visit, he was selected to paint a portrait of Queen Victoria, who had recently succeeded to the throne of Britain, for the Society of St. George in Philadelphia. The Society adopted this resolution: "To memorialize her Majesty to sit for her picture to Mr. Sully for the gratification and use of the Society". Mr. Sully became an American citizen before making this second visit to Europe. The memorial reading "We have been induced thus to petition your Majesty in consequence of the contemplated departure of Thomas Sully, Esq. for England, whom we beg leave to recommend to your Majesty as the most finished artist in portraits in America, who would do ample justice to your picture, and who combines in himself the various recommendations of being an Englishman by birth, an accomplished artist and a gentleman".

The Sully family were thrilled with the expected visit to Europe and in the midst of the excitement of the moment, his daughter in the seventh heaven of delight as the time for leaving approached Thomas Sully received a notification that his son Alfred had been appointed to West Point. It was hard to know who was the most delighted one of this family, Blanche who was to visit England with her father, Alfred who had been appointed to West Point, or the great artist at the prospect of painting the portrait of the young Queen. It was indeed a happy family at this date. Thomas Sully, the happy father, wrote the following letter to his friend who was the Secretary of War:

> "To the Honorable Joel Poinsette"
> Dear Sir:
>
> I have taken passage with my daughter for London and am about to sail on the 10th inst, from New York.
>
> I cannot leave home without the gratification of returning you my grateful thanks for your kindness in appointing my son on trial as a cadet at West Point.
>
> I hope his future good conduct will prove his gratitude for the privilege.
>
> I pray God bless and prosper you.
>
> Very sincerely your friend and obliged
humble S'v't
Thomas Sully.

The artist's son lived up to his father's hopes, graduating in the year 1841 from West Point with high honors—all through the four years as a cadet he stood as an honor man in his classes.

Like his famous father he too was to shed luster on the Sully name. At the termination of the War Between the States in which he was active throughout, he is listed as brevette Major-General of Volunteers, and Brigadier-General in the Regular Army. In acknowledgment of his services to the United States, "Fort Sully" established in 1866 in Dakota Territory was named in his honor.

The trip across was an enjoyable one for father and daughter, and when comfortably located in London, another triumph was to come to Mr. Sully. "The Queen consents to sit most willingly—— think of that! The news coming through Lord Melbourne.——She is now at Windsor Castle passing the Christmas holidays—— and as soon as she comes to town she sends word that she'll gratify Mr. Sully".

Old files of THE TRUE AMERICAN, bearing the date December 18, 1839, on page 2, column 3 we find notices of the arrival of the portrait Mr. Sully painted of the English Queen. The portrait was placed on exhibition and the following newspaper article appared:

> Sully's Victori.a This magnificent full length portrait of Queen Victoria, painted by Sully from life at the Court of St. James, has been received by John J. Haswell of this city, consigned to him by the "Society of the Sons of St. George, established in Philadelphia for the advice and assistance of Englishmen in distress" and we are pleased to learn that Mr. Haswell in conformity with the wishes of that truly benevolent association, will cause the same to be exhibited in aid of its funds as soon as a suitable location shall present.
>
> Report speaks highly of this work of Mr. Sully and it has frequently been stated in the English journals, over the signature of the most eminent artists that Mr. Sully has been most successful in conveying a true likeness of her majesty.

POCAHONTAS PORTRAIT

Excerpts from Letters of Robert Sully to Lyman Draper give interesting history to Students of Early Virginia: Discussion over Picture. (News Leader, April 21, 1934) by Julia Sully.

> From time to time discussion arises as to the famous picture of Pocahontas known as the Turkey Island Portrait. Perhaps the following excerpts from the letters of Robert Sully to Lyman Draper, corresponding secretary of the state historical society of Wisconsin, during the years 1854-1855 may be of some interest to students of this subject.
>
> Robert Sully, nephew of Thomas Sully, was commissioned by the historical society of Wisconsin to paint the portraits of Black Hawk, the prophet and Black Hawk's son when these Indian captives were brought to Fortress Monroe. Many letters passed between the artist and Mr. Draper during the execution of this commission, and a strong friendship was formed which finally determined Sully to leave Virginia and make his home in Madison Wisconsin. In October 1855, the artist started for his new home, but stopping in Buffalo he contracted pneumonia and after an illness of ten days died in that city. The first reference to Pocahontas occurs in a letter dated April 20th, 1854, in which he writes: Permit me to suggest to your society (state historical society of Wisconsin) a little gift I designed for them. Some twenty years ago there existed in Virginia the fragments of a portrait that had always been regarded as an original of "Pocahontas". I copied this picture which excited much interest at the time. My copy was engraved in the Indian gallery got up by

Herring and Longacre. The certificates of many members of the family (her descendants) giving an account of the somewhat interesting manner of its coming to Virginia, etc., I possesss and can send you.

In consequence of its being in the absurd costume of James I, all Indian association was destroyed. I can at any time get access to my own pictures. I propose reproducing or repeating this picture in more ideal style, more in accordance with Indian character, at the same time preserving the features and expressions which are truly fine. I am under these circumstances, to paint one for the Virginia historical society; at the same time I will paint one for your society which I beg will be accepted as a feeble token of my interest and good wishes for your prosperity.

* * * *

It is true the subject is one not having reference to your State (Wisconsin) but surely a memorial of so interesting a being, who twice saved the Colony of Virginia by her heroism and devotion, under circumstances of singular peril and romance, may be regarded as an object of interest any where. The response to this offer must have been a cordial acceptance, for on May 13, 1854 Robert Sully writes as follows. I am glad that you attach so flattering an interest to the Pocahontas, let me explain my idea of treatment of the subject. The classic and correct Beverly, the oldest Virginian historian, alluding to the pastimes and festivities of the Indian girls, the wild gambols of the dance &c. says: "Even the decent Pocahontas did not disdain to mingle in these pastimes. Crowned with a wreath of flowers, as she sometimes led the chases and presided in the dance". That hint I have taken. The details of Indian costume are far from being poetic . . . . I shall represent a beautiful girl, nude to a little below the shoulders, so as to preserve delicate associations with so interesting a subject the only approach to costume, the fur of some animal." This is historical and true, but the wild flowers of the Virginia forest are beautiful and poetic and equally true. My friend Mr. Maxwell, the president of the Virginia historical society, is much pleased with my design as agreeing with his ideal completely.

GREENE.

It is commonly supposed that the name of Green is of Saxon or Scandinavian origin, but it is found that there was a patrician family of this name after the Roman Conquest of England, which suggests that it is of Latin derivation.

In the early part of the thirteenth century, about twelve years before the granting of the Magna Charta, during the reign of King John, there lived in England one Alexander de Boketon. It was his great grandson who took unto himself the name of GREENE, and spelled it Greene. He was created a knight and was a member of Parliament from Northampton Country. Sir Henry Greene, a descendant of this family, became Lord Chief Justice of England.

Crest and Coat-of-Arms of the Greene family.

Katherine Parr, painted 1547. Wife of Henry VIII of England. (Original in collection of the Earl of Ashburton.)

Self Portrait by Thomas Sully

Chester Sully. Portrait by Thomas Sully.

Crest and Coat-of-Arms of the family of Pierre Denis de la Ronde. (Courtesy of Emile Ducros, Historian.) See page 132, Vol. II.

Crest and Coat-of-Arms of the de Dreux family which descends directly from the Comte de Dreux, 5th son of Louis VI of France. (See page 140, Vol. II.). (Courtesy of Mr. and Mrs. Robert Dugue de Livaudais.)

In America the first Greenes settled in New England and Major John Greene was Deputy Governor of the Colony of Rhode Island. Prominent personages of the family in later times were Joseph Warren Greene and William Benton Greene, of Rhode Island. The latter was an eminent clergyman and professor of ethics at Princeton Theological Seminary. Charles Samuel Greene, of California is also a descendant.

WAVERTREE MANOR

Originally attached to this splendid old plantation manor house was a tract of four thousand acres. This was purchased in 1834 by Mr. Elam Bowman, at which time a house was erected which later became a part of the present immense home, which was built for Mr. Bowman in 1857 under the direction of a New York architect, Mr. Eshleman.

Among the large number of slaves owned by Mr. Bowman of the plantation family of that name, was one named Caleb Christopher, who had been purchased in Louisville, Kentucky, for the sum of $3,000.00 and brought to this site to do much of the cabinet work in Wavertree Manor. Caleb Christopher was a finished carpenter and was put in charge of the work. The overhead paneling of porches, etc., was done by another skilled slave. Nothing but choicest cypress was used in the Wavertree manor house, every bit of the woodwork in the place being prepared and built on the spot. An expert in plaster work, Mr. Carkeet, who came from Natchez, did the plastering of the walls inside as well as on the exterior, which, when finished had the appearance of marble. It is still in good condition after a century of wear.

The house, a very large one, was nearly completed when war was declared, and the architect returned to New York. As the slate that had been ordered for the roof did not come, hand-made shingles were substituted for the slate, and rushing the work, the house was completed before the Union soldiers got very far South.

Mr. Bowman's family and his descendants occupied the house from the time it was finished until 1925. Since then it has been empty for part of the time in charge of a care-taker. It was bought by the Moberly Brothers of Tallulah, and then became the property of Mr. L. T. Collins, who was greatly interested in the place and did much to restore the house and improve the grounds. Now it is the home of Mr. Berry who lives there and manages the 1580 acres that are still attached to the manor. Mr. and Mrs. Bert W. Berry, and their family, are social-minded and have the old place gay again, which recalls the hospitality of olden days.

The rooms are immense, the two front ones being twenty feet square, and the hallway between eighteen feet wide. The porches around the house upstairs and down are extremely wide, so much so that measurement of the distance around the porch shows that "seven times around the porch amounts to a mile". The mansion contains some twenty spacious rooms. The splendid furniture that had been ordered when the war broke out never was delivered, but other antiques have filled the rooms. The house is two-storied with an observatory from which one gets a splendid view of the surrounding country.

It has been a great cotton plantation in its day and its acres still afford a large yield of the white fluffy bolls.

The grounds about the house are extensive having a variety of trees surrounded by stately oaks. It has never been permitted to fall into ruin and today happiness reigns there again, recalling the days when the Misses Ivy of England lived there, and named the place after that of their friend, Mrs. Hemans, poetess of England. Located on a road that branches westward from Highway 65, at a point known as the Helena Bridge about two and a half miles from this point the old mansion appears in all its glory, a spot loved by the patrician families of Tensas Parish, old and young for it was a great social center in olden days.

As lights glimmer in the negro cabins at twilight in the distance and the strumming of a banjo with the cadence of negro melodies is wafted to those seated on the broad cool porches, Time is turned backward and one thinks of the Golden Age when plantation life was at its best.

de Marigny de Mandeville.

CHAPTER XVIII.

THE DE MARIGNY—DE LA RONDE—ALMONASTER DE DREUX—VILLERÉ—BEAUREGARD—LANAUX RARESHIDE FAMILIES

de MARIGNY.

FROM the marriage of Pierre de Marigny to Jean Marie d'Estrehan, four children were born. Jean Philippe, who died unmarried; Marie Celeste, who became the wife of Jacques Francois Enoulde de Livaudais; Antoine Marie on account of her ravishing beauty, called by the Duc. D'Orleans, La Perle, who died without issue, and Bernard, the third child. Bernard Philippe de Marigny de Mandeville, born in 1785, died in 1868, married Mary Ann Jones, daughter of Evans Jones of Pennsylvania, who had been American Consul at New Orleans, and Marie Verret. Mary Ann Jones died in childbirth in Philadelphia June 4th, 1808. About eighteen months later Bernard married Anne Mathilde Morales of a prominent Spanish family. His second marriage not proving a happy one, he spent a great deal of his time on his estate in Mandeville, Louisiana.

The children of Bernard de Marigny and Mathilde Morales were five in number, as follows: I. Antoine James, known as "Mandeville" Marigny; who was born in 1811 and married Sophronia Claiborne, daughter of Charles Cole Claiborne, first American Governor of Louisiana. Her death occurred in 1890, her three children by this marriage died without issue. Antoine James (Mandeville) de Marigny died in 1890.

2. Rosa de Marigny, born in 1813, married M. de Sentmanat (who became involved in a plot against Santa Anna) issue three daughters; one became Madame Nevil Soule, son of Pierre Soule; another married Allan Eustis, (descendants residing in Europe), and the third became Mrs. Philippe Villere, no children.

3. Angela de Marigny, born 1817, became Madame F. Peschier, who was Swiss consul in New Orleans. Became the parents of several one of their daughters becoming Mrs. Leon Joubert de Villemarest.

4. Armand de Marigny.

5. Malthilde de Marigny, born 1820, became Mrs. Albin Michel de Grilleaud, a son of the French consul in Louisiana. When Prosper de Marigny, the great grandson of Bernard de Marigny and Mary Jones (Evan Hall Plantation) died in Mandeville, La., 1910, the name of Marigny became extinct in Louisiana, where it had occupied a prominent position for over two centuries.

The children of Pierre Philippe de Marigny, the elegant aristocrat and multi-millionaire who died in 1800 were five in number as follows: Antoine, born 1773; Jean, born 1781, no children; Bernard, born 1785; Marie Celeste, born February, 1786, who married Jacques Enoult de Livaudais; Antoine, born in 1787, no children.

GENEALOGY OF THE DE LA RONDE FAMILY.

(From the authentic notes compiled by Joseph Emile Ducros, Historian, Mandeville, Louisiana.)

Jacques Denis de la Thibaudiere, son of Jacques Denis de la Thibaudiere and of Marie Cosmier, was a Captain in the troops and subsequently quartermaster General of the armies of Louis XIII and XIV. During the wars of Candis and Crete (1645-1674) between the Turks and Venetians, Venice calling loudly to

Christendom for assistance and Christendom replied in the persons of thousands of French soldiers and sailors who volunteered secretly for Malta and Venice, as there was no open war between Turkey and France. In some cases they actually deserted the royal service in order to go. Jacques Denis responded to the urgent appeal and took service with Malta. He was killed at Chios in the terrific naval battle between the celebrated Anne Hilaire de Contentin, Count of Tourville assisted by Honore de Mouchy d'Hocquincourt, who with three hundred men in a fine 36-gun frigate defeated twenty-four Turkish galleys.

Hugues Denis de la Thibaudiere, brother of the foregoing, was an officer in the Regiment of Royal Guards. He was killed in Italy. Marie Denis de la Thibaudiere, daughter of Jacques Denis and Marie Cosmier, first married Mons. de Norvaise and left no children. In her second nuptial with Robin Seigneur du Bourg Desure in Touraine, she left two daughters. Francoise Denis de la Thibaudiere, daughter of Jacques Denis and of Marie Cosmier, married Monsieur Robin, Provincial Provost and Intendant of Gabeles (exciseman). They left several children— Simon Denis, Ecuyer, Sieur de la Trinite in Canada, brother of Nicolas Denis (Royal Governor of Acadia, etc.) great-great-grandfather of Pierre Denis de la Ronde of Versailles plantation.

As one of the first settlers of America, he set an example for his descendants to emulate. Neither the biting winds of the Northern forests, nor the treacherous red enemy that was perhaps hiding behind many of the ice-clad trees, when in the depths of winter he trudged through the piling snow drifts to uphold the glory of the Lilies of France and extend the dominion of his King, daunted him. Born in Tours, Touraine, France, in 1599, he was baptized in the church of St. Vincent of Tours. He was the founder of the family in New France (Canada) and became one of the distinguished officers of the celebrated Carignan-Salieres regiment sent to Canada by Louis XIV, holding a commission as Captain in this famous fighting unit. The men that comprised it had won their spurs on foreign fields, and they accomplished in Canada still mightier achievements. They were sent to America to subdue a treacherous ever-aggressive and bloodthirsty foe, the Iroquois, who as early as the first settlement of Quebec by Champlain in 1608 had harassed the French. The Carignan-Saliere regiment fought with dash and distinction in the European and Turkish wars under the great Turenne.

Pierre Denis, Esq. Sr. de la Ronde (the progenitor of the Louisiana family), son of Louis Denis de la Ronde, and Marie Louise Chartier de Lothiniere, was born at Quebec on Nov. 11, 1726. He was an officer of the French Navy, detached therefrom by the King and assigned to duty as a lieutenant of foot soldiers in the Infantry of the Marines (a training corps d'elite, an exclusive, military, nobly born body, intensely punctilious aloof and superior, the "Great Corps") sent to Louisiana prior to Feb. 26th, 1748, when he was twenty-one years old. He was a Knight of the Royal and Military Order of St. Louis and member of the early Cabildo as Regidor. About 1755*1757 he married Marie Madeline Broutin (widow) of Louis Xavia Martin de Lino, ecuyer, Sieur de Chalmet, formally a lieutenant of infantry in the French marine, of the Natchez Post in 1751. A daughter of Ignace Francois Broutin, one of the Colony's royal engineers, also Captain and Commandant of the Natchez Post.

Pierre Denis de la Ronde became the father of four daughters and one son, all of whom married persons of distinction as shown hereinafter. Louise de la Ronde, born in New Orleans, July 25th, 1758. She was married in St. Louis church, March 20th, 1787, to Don Andres Almonaster y Roxas, a native of Mayrene, in the Kingdom of Andalusia in Spain, son of Don Miguel Jose Almonaster and Dona Maria Juanna de Estrada Y. Roxas. Her second marriage was to Jean Baptiste Victor Castillon, a native of Tarnos in the Lower Pyranees, France, born in 1765, the youthful and dapper French Consul at New Orleans, son of Etienne Castillon and Isabelle Lasserre.

Therese Josephte de la Ronde, born Sept. 14th, 1759, was married in the church of St. Louis, April 25th, 1778, to Don Juan Pristo (an officer of the Spanish Troops who came in the train of General O'Reilly), son of Don Pedro Pristo and Francisca de la Bargos, both natives of Havana, Cuba. Marguerite de la Ronde, born June 10th, 1761, was married (as evidenced by the de la Ronde papers in possession of the Misses de Hoa Le Blanc) to Francois Xavia Dagobert de Verges, Sieur de St. Sauver, and Marie Pinau. Pierre Denis de la Ronde was born April 20th, 1762. As a cadet in the second company, first battalion, First Regiment of Louisiana Infantry (maintained by his Catholic

Majesty the King of Spain), he participated under Governor Galvez in the campaigns against Baton Rouge, Mobile and Pensacola, 1779 - 1781, during the conquest of West Florida. For valiant services rendered in that campaign, he was promoted by the Governor to a lieutenancy in the same company. Prior to Feb. 28th, 1748, when he was twenty-one year old, he was a knight of the Royal and Military Order of St. Louis and a member of the early Cabildo as Rigidor.

Pierre Denis Seur de la Ronde, born in the City of Quebec on the 11th day of October, 1726, was the son of Louis Pierre Denis de la Ronde and Marie Louise Chartier de Lothiniere. He married Madeline Broutin, whose father was the wealthy and prominent royal engineer under Bienville. Pierre Denis de la Ronde's family had a patent of nobility accorded in Quebec in 1691.

The children of Pierre Denis de la Ronde and Madeline Broutin were four in number, one of whom, Louise de la Ronde, who was born in New Orleans, July 25, 1758. On March 20, 1787, at the age of twenty-nine she became the wife of Don Andres Almonaster y Roxas. Of this marriage, one child was born, named Micaela Almonaster, who later married Celestin de Pontalba, and left New Orleans to live in France at the Chateau Mont. L'Eveque. The bride inherited not only her own share of her father's estate, but also that of a sister, who had died before her father, and again at her mother's death, she inherited another vast fortune.

A spoiled child with every wish gratified and untold millions at her command, Mme. Pontalba wearied of the solitude of the country, and longed for the excitement of city life she had always known. Bored to death by the quiet home-life at the chateau and her husband's dull relatives, she sought an outlet for her attacks of nerves by directing her own private theatre. There she and her friends gave theatrical performances much to the annoyance of her husband and his family, who incessantly chided her for her continuous extravagancies. It was not long before a separation occurred, so managed that scandal was avoided. She made a visit to Louisiana to attend to business matters and the succession of her mother. On returning to Paris she secured her freedom from her husband.

On an October morning in the year 1834 at the Chateau Mont L'Eveque screams were heard coming from an apartment and servants, aroused by this disturbance in the early hours, rushed in to find the Baronne de Pontalba moaning and apparently in a dying condition, as blood was pouring from the pistol wounds that rent her body. A surgeon was summoned and almost by a miracle saved her life. Her father-in-law, the old Baron de Pontalba, was found dead in an upright position, his hand clinging to a pistol and resting on the chair in which he sat.

His descendants say that the wilful waste, as he considered it, of the fortune which should have been saved for her children, had driven the eighty-year-old man insane. Even this tragedy did not curb her extravagance, for when she learned that the marble palace that had been built by King Louis XIV for the Duke of du Maine was to be demolished, she purchased the palace and attempted to live there. But she soon found that even her millions could not maintain so grand a palace. Its rooms numbered four hundred, and repairs were greatly needed, so after a consultation with architects, the chateau was demolished. The marble and statuary, carved and paneled woodwork, and other materials were salvaged and used in rebuilding for her a smaller chateau, more in keeping with her income.

Here she lived the life she liked—an incessant round of gala balls and fetes, banquets, etc., to which the most exclusive of the aristocrats of the exclusive Faubourg St. Germaine came. Later, she again visited New Orleans where, as usual, she was warmly greeted by her large circle of friends and relatives. It was then that she carried out her plan to build the two rows of beautiful old Pontalba buildings that make of Jackson Square one of the finest of its kind in America.

It was in the Pontalba house that Jennie Lind stayed while in New Orleans, as the guest of that distinguished lady. Mme. Pontalba also contributed freely to the erection of Jackson Monument, and financed the remodeling of the Place D'Arms into the beautiful square we see today. After lying empty half a century, the ancient Pontalba Buildings are again homes of distinguished and cultured people.

Pierre Denis de la Ronde II built the beautiful Versailles plantation mansion, the handsomest in the state at that date. From letters written when the de la Rondes lived at Versailles, we judge it to have been the leading salon in the state, as all the

Micaela Leonarda Baronne de Pontalba (neé Almonaster.)

Baron de Pontalba, Sr.

The Baronne Celestin de Pontalba in old age.

Baron Celestin de Pontalba in old age.

(All pictures courtesy of Mrs. Edwin X. de Verges.)

Don Andres Almonaster.
(Courtesy Louisiana Museum.)

The Duke of Orleans, who later became Louis Philippe, King of France. While in exile in America with his two brothers were entertained and befriended by the wealthy aristocrats of Louisiana in 1798.

Antoine Marie de Marigny de Mandeville, called "La Perl" because of her great beauty. (Courtesy of Mrs. R. G. Dugue.)

Bernard de Marigny, who set the standard of high living, while wasting fortunes, always remained a gentleman.

brilliant people of the day gathered at the banquets given by this distinguished family.

Pierre Denis de la Ronde II was a member of General Andrew Jackson's staff at the time of the Battle of New Orleans, the greater part of the fighting being done on the Versailles plantation. Later he was made a Major General of the militia of the State. When the English invaded Louisiana, coming by way of Bayou St. John, through the Villere Canal in 1812, Colonel Pierre de la Ronde, who had just returned from Chef Menteur, was met by de Villere who had escaped from the English, informing him that the Red Coats had landed. Both hastened at once to General Jackson in New Orleans, who decided to fight that night— a decision resulting in victory. Most of the fighting took place on the de la Ronde plantation, although the Chalmette plantation has always been said to be the scene of the heaviest fighting. Beneath the great grove of the de la Ronde oaks the next morning a large number of dead Englishmen were found.

With the death of Colonel Pierre Denis de la Ronde at Versailles in 1820 ended the name in Louisiana. But he left nine daughters who all married, leaving a large number of socially porminent descendants.

The other children of Pierre Denis de la Ronde and Madeline Broutin were (2) Marie Theresa de la Ronde, born Sept. 4, 1759, died April 20, 1817, having married on April 25, 1778, a son of Don Pedro Prieto named Juan Prieto of Havana, Cuba. (3) Margaret de la Ronde, born June 10, 1761 and who became the wife of M. deVerges de St. Sauveur. (4) Pierre Denis de la Ronde, Jr., born in New Orleans, April 20, 1762, married Mademoiselle Eulalie Guerbon, a daughter of M. Alexander Guerbon and Elizabeth de Trepagnier, whose family owned a number of plantations on the west bank of the Mississippi River. He died Dec. 1, 1824. He had one son and this son died without issue, so the name became extinct in Louisiana.

Pierre Denis de la Ronde III, born Jan. 1st, 1801, and died March 12th, 1840, the only son, who wedded Malvina Roche on May 22nd, 1828, a daughter of Don Nicolas Roche and Dona Louisa Sigur. Adelaide Adel de la Ronde, born Dec. 24th, 1803, and died the 22nd of October, 1837, who was married on April 15th, 1820, to Pierre Adolph Ducros, son of Joseph Rodolph Ducros and Marie Lucie de Reggio, daughter of Francois Marie de Reggio and Helene de Fleuriau; issue as follows: Elisabeth Adel Ducros, whose husband was Gabriel Erieville Villere; Pierre Adolph Ducros,, Jr., born Mar. 16th, 1827, died June 20th, 1905. A graduate of Harvard University and became one of the leading legal lights of the New Orleans bar of which he was a member for fifty-six years. He married Coralie Auguste Louise Fernet, daughter of Louis Fernet and Francoise Victoire Webre, who was born in France, and Villere, unmarried.

Elizabeth Celeste de la Ronde, born June 15th, 1791, died Sept. 1st, 1822; she married Maunsell White, a native of Kentucky, who was born in Ireland in 1784, and died Dec. 17th, 1863. His parents were Lawford White and Anna Maunsell. She had one child named Eliza who became Mrs. Cuthbert Bullit, her husband being a native of Kentucky, issue one child that died in childhood.

Heloise de la Ronde, born Dec. 11th, 1792, and died on the 14th of November, 1867, who after the death of his first wife married Maunsell White. Issue three children: 1st, Anna White who became the wife of Dr. Hugh Kennedy of Louisville, Kentucky. Issue—Heloise Kennedy, who became Mrs. Malcolm Bullit; Clara Kennedy, who became Mrs. Aleck Bullit, and Anna (Nan) Kennedy, unmarried.

Clara White, daughter of Heloise de la Ronde, married Carl Kohn, a New Orleans banker, and became the mother of six daughters; Hilda Meyer, unmarried; Clara Meyer, who married Louis M. McCaleb; Evelyn Meyer, unmarried; Mildred Meyer, unmarried; Leonora Meyer, who became Mrs. John Hickey; and Virginia Meyer, unmarried.

Maunsell White, Jr., who married Elizabeth Porter Bradford, a niece of Jefferson Davis. Issue—Sidney Johnson White, who married Elizabeth Tobin; Anna White, who became Mrs. Thomas H. Anderson; Lucie White, who became Mrs. (Dr.) Clement P. Wilkinson; Mary White, who became Mrs. A. Ringgold Brousseau; Elizabeth White, who became Mrs. Edwin W. Rod; Carl White, who married Mary Mitchell, and Maunsell White who died unmarried.

Josephine Pepita de la Ronde, born June 21st, 1796, died Aug. 11th, 1851, whose first husband was Thomas S. Cunningham, of the U. S. Navy; became the mother of seven children, as follows: Christian Louis Ducros, who died in childhood; Victoria Louise Ducros, died in childhood; Delaronde Pierre Ducros, who went to Central America, establishing himself in Bluefields, Nicaragua, later dying there; Louis Henry Ducros, who never married; Adolph Victor Ducros, unmarried; Joseph Emile Ducros, born on Pecan Grove plantation, Feb. 15th, 1865, whose wife is Florence Olivia Patton and became the parents of five children; Fernet Octave Ducros, born July 7th, 1869, who was married April 12th, 1887, to Henri Jules Stouse, and became the mother of eight children.

Marie Felicete de la Ronde, born Sept. 28th, 1805, died 29th of September, 1842, became Mrs. Jayme F. Jorda, wife of the son of Jayme J. F. Jorda and Mlle. Helene de Reggio. Issue nine children.

Isabelle Emilie de la Ronde, born 6th of August, 1807, died March 18th, 1890, became Mrs. Pierre de Hoa Cacho, born 16th of September, 1802, died Nov. 2nd, 1866; Pierre de Hoa Cacho's parent were Don Manuel de Hoa. Emilie de la Ronde bore him three children, as follows: Amalie de Hoa, who became Madame Uubain Forestier, issue one child, Albert Forestier; Appoline de Hoa, who became Madame Belgarde Lacoste; Eulalie de Hoa, who became Madame Charles Emile LeBlanc. Issue seven children.

Magdalina Azelie de la Ronde, born 21st of May, 1809, and died 1st of July, 1872, became Madame Pierre Urbain Forestier. Issue two sons named as follows: Urbain Forestier, whose wife was Amalie de Hoa; issue one son who died unmarried. Louis Forestier, born 25th of December, 1833, died 6th of April, 1862. His wife was Felicete Jorda. Issue three daughters, named Amalie Forestier, Louise Forestier and Gabrielle Forestier. Pierre Denis de la Ronde, born in the city of New Orleans on April 20th, 1762, and died Dec. 1st, 1824. He married on Jan. 31st, 1788, Eulalie Guerboise, a daughter of Louis Alexander Guerboise and Elisabeth Trepagnier. Of this union ten children were born, nine girls and one boy. Among the host of friends of the de la Ronde's, this plantation home, when the tenth child was born, became known as "Parnasse" and the girls were referred to as the nine muses, while the son was called "Apollo". While the male members of the coterie sipped their rare wines and brandies, the ladies as befitted, sipped nectar, eau sucre, or orange flower water.

DeDREUX

In the archives of this notable family one finds that the family runs in an unbroken chain to the fifth son of King Louis VI of France known as the Comte de Dreux (1108-1113). It is an interesting document, the genealogical record of this ancient family stemming to the Royal Family of France. As one reads, the names of Kings of France and Dukes of Brittany recall thrilling episodes, wars and events that make French history. Finally one comes to the Marquis Dreux-Breze, who had the exalted position during the reign of King Louis XIV.

The American branch, which settled in Louisiana, starts with Mathurin Dreux, a son of Louis Dreux-Breze and Francoise Harant, his birthplace being Savigny, Province of Anjou France, and the year of his birth 1698. He came to Louisiana in 1718. He was a close friend of Bienville, and according to family records was one of those who accompanied Bienville when he selected the site of the present city of New Orleans. Allowed to choose the site for his plantation, unlike Bienville, he selected land in the area of Bayou St. Jean instead of on the Mississippi River, noting that the land there was higher and in less danger of overflow, as well as having a thicker growth of trees better suited for cultivation when once cleared.

The wooded land greatly appealed to them, for as soon as a brother, Pierre, joined him they started a saw-mill and brick-kiln, burning shells to make lime. They realized that settlers would need all these commodities once the town was laid out. Having some means it was easy for them to obtain labor, and before long became wealthy. With numerous slaves, and herds of cattle they were soon supplying the community with meats and milk products. Their own plantation was called Gentilly, which is not a corruption of Chantilly as is stated in some guide books of the city, but named after Gentilly, a commune in the department of the Seine in France. They became known as Sieurs de Gentilly, as one finds on old documents in the Cabildo and St. Louis Cathedral.

In the early church records one finds the following, dated 1732: "Mathurin Dreux, resident of Gentilly, Son of Louis Dreux, a native of Savigny Anjou, an officer of the militia of this province and demoiselle Francoise Harant native of Savigny diocese of Anjou (his mother) and demoiselle Claudine Francoise

Hugot, daughter of the deceased garde magazin general of the concessions of Monseigneur Le Blanc and Francoise Martin, widow of Sieur Moriset". A year later Mathurin's brother also took to himself a wife. He too was an officer in the militia of the city and his choice was demoiselle Anne Corbin Bachemin, a daughter of Jean Corbin Bachemin and demoiselle Ann Marie Judith le Hardy, who had come from St. Malo.

At that time there was a wide roadway leading from the rear gate of the moated and palisaded town to the estate of Gentilly belonging to the Dreux family and the settlement along Bayou St. Jean. For two centuries it has been a picturesque thoroughfare with a number of old plantation homes erected a short distance back. This Bayou Road was the main driveway out of the city until the coming of the Americans after 1803, and still bears the name "Bayou Road". The home that the Dreux brothers built on their land was a large and well built one, and the Marquis Marigny de Mandeville copied the plan for his house later. While this home of the Dreux brothers was being erected crowds of city residents would drive out to see it, and it was so attractive that for many years strangers were taken out to see it. Here they lived and reared their families, living like a noble in his chateau with a band of house slaves and field hands by the hundreds. Their children, as one would expect, married into the aristocratic wealthy families of the colony. One married a de Llome, another a Beauregard, and others into the Bermudez, Soniat du Fossat, de Fazende, de Logny, Dugue, de la Vergne, Joumoville, de Villere, de Freneuse, and other families. In fact the Dreux family has married, or can be traced in the genealogical records of almost every one of the early aristocratic families of New Orleans.

ROUYER de VILLERAY
St. Bernard Parish.

ROVERE,   LA ROUYER,   ROUERE,   ROUER,
RAYMOND de ROUER

All these names we encounter in our research into the genealogical records of the Villere family which has branches in Italy, France, Canada and United States.

The family has furnished Cardinals, Bishops and many lesser religious members to the Church, sovereign princes to Italy and statesmen to the Republic of Genoa. It has always been foremost in civic and military affairs.

When the terror of the French Revolution was in full sway, the Marquis de Rouyer de Villere, burnt the genealogical records of the family in his Chateau at Havre, before fleeing from that place in order to keep the members of the family off the list of those to be guillotined.

VILLERE.
(ROUYER DE VILLERÉ).

The first Villere to come to Louisiana, was Etienne Roy Villere. He joined the band of Canadians that had been furnished for the trip. Among these Canadians were some members of the Chauvin family to whom Etienne Roy de Villere was related through marriage. The church records of Montreal in 1695 show that Jacques Nepveu, a son of Philippe Nepveu and Marie Denise Silvestre, married Michelle Chauvin, daughter of Pierre Chauvin and Marie Antreuil. The records show also that Etienne Roy de Villere was married in the city of Montreal to Marie Nepveu, daughter of Jacques Nepveu and Michelle Chauvin. Their son, Joseph Roy Villere, became a maritime notary, later marrying Margurite de la Chaise on October 12th, 1759, the marriage ceremony solemnized in the church that was replaced by the present St. Louis Cathedral in New Orleans, La. The marriage settlements on both sides were generous, and the young couple lived with the bride's parents for three years, as was the custom of that day. At the end of the allotted three years, they moved to a simple plantation home close to the plantation of the bride's grandfather, Chevalier d'Arensbourg, on the German Coast.

Roy Villere was made a captain of four hundred German troops by his wife's grandfather. In 1761 a son was born, who was named Jacques Philippe Roy de Villere, and in 1764, daughter was born, who was called Louise. In the same year the colony was shocked by the news that France had ceded the colony to Spain. Nicolas Chauvin fils (de la Frenier) who had been born in New Orleans, at this time occupying the position of Attorney-General, feeling that it was the Canadians that had founded the Colony, called a meeting of the citizens of the city and parishes to protest against the colony being transferred to Spain. Joseph

Roy de Villere was one of the most enthusiastic supporters of this protest. When the assembly was called again to support the resolution to expel the Spanish representative, Captain Villere from the German Coast with his band of four hundred well trained and fully armed German soldiers, confident that they were powerful enough to resist the Spanish Government, marched to the city, seized the Tchoupitoulas gate and continued on to the place of meeting to rally to the support of La Frenier. When General O'Reilly, the Spanish representative, soon arrived from Cuba with a large force of soldiers to suppress the rebellion, Villere and all concerned realized how powerless they were. Villere's first thought was to flee with his family to a place of safety, but when assurance was brought him that General O'Reilly intended to be lenient with all the offenders, and he had also learned that some of his friends and relatives were imprisoned, he decided to throw himself on the mercy of General O'Reilly. His wife begged him not to be so foolish. His family and friends implored him to run away, all to no avail, for he presented himself to O'Reilly, and upon reaching the Tchoupitoulas gate was seized, placed under arrest and taken aboard a Spanish frigate lying in the river in front of the city. Various versions of how Joseph Roy Villere met his death have been given, but Judge Martin, a Louisiana historian of the early 19th Century, and a close friend of the Villere family gives the version as told by the wife of the murdered man.

When Madame Villere learned that her husband had been arrested and taken aboard the Spanish vessel, she immediately had her slaves row her out to the vessel in a skiff. She made herself known to an officer of the ship after her skiff had been tied to the Spanish frigate, and asked to be allowed to speak to her husband, which request was ignored. Villere, recognizing his wife's voice, made an effort to get away from his captors to speak to his wife, and in the scuffle that ensued fell transfixed by a bayonet. His bloody shirt was thrown down to the skiff that Madame Villere might know that no longer had she a husband. Then Madame Villere sought the protection of her grandfather's home for her children and herself, for the Spanish Crown later seized her plantation, home and contents.

Some years later her son, Jacques Philippe Villere, born in 1761, was sent for by King Louis XIV to be educated at the French

Court, and when he reached the age of eighteen, received a commission in the French Army with the rank of Lieutenant, and was sent to San Domingo. Learning of the death of his mother, he returned to Louisiana where he remained, marrying in 1784 Mademoiselle Henriette Fazende, daughter of Gabrielle Fazende, in the same church in which his father and mother had been married.

From the marriage were born Rene Gabriel, who married Eulalie de la Ronde, issue five children. Jules Villere became the husband of Pearle Oliver, issue three children, their daughter marrying General Gustave Toutant Beauregard; their children being: Rene, Henri, and Laure, who became Mrs. Charles Larendon, her husband being a native of Atlanta, Ga. Of this marriage one daughter is living, Miss Laure Beauregard Larendon, who now resides in Atlanta, Ga. Delphin married Delphine Bienvenue, issue eight children. Anatole became the husband of Felicie Elmina Forstall, issue six children. Adele became the wife of Hughes de la Vergne, issue six children. Leocadie married first, Cyril Fazende; second, Paul Launausse. Jacques P. Villere had a brilliant record at the battle of New Orleans, and in 1816 was elected to succeed Governor Claiborne as Governor of Louisiana. Becoming governor at a time when the state was beginning to develop its full measure of wealth Governor Villere proved to be the man for the occasion, having accomplished much for the state during his term of office He died in 1830 and is buried in the old family tomb in the St. Louis Cemetery. All of his children survived him. Old plantation sites below the city of New Orleans mark the places of his own and his sons' plantations. Later in life Villere purchased from Soniat duFossat the plantation known as "Conseil" thereby enlarging his plantation holdings, and giving the family a larger plantation residence. During the Battle of New Orleans it was used as a hospital, being located near the scene of battle. According to Mrs. George Alfred Lanaux of New Orleans, the plantation known as Conseil, may be described as a spacious cottage, brick between posts, with galleries on three sides. The dining room was in a separate building connected with the mother house by a passageway covered to keep out the cold and rain, this apartment measuring 20x40 feet with a huge pantry in the rear. It might be mentioned that a brick paved gallery extended around this room as well as around the

A.P. monogram on the Pontalba buildings, New Orleans, La.

Race of the Robert E. Lee and Natchez

Typical plantation home of a wealthy planter

Evergreen Plantation Home

rest of the house, and three large bed-rooms were planned in the space upstairs. An oak avenue was in the rear and the outbuildings and slave cabins scattered about the rear grounds. The illustration of this old plantation gives a good idea of the Conseil plantation mother house. It became a social center of that section the Villere's being related to numerous families of the vicinity.

TOUTANT DE BEAUREGARD.

Jacques Toutant Beauregard was the first of the name to come to America. He was commandant of a flotilla bringing supplies, troops, etc., for the colony in Louisiana, sent by King Louis XIV of France. His instructions were to bring back timber to be used for naval construction on his return trip. His mission having been accomplished with such gratifying results he was decorated with the Cross of St. Louis.

The family of Beauregard reaches back, according to records in the family, to Wales when as early as 1290 a belligerent Welchman bearing the name of Tider (Young) lead a number of his comrades antagonistic to King Edward the 1st of England against that monarch. Routed by overwhelming numbers, Tider fled to France where Philip the Fair summoned him to appear at his Court. His winning personality gained for him as wife, Mademoiselle de Lafayette, one of the King's sister's maids of honor. Later Tider was promoted to a post in the English possessions in France, which unfortunately was not administered in a manner pleasing to the King, Tider returning to French service where he lingered until his death near Tours.

His son returned to the scene of his father's failure because the family still had great influence, which he brought to bear in obtaining a noteworthy position under the Crown of England. The name Tider was changed to Toutank, less odious to the King, and eventually Toutank became Toutant. Later, a daughter married one Sieur Paix de Beauregard—eventually a hyphen was substituted for the "de" and we find the name as we know it today.

Jacques Toutant-Beauregard, now a chevalier of St. Louis, returned to Louisiana and marrying Mademoiselle Madeline Cartier, settled in the state. Three sons were the issue of this marriage.

Louis Toutant-Beauregard, who married Mademoiselle Victoire Ducros, a daughter of a St. Bernard planter. Planter Ducros was a man of importance in the colony, having with honor filled a number of offices of responsibility and trust under the French and Spanish Dominations in Louisiana. Of this marriage a daughter and two sons were the issue. It is with the younger son who married Helene Judith de Reggio we are concerned. Of this marriage several children were born, the third oldest named Pierre Gustave Toutant-Beauregard, who later became the celebrated Confederate General.

The General's mother's family, stems back to the Duke of Reggio and Modena, springing from the ancient and illustrious house of Este. Coming to Louisiana with his command after having a captaincy given him by King Louis XV for having distinguished himself while fighting under the Duc de Richelieu, Francois Marie Chevallier de Reggio was a relative of the reigning Duke at that date. Chevallier de Reggio received the appointment of Royal Standard Bearer, or Alfrez Real, when the Spanish took over Louisiana. He married Mademoiselle Fleurian—two sons were the issue; the youngest son marrying Mademoiselle Louise Judith Oliver de Vezin. She it was who became the mother of the lady who in turn was to become Helene Judith de Reggio, mother of the future Confederate General.

General Beauregard first saw the light of day May 28, 1818 on his father's plantation below New Orleans in St. Bernard Parish. This plantation home was burned down many years ago, according to his grand-daughter, Miss Laure Beauregard Larendon. Shortly after graduating he was married to Mademoiselle Laure Marie Villere, a grand-daughter of the patriot whose bloody shirt was thrown to his wife by the Spaniards. Mademoiselle Villere was a daughter of Jacques Villere, the first Creole to become Governor of Louisiana. Of this marriage three children were the issue—Henri and Renée, and a daughter Laure. Renée became the owner of the plantation known as Bueno Ritero, originally built for the Marquis de Trava. He was a judge in the parish of St. Bernard, filling the position with credit and ability. Henry later left New Orleans. Laure married Charles Larendon, a wealthy gentleman from Atlanta, Georgia. She died at the time of the birth of her daughter Laure Beauregard Larendon.

General Beauregard married a second time, choosing another aristocratic Creole, Mademoiselle Caroline des Louder, a daughter of a prominent Louisiana planter; she died during the Civil War. General Beauregard lived until 1893, and is buried in the tomb of the Army of Tennessee. A large funeral procession following the body to the grave, where military honors were accorded him. Close by in another vault, his son Renée rests, and but a short distance away in the handsome Larendon tomb, with her husband and an earlier daughter, in this beautiful cemetery, rests his idolized daughter, Laure.

LANAUX.

Philippe Lanaux, native of Nantes, Bretagne, France, son of Pierre Lanaux and Jeanne Guivaux, both of Nantes, married on the 19th of October, 1783, Angela Bossonier—born in New Orleans, daughter of Antoine Bossonier and of Lorenze Gache, both of the city of Dampierre, Provence du Dauphine, France. (Note— In the registers of the Parish of St. John the Baptist, La., it is recorded that Antoine Besonier of Marmillion, native of Dampier in Dauphine is married to Dame Lorenza Gache, native of Montmelien, Chef-Lieu de Canton en Savoie). Died July 2, 1814, aged 50 years. She must have been born in 1764. Her death notice bears "Daughter of Antoine Bozoiner de Marmillion and of Lorenzo Gachet".

Of this marriage were born: 1. Antoine Philippe Lanaux, Oct., 1790, died in New Orleans. Children: 2. Charles Julien Lanaux, March 14, 1792, died in Havana, June 26, 1826. Children: Jean Fois Phil Lanaux, born Dec. 30, 1793, married Clara Lange; Henriette Lanaux, born Aug. 6, 1795. 3. Arnaud Lanaux, born Feb. 9, 1797, married June 17, 1847. Children: Santiago Lanaux, born Jan. 16, 1799; Pierre Julien Lanaux, born April 7, 1801. 4. Senville Devis Lanaux, born June 12, 1802. Children. (Euphosine Lanaux) twins born June 12, 1802. Joachim Jean Lanaux, born Jan. 6, 1810, died in France, left some children. (Note— Five of the children of Philippe Lanaux have left a posterity— the others did not have any children. All preceding data is taken from the archives of the St. Louis Cathedral, New Orleans, La. The orthography of the names are exactly as taken from the registers).

The mother of Philippe Lanaux is named Jeanne Guivaux in the marriage certificate—and in a few instances the certificates of birth or baptism of Philippe Lanaux's children she is named Jeanne Gérot or Jeanne Gérard. The wife of Philippe Lanaux is named Angéla Bossonié in the certificate of marriage, and in her mortuary notice she is named Angélique Bozonier, fille d'Antoine Bozonier de Marmillob et de Lorenza Gachet, and in the birth notices of her children she is named Angelique Bozonier, fille d'Antoine Julie en Bozonier et de Lorenza Gachet. (Great great grandfather of Mrs. John F. Coleman nee Valentine Lanaux) who compiled this record).

Her great grandfather was Charles Julien Lanaux, who married Aime Aglaé Roussel, daughter of George Roussel and of Adele Haydel. (Note: This marriage must have been celebrated in the parish of St. John the Baptist, La. See register). Of this marriage were born: George Charles Lanaux, born Aug. 16, 1816, died 1888; Philippe Alfred Lanaux, born 1820, died 28th of August, 1835 (C. St. L.). Theodore Lanaux: Angéle Lanaux, born 1820 or 1821, died Aug. 25, 1822; Angéle Lanaux, born 1822 or 1823, died July, 1825; Marie Caroline Lanaux, born April 19, 1825, died April 25, 1867.

George Charles Lanaux, born Aug. 16, 1817, married Jeanne Odile Lanaux, born July 9, 1817, died Sept. 24, 1885. Of this marriage were: Marie Léonide Lanaux, born Nov., 1839; George Alfred Lanaux, born March, 1841, who married Eulalie Valentine de Villere; Florian Lanaux, born July 30, 1842, died June 6, 1843; Georgine Lanaux; Marie Georgine Lanaux; Jean Arnaud Lanaux, born July 9, 1847, died June 25, 1881. George Lanaux: Marie Adelaide Lanaux, born June 19, 1852; Marie Odile Lanaux, born Feb. 5, 1854; Charles Lanaux, born May 17, 1858.

On March 19th, 1862, George Alfred Lanaux married Eulalie Valentine de Villere, daughter of Eréville de Villere and of Adéle Ducros. Of this marriage were born: Florian Jean Lanaux; Laurence Lanaux; Gabrielle Laurence Lanaux; Marie Bianca Lanaux; Alfred Lanaux; Alfred Lanaux II; Louise Valentine Lanaux; Marie Adel Lanaux; Marie Rita Lanaux; Henrie Lanaux; Marie Beatrice Lanaux; Joseph Henri Lanaux.

"POUR DIEU ET LE ROI".
BARONS POUJAUD DE JUVISY.

Francis Brice Poujaud, Lord de Juiisy-Baron de Louvie—Intendant of the Royal Domaine under Louis 16th. (Born at Paris,

Miss Laure Beauregard Larendon

Where Gen. P. T. G. Beauregard is buried, Metairie Cemetery, New Orleans. Tomb of the Army of Tennessee, with statue of Gen. Albert Sidney Johnson on horseback. (Courtesy of Miss L. B. Larendon)

Mrs. John F. Coleman (Valentine Louise Lanaux.)

Charles Alfred Lanaux Rareshide

Crest and Coat-of-Arms of the Rareshide family. (Courtesy of Mrs. John F. Coleman)

Crest and Coat-of-Arms of the Poujaud de Juvisy family.

France, left France during the "Reign of Terror" and came to the United States in 1791, at Baltimore). Married at Paris, France, to Marie Françoise Nicol de Bessy de Neuville (Daughter of a Duke de Neuville—Royal blood of the "Legitimist Branch of the House of Bourbon").

Issue: Marie Antoinette Poujaud, born at Juvisy, France. (Her father being of the household of Louis XVI and Marie Antoinette, the latter was her Godmother and Namer). She married at Paris, France, during the Reign of Louis XVI, Henry Wilson, who was born in 1773. (Private Secretary to President Monroe who was at that time Minister to France).

Issue: William Many Wilson, born at San Domingo, Dec. 4, 1796, who married at Pensacola, Fla., Sept. 16, 1829, to Emma Billington Abbott, born at Philadelphia, Pa., Feb. 8th, 1813.

Issue: Emma Florence Wilson, born at Pensacola, Fla., Feb. 26th, 1837, who married at New Orleans, La., Nov. 30th, 1858, John Henry Emile Rareshide, who was born at New Orleans, La., Feb. 2nd, 1837.

Issue: Clarence Wolff George Rareshide, born at New Orleans, La., Dec. 1st, 1861, married in New Orlenas, La., Feb. 8th, 1897, to Miss Louise Valentine Lanaux.

Issue: Charles Alfred Lanaux Rareshide, born in Houston, Texas, Dec. 5th, 1897, was married in New Orleans, La., Sept. 9th, 1930, to Miss Henryetta Castillo Bayle.

Issue: Clarence Rareshide, born at New Orleans, La., April 1st, 1932. Lanaux Jules Rareshide, born at New Orleans, La., Dec. 5th, 1933. Henryette Bayle Rareshide, born at New Orleans, La., Dec. 10th, 1934.

—*Herald Bureau, New Orleans, La.*

VIS * VIM * REPELLITE.

RARESHIDE.

Arms. Or a bend gules, between two Lions' heads eraged, sable. Crest. Out of a mural crown or, a demi Unicorn rampant, sable, crined and unguled or. (Amoral de Z.)
(Confirmed at Visitation of Heralds at Somersetshire, 1697 E.)

The Rareshide family was originally from Somersetshire, England. They settled in New York State and Pennsylvania. Since

1812 the family has resided in New Orleans, La.. Michael Rareshide— a native of New York State, married about 1808 or 1809, Hester (Esther) Fitley of New York (She was of the Fitley family who were Quakers and originally settled in Pennsylvania and New York State. Issue: John Rareshide, born in the city of New York in 1810, who married at New Orleans, La., in 1830, to Rosina Louise Florance, who was born in Charleston, S. C., June 6th, 1812.

Issue: John Henery Emile Rareshide, born in New Orleans, La., Feb. 2nd, 1837, who married in New Orleans, La., Nov. 30th, 1858, Miss Emma Florence Wilson, born in Pensacola, Fla., Feb. 26th, 1837.

Issue: Clarence Wolff George Rareshide, born in New Orleans, La., Dec. 1st, 1861, who married in New Orleans, La., Feb. 8th, 1897, Miss Louise Valentine Lanaux.

Issue: Charles Alfred Lanaux Rareshide, born in Houston, Texas, Dec. 5th, 1897, who married in New Orleans, La., Miss Henryetta Castillo Bayle. Miss Bayle is a daughter of Mr. and Mrs. Jules Bayle of New Orleans, Mrs. Jules Bayle having been a Miss Lina Baker, a daughter of the late Judge Joshua G. Baker, who was ex-Justice of the Supreme Court of Louisiana, famed for his fearless rulings, having served 38 years on criminal bench and two on Supreme Court. He was born August 3, 1852, on the plantation of his maternal grandfather G. L. Fuselier de la Clair, nine miles above Franklin, La. He being the son of Anthony Wayne Baker and Emma Fuselier de la Clair. During his early education he had private tutors, and later attended schools in Hampton, Conn., and Gonkus, New York. He graduated from the Bellevue High School, Bedford City, Virginia, in 1871. Returning to the home of Governor Baker at Fairfax in St. Mary's Parish, shortly afterwards moving to New Orleans, where he lived until his death. He studied law in Louisiana and in 1874 was licensed to practice law. His first wife was Miss Susan Henryetta Castillo, grandmother of Mrs. Clarence Alfred Lanaux Rareshide of New Orleans, La. His second wife being the former Mrs. Mary Monroe Vincent, a sister of the late Chief Justice Frank A. Monroe of the Supreme Court of Louisiana.

G. L. Fuselier de la Clair, grandfather of Hon. Joshua G. Baker, was a close relative of the immensely wealthy plantation family of the name Fuselier de la Clair, whose splendid early type Louisiana plantation home at Grand Coteau, was burned by the Federal troops when they failed to trap the Confederate officers attending a banquet given them by the old planter Fuselier de la Clair. The Chrétien family of Chrétien Point also are related to the Fuselier de la Clair family by marriage.

Chapter XIX.

THE ALSTON—PIRRIE—BOWMAN—MATTHEWS FAMILIES

THE first Alston of the English branch that settled in the Felicianas, to come to America was John Alston, who married Mary Clark, daughter of John Clark and Mary Palin. His son, Solomon Alston, married Anne, nicknamed Nancy Hinton, daughter of Colonel John Hinton of Chowan, in the colony of Carolina. Their son, John Alston, born in Carolina on the 18th of April, 1733, like his father and grandfather, was a loyal English subject and proud of his patrician ancestry and his distinguished forebears. His life was a succession of hazardous adventures, and his stately figure of over six feet four inches, made his great courage fully appreciated by his antagonists. After coming to Louisiana he married Elizabeth Hynes, a member of the family for whom Hynes county was named, and became the father of five children. At the time that the dissatisfied colonists were bringing their grievances to a point where rebellion was manifest and their attitude towards the rule of King George III was plain, John Alston made no attempt to hide the fact that he was a Tory, and not in sympathy with the revolutionary spirit sweeping the colonies. In 1770, disposing of his property, with his wife and their four children, he abandoned Carolina, and like many other loyal English subjects, came South to the Natchez Country of west Florida still under the British Flag. He bought a plantation near Natchez and being wealthy, had a comfortable home built called "La Grange". He engaged tutors for his children, and lived as he had done in Carolina on his father's plantation. In 1772 a child was born, a daughter that they named Lucretia, who later was known as Lucy, the last child of this marriage.

The Declaration of Independence had taken place, and in the year 1779 Don Bernado Galvez, then Spanish Governor of Louisiana, with his troops compelled the English to depart, and prevented them from taking Fort Bute at Manchac, and New Richmond, as Baton Rouge was called at that time. Notwithstanding all this, John Alston still remained loyal to the English. In 1781 when the Spanish under Galvez were engaged in overcoming the last stronghold of the English at Pensacola, Florida, a message was brought that English ships were in the Mississippi River, on the way to recapture Natchez. Under the leadership of General Lyman, many planters rallied to the British cause and planned to recapture Natchez and its fort by overcoming the small number of Spaniards guarding it. Encouraged by the report that the English had badly defeated the Spaniards, about one hundred men with John Altson amongst them, started a siege on the 22nd of April, 1781. It lasted seven days before the Spanish garrison surrendered. Once again Natchez was English, and with joy the British Flag flew in the breeze. Happiness again reigned, but only for a brief period.

Joy was soon turned to terror when it was learned that the message that they had gotten was a false one, as it was the English who had been defeated, and no English vessels were coming to their aid. At once the Union Jack was pulled down, and the Spanish flag flown from the flag-staff again while those who had taken part went into hiding, remembering how "Bloody O'Reilly" had executed the revolters in New Orleans some time before. Don Carlos de Grand Pré, lieutenant-colonel of His Majesty's Spanish forces arrived on the 29th, carrying with him documents showing his appointments as Civil and Military Commandant of the district of Natchez. Immediately he began a detailed investigation, and obtained a list of the names of those connected with the seizure of the fort. There began arrests, seizures, and confiscation of the properties belonging to the Englishmen who had taken part in the retaking of the Fort at Natchez.

A number of British subjects who were connected with the affair made an attempt to reach the closest English post located on the Savanna River. Determining to remain with his two oldest sons and see what the outcome would be, John Alston sent his wife and three youngest children well supplied with necessities for the journey, and a number of trustworthy slaves on an overland trip to this English settlement on the Savanna River. When out but two days Mrs. Alston who was on horseback, was critically injured when the horse on which she was mounted slipped, and in falling Mrs. Alston fractured several of her ribs. She developed complications, dying in a few weeks, after her children and faithful slaves had brought her back to the plantation where all that lay in their power had been done to ease her suffering.

Learning of his wife's death, John Alston and his sons, William and Lewis, made an attempt to escape. The sons succeeded, but John Alston was not so fortunate. He was found guilty and condemned to imprisonment in Moro Castle, Cuba, for life.

A faithful slave who had taken care of Mrs. Alston since birth, having been a house slave in her parents home, "Mammy Pratt", she was called, was again to show her devotion. In the hour of need she became the protector of her dead mistress' little children. Realizing that he might be retaken any moment while he was in hiding in an Indian settlement, John Alston had visited his friend, Dr. Farra, whose plantation in the vicinity of False River on the west bank of the Mississippi River, was not far from the Indian settlement. He had asked his friend to aid in protecting his children. In the swamp where faithful Mammy Pratt concealed her charges was a little cabin with but one room, here all of them lived an entire year, and on the scanty meals that the old slave could obtain from neighboring plantations. The oldest child, Solomon, who was twelve years of age, fished and hunted, and in this manner they managed to survive.

Alexander Stirling, a young Scotchman from far Augushire, North Britain, who was plantation manager for Dr. Farra, became a devoted friend of the children, sympathizing with them in their plight. He fell in love with Ann, and she with him, and on the 26th of May, 1784, they were married, and in later years settled in Feliciana on Rio Feliciana at a place known as Murdock's Ford, called at present Thompson's Creek. Alexander Stirling, of good parentage, opened a small store, and his genial manner won for him customers from far and near, with the result that he soon became independent, and both soon were able to take their rightful places socially in the community. Both of John Alston's sons, now grown a little older, had been pardoned owing to their ages. They were allowed to return to the place of their birth, here in the Tunica section, where they laid out plantations, later becoming successful planters.

In the winter of 1793, the future William IV of England, while visiting Cuba learned that in damp and dismal dungeons of Moro Castle in Havana, Cuba, were imprisoned English subjects under sentence of death. He pleaded for their release, and as a result of his intercession, John Alston was released under the promise that he never again would enter Spanish territory.

A reward of $5,000.00 was offered for any one finding him in the Spanish Possessions, and, as a final chapter in the life of this loyal Englishman, hearing that his children were in want, and suffering, John Alston surprised Governor Galvez by a visit, at which time he told his Majesty's representative that he had come to claim the reward, and was ready to give himself up, wishing the money for his children whom he understood were destitute. The Spanish Governor overcome by the love of this father for his children, gave him an absolute pardon, requiring only that he never again bear arms against Spain or her possessions. John Alston remained true to his word, for up until his death in Louisiana in 1802, he never again made any attempt to oppose the Dons. He found his daughter Ann happily married and a mother, and also learned that Lucretia was in a convent in New Orleans being educated. Then he found William and Lewis on their plantations on Tunica Bayou doing well. Finally he got back some of his old slaves, and by unending energy again rose to be wealthy, owning large tracts of valuable plantation and timber land at his death.

The children of John Alston and his wife Elizabeth Hynes, whom he married in 1761 were: (a) William Alston, whose wife was Mildred Wells, a native of Rapides Parish, Louisiana. (b) Louis Alston, who married Mary Anna Gray, who died childless; for his second wife, he took Rebecca Kendall, who bore him four children. (1) Isaac Alston, who remained single. (2) Louis Alston, whose wife was Lydia Adams, who had one son that settled in Pointe Coupee, La. (3) Anna Maria, who married Abraham Gray. Their children were: Charlotte, who married John Baker; James, who married Sarah Dohety; Ruffin, who married Lucy Davis; Elisabeth Alston married Arthur Adams, no issue; Anna Alston married Alexander Stirling and became the mother of nine children. (4) Solomon Alston remained single. (5)

Lucy Alston, christened Lucretia, was born at her father's plantation in Homochito, Miss., in 1772, and died in 1833; her first husband being Ruffin Gray for whom Oakley plantation was laid out and its manor built. Ruffin Gray later returning to Homochito because of illness, and died shortly afterwards. His widow later on married James Pirrie, a member of a distinguished patrician Scotch family. He having been an alcalde, under the Spanish Rule and living in Feliciana at the time of his marriage. He was born in 1769, and died on March 7th, 1824.

The children of Lucy Alston by her marriage to Ruffin Gray were four in number: (1) Elisabeth, who died in infancy; (2) Ruffin, who died in infancy; (3) Mary Ann. Of the children by her second marriage, there were three in number, two of them dying in infancy. Eliza, who was born on October 6th, 1805, became a great beauty and social celebrity, on account of her vivaciousness, rare wit, charm of manner and wealth.

Mary Ann, sister of Eliza, first married Jedidah Smith, a native of Adams County, Mississippi, issue: Catherine and Sarah. Her second husband was Dr. Ira Smith, no issue from this marriage. Beautiful Eliza Pirrie became a bride on three occasions: her first husband being the handsome and wealthy young Robert Hilliard Barrow of magnificent Greenwood Plantation, undoubtedly having the most beautiful Greek Revival type of plantation manor in the state of Louisiana. Issue: Robert Hilliard Barrow II, born after his father's death, who married Mary E. Barrow, daughter of David Barrow, builder of Afton Villa. Nine children blessed this union, Rosale Plantation a bridal gift of David Barrow, was one of the fine plantation homes in Feliciana, it being destroyed by fire in 1880.

The children of Robert H. Barrow who survived infancy are: Charles Barrow, Sarah Barrow, Eliza Barrow, Bennet Barrow, Robert Barrow, Isabelle Barrow, and Samuel Barrow. Eliza Pirrie Barrow, later married Reverend William Robert Bowman, who was a rector of Grace Episcopal Church at St. Francisville, La. He was a native of Brownsville, Penn., and was born Dec. 7th, 1800, and died Aug. 30th, 1835. Issue of this marriage were two children, Isabelle Bowman, who became the wife of William Wilson Matthews; issue of this marriage were six children: 1st Robert Bowman Matthews; 2nd, Cora Slocum Matthews; 3rd, Lucy Pirrie Matthews; 4th, Ida G. Matthews; 5th, Leonard Finlay Matthews; 6th, William Wilson Matthews. James Pirrie Bowman, son of Eliza Pirrie and Rev. Bowman, who married Sarah Turnbull, daughter of the builder of the beautiful plantation home on Rosedown Plantation near St. Francisville, La. Ten children were the issue of this marriage, all of them born in the old mansion.

They are Martha Bowman, (2) Eliza Bowman; (3) Sarah Bowman; (4) Anna Bowman; (5) Daniel Bowman; (6) Mayme Bowman; (7) Minna Bowman; (8) James Bowman; (9) Carrie Bowman; (10) Belle Bowman. Eliza Pirrie's third husband was Henry E. Lyons of Philadelphia, Pa., which occurred five years after the death of Rev. Bowman; issue of this marriage, (1) Lucy Lyons; (2) Cora Lyons, who became the wife of Captain Richard Floyd; (3) Eliza Lyons, who died in infancy.

The memory of Eliza Pirrie Barrow Bowman Lyons lingers in the beautiful Feliciana country, like a tuneful melody which never fails to evoke recollections of a pleasant nature when heard. So thoroughly has her history been interwoven with the history of the plantations of this area, that it is a hard matter to write about the one without including the other. Under the circumstances it seemed but fitting that when she died on April the 20th, 1851, that she should be laid to rest beside her husband the Rev. William Robert Bowman in a grave close to that of some of her own, in the little cemetery on Beechwood plantation in Feliciana, which country she loved, and where she was loved so dearly.

When one visits Verona, Italy, one unconsciously thinks of Juliet. So too, when Louisianians visit the Felicianas, their thoughts wander to Eliza Pirrie. Not to the gracious matron, but to the Eliza that Audubon knew, and of whom he wrote in his diary "My beautiful Miss Pirrie of Oakley". The beautiful vivacious girl whom all idolized.

Rathbone

CHAPTER XX.

THE RATHBONE—DE BUYS—HICKY—DUGGAN
DE MACARTY FAMILIES

AMERICAN BRANCH OF THE RATHBONE FAMILY.

*(Copied from Family Tree, courtesy of the de Buys Family
of New Orleans).*

JOHN RATHBONE of Block Island, married Margaret * * * *
Their children: William; Thomas; John, who married Anne Dodge, Jan. 10, 1688; Joseph; Samuel, born Aug. 1672, died 1757; Sarah; Margaret; Elizabeth.

The children of John Rathbone who married Anne Dodge were: Mary, who died Oct. 3, 1688; Jonathan, born May 22, 1691, died April 1, 1766; John, born Dec. 23, 1693; Joshua, born Feb.

3, 1636, married first, Mary Card, issue one son; married second, Mary Wightman, born Feb. 16, 1724: Benjamine III, born Feb. 11, 1701; Annan, born ———— 9, 1703; Nathaniel, born Feb. 11, 1708; Thomas, born March 2, 1709.

The children of Joshua, who married Mary Card and later Mary Wightman, were: Joshua A; Valentine Wightman, born Dec. 23, 1724; Mary, born ———— 17, 1726; Martha, born Mar. 1, 1728; John (Rev.) married June 26, 1729, near Stonington, Conn.; Content Brown; John, born Oct. 20, 1751, died March 14th, 1843; Martha, born Aug. ——, 1753, died Dec. 1, 1837; Daniel, born July 14, 1755, died in infancy; Prudence, born Jan. 31, 1757, died Aug. 16, 1827; Marion, born Feb. 27, 1759, died Jan. 5, 1852; Valentine W., born May 13, 1761, died 1813; David, born May 29, 1763, died Aug. 2, 1823; Joseph A., born June 16, 1765, died Jan. 18, 1813; Aaron, born July 25, 1770, died May 13, 1845; Moses, born July 25, 1770, died in Batavia; Edward, born Nov. 1, 1773, died young; Samuel, born July 1, 1776 at Stonington, Conn. Married Mary Turner of Montville, Conn., 1800, April 13th, died about 1814 at Buffalo, N. Y.; Content, born Mar. 26, 1778, died July 30, 1779.

The children of Samuel Rathbone and Mary Turner, were: Marie Theresa, born Feb. 1801; James Hammer, born July 14, 1802, died Aug. 17, 1853; Henry Alanson, born Dec. 27, 1803, married first, Annie Powell, of Tennessee, issue: Geo. Powell, who died in 1853; married second, Marie Celeste Forstall of New Orleans, and died March, 1867; Samuel, Jr., born Aug., 1809, died Nov. 6, 1834; John R., born Dec. 3, 1810, died in infancy; Juliet Content, born April 8, 1812; Sarah Ann, born Sept. 30, 1814; John E., born May 26, 1816, died July, 1867; Charles Edward, born Dec. 17, 1818; Isaac T., born July 26, 1821, died June 12, 1819. The children of Henry Alanson Rathbone and Marie Celeste Forstall were: Marie Celeste Emma, who married John B. de Lalande de Ferieres of New Orleans, born Dec. 27, 1840; Paul Henry, died in infancy; Marie Pauline, married Peter Labouisse of New Orleans; Francis Henry, died in infancy; Elizabeth Marie Stella, married M. James de Buys of New Orleans; Marie Laure, died in infancy; Marie Louise Alice, married William Phelps Eno of New Orleans; Marie Rita married Edgar dePoincy of New Orleans.

The children of Marie Celeste, who married John B. Lalande de Ferriere are Marie Juanita; Marie Rubie; Marie Ethlyn; Marie Roy; Marie Rathbone; Marie d'Assise Gayoso.

The children of Marie Pauline, who married Peter Labouisse are: Peter and Edith; Elizabeth Marie Stella Rathbone and James de Buys' children are: Rathbone Emile; James Temple; Walter Lawrence, and Lawrence Richard.

De BUYS.

The first member of this distinguished family whose name appears in early Louisiana annals, is Gaspard Melchior Balthazar de Buys, son of Pedro de Buys and Micaela Lion, according to the records of the St. Louis Cathedral, who was born in DunKirk. The older generations of the family had sailed their own vessels protected by Louis XIV, and aided the French in their wars against England. Serving under Count de Grasse, Gaspard de Buys was a captain of a man-of-war in the War of 1776, but having become infected with yellow fever while in the West Indies, de Buys handed in his resignation to the navy and sailed for Louisiana, landing in New Orleans, at that time under the rule of Spain. A little later while in Louisiana he married Eulalie de Jan, or de Jean, daughter of Antoine de Jan, a native of Bordeaux. Her mother being Angele Monzey de Montjean, a native of New Orleans. According to the family record of Dr. L. R. de Buys, Angele de Montjean's mother was saved from being killed by the Natchez Indians by an Indian nurse who carried the child through the forest from Natchez to the settlement at New Orleans. After being educated by the Ursuline Nuns in New Orleans she later married a business man of the city named Claude de Jan.

Gaspard de Buys' name occurs on the records of the first Legislative Council by the President of the new American government. The children of Gaspard de Buys and Eulalie de Jan were four in number, named as follows: Pierre Gaspard, William, Manette, and Adele.

Pierre Gaspard, married Jeanne Clement, daughter of Antoine Viel and Jeanne Rosa Dupuy. Pierre Gaspard de Buys was such an ardent republican in his feelings, that he celebrated a christening feast by inviting all of his friends to the feast requesting that they bring their patents of nobility. On the festive board stood

Crest and Coat-of-Arms of the de Buys family.

Crest and Coat-of-Arms of the
Forstall family.
(Courtesy of the de Buys family.)

Gaspard de Buys   Henry A. Rathbone

James Mather (1807), Great, great, great grandfather of Mrs. L R. de Buys, Sr.

a large chafing dish. The patents of nobility were placed upon it, fire lighted underneath, and the infant Pierre was passed over the smoke of the burning family titles amid the cheers and clapping. They named their other children in a manner which displayed a generosity of feeling. Marie Elizabeth, Eugenie, Paul, Emile, Marie Antoinette, Odille, Lucien, Napoleon.

Gaspard served on the staff of General Andrew Jackson at the Battle of New Orleans, and following the war he was elected to the Legislature, becoming Speaker of the House in 1846. He is remembered as general of the Louisiana Legion, which developed from the famous aristocratic old "Battalion d'Orleans" and were praised by Andrew Jackson. Later when called to colors by General Taylor to advance to the Rio Grande area during the War with Mexico the Legion responded at once, readily furnishing the required contingent. An old newspaper notice of that date states, "That Mr. William de Buys, (On account of advanced years), being replaced by a younger officer had been noticed walking in the ranks beside his two sons, shouldering a musket and chatting gaily as he marched along".

As Mr. de Buys advanced in years he developed his talent for painting, being especially clever in water color work. He spent much time at his country home sketching the lanscapes in its vicinity and about Biloxi, Miss. He was also a great fisherman and hunter, and when he died, not only his large host of friends, but all who knew him in the area of his summer home displayed real sorrow for his genial disposition had endeared him to all he met. His family at his death consisted of his widow who had been Miss Corinne Andry, and his four children—Felicie, Gaspard, Ovide, and Corinne. An adopted son known as John de Buys, who was taken when his mother died of cholera, grew up to be a great duelist. Of Irish descent he had all of the daring, wit, and agility necessary to carry that art to perfection.

Mlle. Manette de Buys, eldest daughter of Gaspard Melchoir de Buys, and Eulalie de Jan became the wife of Pierre Victor Amedée Longer, a gentleman of Rouen, France, noted for his elegant appearance and distinguished bearing. Madame Longer, a grande dame of French tradition, her household is cited on all occasions when the aristocracy of old New Orleans becomes the topic of conversation by those who know their New Orleans. Her daughters all made brilliant marriages: Eulalie married Samuel

Bell; Adele became Mrs. Florian Hermann; Odile, Mrs. Michel Musson; Armide became Mrs. Amedée Saules; Amélie, Mrs. James Behn; Angele, became Mrs. Evan Jones McCall; Heda married Charles Kock; Helena, Mrs. Luling, whose daughter became Lady Alice Ben, wife of Sir Arthur Ben, Member of Parliament, London.

Madame Gaspard de Buys, to the end of her days remained the great lady of her younger years—living in the fine old home of her daughter, Mrs. James Behn on South Rampart Street, between what is now Tulane Avenue and Canal Street. Yearly during her lifetime her large family gathered here, those in Europe coming for the occasion. Gaspard de Buys died in 1827, Madame de Buys living about fifty years longer.

Felicie de Buys, eldest daughter of General de Buys, became Madame A. J. Mummy, of France the mother of two daughters; one married M. Schroder, Consul General for Germany in France; the other became the Countess de la Gerronniére, of Haute Vienne, France.

Marie Elizabeth de Buys was married first to Hypolite Tricou. Her second husband was Samuel Hermann. She was a sister of General de Buys. Estelle Tricou, daughter of Hypolite Tricou, became Mrs. Bernard Peyton of Virginia, their son, William Charles de Buys marrying Anne Dupont. Alice Hermann, daughter of Marie Elizabeth de Buys and Samuel Hermann, married Henry Palmer, and their daughter May married Honorable Chauncey Depew. Her sister Louise who was the second daughter of Samuel Hermann, became Mrs. Hall McAlister of Georgia.

Paul Emile de Buys, son of Gaspard de Buys and Elizabeth Viel, married Emma Forstall, a daughter of Placide Forstall of New Orleans, who had large plantation interests on the West Bank of the Mississippi River. Gaspard James de Buys, their son, married Stella Rathbone, and became the forbears of the de Buys brothers, four in number, who have become prominent in their various vocations: Rathbone, who has made a name for himself in the architectural world, also an able archivist; Laurence Richard, chronicled in "Who is Who" as an eminent physician and child specialist; Walter and James.

Marie Antoinette Odille de Buys became the wife of Joaquin de Vignier, a native of Havana, her second husband being Foster Elliot of New York. Their issue for several generations survive: Pierre Victor Amédee married Cécile Denis, a daughter of Henry

Denis of New Orleans, issue two children, Alfred, and Amélie who married George C. Préot.

Lucien N. E. de Buys married Lucille Elizabeth Enould de Livaudais, whose home became a center where gathered for many years the noted families that gave to New Orleans of her era the reputation of a cultured city. Her family was a large one consisting of fifteen children, three sons and twelve daughters. Her latter years engaged in the collection of the family records, memoranda, arms, photographs, etc. She has left to her descendants beautifully drawn, correctly planned and carefully checked family trees of the many noted aristocratic families from which her children descend and have married into. With these are numerous beautifully illuminated crests and coats-of-arms granted to these noted families.

Mrs. Laurence Richard de Buys, is the daughter of the late Joseph H. Duggan of New Orleans who as a State Senator was mainly responsible for the ousting of the Louisiana Lottery. She is also the great granddaughter of Colonel Philip Hicky of "Hope Estate" plantation. Colonel Hicky, Howard Barrow, Steele, Morgan, Mather and several others were concerned in the revolution of the Florida Parishes in 1810, and were instrumental in turning them over to the United States Government, according to Stanley Arthur in the Louisiana Quarterly, Jan. 1938 vol. 21, No. 1.

A Cane Cutter

In her memoirs of "Old Plantation Days", the late Mrs. Eliza Ripley in writing about beautiful old "Hope Estate Plantation" recalls a faithful old negro mammy named Milly Turner, who had nursed five generations of the Hicky family. "Who of us that lived within a day's journey of Col. Hicky, but remembers his Milly, the Mammy of that grand, big household? Colonel Hicky lived to see his great grandchildren grow up and Milly mammied at least three generations at Hope Estate. She was a famous nurse, mind you, this was decades before nurses arrived on the stage. How many of us remember how tenderly and untiringly Milly nursed some of our invalids to health? Her services were tendered, and oh! how gratefully accepted.

With a sad heart I recall a sick baby I nursed until Milly came and put me to bed and took the ailing child in her tender arms. For two days and nights until the end she watched the little fluttering spark. This faithful negress nursed her old master in his last illness, grieving at his death as if a member of her own family had died."

The land on which the old arsenal and surrounding acreage, comprised originally, was a part of the immense land holdngs of Col. Philip Hicky. The Colonel, in early days having given it for military purposes and the erection of an arsenal. Later it was turned over by the state to the Louisiana State University.

BIRTHS (Diary of the Hope Estate)

Daniel Hicky—born February 1740, Ernis County Clare and Province of Nunster, Ireland.

Martha Hicky, London, England.

Philip Hicky (son of Daniel and Martha Hicky), born in Manchac Dist., Florida, then under the Government of Great Britain on the Bank of the Mississippi—was born 17th June A.D. 1778.

Anna Hicky (daughter of James and Francis Mather— born in New Orleans, March 4, 1781.

Martha Francis Hicky—born in New Orleans, 1st April 1802.

Eliza Constance Hicky—born in New Orleans, 26th March 1804, Monday at 5 o'clock A. M.

Adele Hicky—born on Hope Estate Plantation, East Baton Rouge, 15th August 1806.

Aurone Hicky—born in New Orleans, May 24, 1809.

Caroline Sarah Hicky—born in New Orleans, 4th June 1812.

Mrs. Pierre Charles Forstall, neé de Lavillebeuvre, mother of Placide Forstall (father of Mrs. Henry Rathbone).

Mrs. Gaspard de Buys, neé Dejan, mother of Pierre de Buys.

Mrs. Henry A. Rathbone, neé Celeste Forstall, mother of Mrs. Jas. de Buys, neé Stella C. Rathbone.

Mrs. Claude Dejan, mother of Mrs. Gaspard de Buys.

Dr. Lawrence Richard de Buys.
(Portrait by Edith Duggan.)

Mrs. Lawrence Richard de Buys (Miriam Duggan.)
(Portrait by Edith Duggan.)

Mrs. Joseph H. Duggan, neé Miss Ida Adele Fowler, mother of Mrs. L. R. de Buys. (Portrait by Edith Duggan.)

Miss Edith Duggan, Portrait Painter.

Crest and Coat-of-Arms of the Lopez family.

Donna Bettie Capomazza, neé Miss Bettie Hardy, Vial Pareoli 54, Rome, Italy. (Portrait by Edith Duggan.)

Miss Langhorne of Virginia. (Portrait by Edith Duggan.)

William Eno de Buys, son of Dr. and Mrs. L. R. de Buys. (Portrait by Edith Duggan.)

Miss Grace King. (Portrait by Edith Duggan.)

Daniel Hicky—born in New Orleans, 11th April, 1814, at residence of A. L. Duncasse, Easter Monday, ½ part of A. M.

Philip Hicky—born on Hope Estate Plantation, East Baton Rouge, 19th October, 1817, A. M.

Maria Louisa Hicky—born Hope Estate Plantation, East Baton Rouge, 18th January, 1821.

Francis Hicky—born Hope Estate Plantation, 8th August, 1823—Dr. C. E. French, present.

Mary Scallan—daughter of James and Eliza Scallan, born Hope Estate Plantation, 25th October, 1823, Tuesday morning, Dr. French present.

Louisa Walsh—daughter of Simon and Martha Walsh, born at Hope Estate Plantation.

Philip Richard Walsh.

Elisa.

Harry Simon Hicky Walsh—son of Simon W. Walsh and Martha Francis Walsh, born on the 20th December, 1832, at Hope Estate Plantation, East Baton Rouge.

Morris Barker Morgan, son of Caroline Hicky LeMoine Morgan, born 25th September, 1835.

Aurone Hortense Morgan—born 30th May 1838.

Mary Morgan—born 15th January 1841.

Gibbs Henry Morgan—born 1st October 1843.

Hicky Waller Fowler, son of Henry Waller Fowler and Adele Hicky, born 31st July 1837, at Hope Estate Plantation.

Eugene Fowler—born 24th April 1841, at Hope Estate Plantation.

Philip Richard Fowler—born 24th November 1843, at Hope Estate Plantation.

Adele Ida Fowler—born 22nd December 1845.

James Mather, son of James Mather and Mary Scallan, great grandson of Philip and Martha Hicky, born 25th April 1843, at Hope Estate Plantation.

Philip Hicky, son of Daniel Hicky and Mary Fowler Hicky, born at New Hope, West Baton Rouge, 30th December 1849, ½ past 11 o'clock.

Tuesday, 10th February, 1824 at 12 o'clock on this day Mrs. Miriam Ayers was safely delivered of a son, Dr. C. R. French and midwife Maryann, present at House of P. Hicky Hope Estate.

Adele Hicky Fowler, wife of Henry W. Fowler, safely delivered of a fine boy, on the morning of the 3rd of April, 1841, at about 7 o'clock. Boy named Eugene.

MARRIAGES

July 6th, 1840, *Miss Maria Louisa Newcomb* safely delivered of a daughter at 2 o'clock in the morning with assistance of Dr. French and Ma Maryann.

Philip Hicky and Anna Mather—married Monday, 24th April 1800, in the Church of the Parish of St. Charles, La.

Elizabeth Constance Hicky to James Scallan—at Hope Estate Plantation, Thursday 26th October, 1820.

Martha Francis Hicky to Simon W. Walsh—at Hope Estate Plantation.

Caroline Sarah Hicky to Morris Morgan, December, 1832, at Hope Estate.

Adele Hicky to Lieutenant Henry Waller Fowler, 2nd March, 1835, Hope Estate Plantation.

Mary Scallan to James Mather, 17th June, 1841.

Daniel Hicky, son of Philip and Ann Hicky, *married to Mary Fowler*, at Mrs. Fowler's, Parish of Iberville, 24th April, 1848, State of Louisiana.

Louisa Walsh, daughter of Simon and Martha Walsh, *married to Charles Mather*, son of George and Aurone Mather, at Hope Estate 26th April, 1848.

Saturday, 6th March, 1824, was married at the House of Philip Hicky (Hope Estate) *Mi. Mary Antonette Fowler to Wm. ——————— of New England.*

DEATHS

Martha Hicky, wife of Daniel Hicky, at Hope Estate, November, 1794.

Daniel Hicky, at Hope Estate, February, 1808.

George Mather.

Maria Louisa Hicky, at Baton Rouge, Mrs. Wikoffs, Friday night 5 minutes before 10 o'clock, 5th September, 1822.

Melinda Fowler—adopted daughter, at T. A. Morgan's, in Baton Rouge, October, 1830.

James Scallan, in Baton Rouge, 2nd January, 1832, half past 11 o'clock A. M.

Thomas Mather, at Hope Estate.

Isaac Wooter, from New England, 12th September, 1831.

James Mather, a cousin of Mrs. Hicky, at the Lausade Plantation, joining Hope Estate, died of Cholera on the —— September, 1832, at 8 o'clock A. M.

Martha Francis Hicky—wife of Simon W. Walsh, on the morning of the 3rd February, 1834, aged 33 years and 10 months.

Anna Louisa Hicky, daughter of Philip and Ann Hicky, 2nd of January, 1832.

George Mather, son of James Mather, aged about 54 years, died at his plantation in the Parish of St. James, La., at about 9 o'clock A. M., 26th day of May, 1837.

1839, Oct. 2.—Died at Hope Estate, a man by the name of *Daniel Dirwin*, a laborer, native of Ireland, interred in the Catholic burying ground. Died in the afternoon of Saturday, 15th October, 1812, say about ½ past 5 o'clock, *Philip Hicky*, aged 25 years and 4 days, after a short illness of only 6 days said to be —————— fever. Died on Monday, 24th October, at 10 M past 1 o'clock in the morning, *Francis Hicky*, aged 19 years, 2 mos. Died at Hope Estate on Monday 11 o'clock P. M., 1st October, 1843 *Aurone Hicky*.

Martha Hicky, wife of Daniel Hicky, at Hope Estate, November, 1794.

Daniel Hicky, at Hope Estate, February, 1808.

Anna Louisa Hicky, daughter of Philip and Ann Hicky, 2nd of January, 1832.

Martha Francis Hicky, wife of Simon Walsh, 3rd February, 1834.

Philip Hicky Junior, died Saturday, 15th October, 1842, only sick 6 days, aged 25 years.

Francis Hicky, died Monday, 24th October, 1842, aged 19 years and 2 months.

Aurone Hicky, died Sunday, 1st October, 1843, Hope Estate.

James Mather (London Mathers), died 30th May, 1832, at the Lausade Plantation.

MISS EDITH DUGGAN.

The late Miss Edith Duggan, another daughter of the late Judge Joseph H. Duggan—was during her lifetime one of the most noted portrait painters in the South. Her portraits were numerous, comprising among her sitters many of the most prominent members of the social life of this section. Her portarits recalling the beauty of the English School, having about them the charm of coloring, pose, and beauty that has made the British School so distinctive in the Art World. Miss Duggan possessed a wonderful personality, was a serious art student, and has left a great number of beautiful well painted portraits which tell of her great interest in her work. Her miniatures too, claim recognition, having about them a beauty freed from the stilted drawing so often found in this type of work. She studied with Andres Molinary, portrait painter, Poincy, and other notable portrait painters in New Orleans, and at the Chase Studio in New York. Her early death was a great loss to the Art World of the South where she had become so prominent and loved in the circles in which she moved.

de MacCARTHY Mac TAIG.

Major General de Marine Chef de Division du Departement de Rochevort is the first one of this ancient patrician family found in the American records. He was the father of Jean Jacques (Jean Baptiste) de Mac Carthy - Mac Taig: in service de la France envoye a la N. O., La. vers 1730 Commdt, un corpsde tache de Marine. Chevalier de St. Louis. Epouse Dame Francoise de Trepagnier. 2. Barthelemy Chevalier deMc.Carthy: passa en Amerique en meme temps que Jean Baptiste de McCarthy—Lieutenant dans le corps command epar J. B. Epouse Dame Francoise Helen Pellerin. 3. L'Abbe de McCarthy Cure de Verruge. 4. Eleanore Chanoinesse a Paris. 5. Francoise Chanoinesse a Paris.

The children of Jean Jacques McCarthy, who married Dame Francoise de Trepagnier, were: (1) Jean Baptiste ne ala N. O. envoye en Europe prend la service en France dans marine Royale en 1787, Major General de Marine, Chevalier de St. Louis du Port de Rochefort 1788. Commdt. de Voisseau Achille a la Rochelle le 2 Dec. 1798. (2) Ne a la N. O. le 5 Mai 1745. Augustin Guilliume prende service entrance dans la maison du Roi com-

Crest and Coat-of-Arms de Macarty family, de Macarty Plantation Home.

Mammy Millie Turner and Lawrence Richard de Buys, Jr., one of the 5th generation she has nursed. (Photo taken when she was 75 years of age. Page 163, Vol. II.)

panique des Mousquetaires a Cheva. le 17 Avril 1766. Retournee a la N. O. Epouse dame Jeanne Chauvin veuv reposse dans France 1781 sous le Comte d'Esting. Sous aide Major a bord le Fendont a la N. O. 1793.

Their children two in number, Augustin Francois. Ne a la Nouvelle Orleans le 10 Janvier 1774. Jean Baptiste Ne en 1776 en 1797. The other three children of Jean Jacques Mac Carthy and Dame Francois de Trepagnier were: (1) Catherine Ursule ne a la N. O. a la Rochelle le 20 Aout 1803. (2) Elizabeth ne a la N. O. A la Rochelle 11 Oct. 1805. (3) Jenne Ne. a la N. O. 8 Aout 1822.

The children of Barthelemy Chevalier de Macarthy and Dame Francoise Helene Pellerin were: (1) Jean Baptiste Ne a la N. O. le 7 Mars 1760. Servit dans l'Armee Francoise lors de la session de Armee Espagnel. Epouse Dame Fazende. * * 1805. (2) Louis, Ne a la N. O. Epouse; Dame veuve Lecoate. (3) Eugene Ne a la N. O. (4) Theodore Ne a la N. O. 1773.—Helene Ne a la N. O. (Mme. Le Breton ouis Mmme. Conway. Catherin Ne a la N. O. (Mme. la Comptesse Fabre de la Jouchere. Marie Celeste Ne a la N. O. Mme. la Comptesse de Miro— Mont l'Eve'que. Briggitts, Ne a la N. O. Mme. Nicolas D'Aunoy.

The children of Jean Baptiste de Mac Carthy and Dame Fazande were Barthelemy Ne a la N. O., Edmond, Ne a la N. O., Epouse Mlle. D'Estrehan. Celeste (Mme. Lanausse) Ne a la N. O. le 2 Dec. 1785 Sept. 1863.

The children of Louis de Mac Carthy who married Dame veuve Lacoate were Louis Barthelmy Ne a la N. O. 1783-1850. Delphine Ne a la N. O.—Mme. Lopez. M. Don Roman Lopez Y Angula.

The children of Delphie de MacCarthy and M. Don Roman Lopez Y Angula were Marie Francoise de Borja Delphine de Lopez Y Angula, married Francois Placide of New Orlens, May 31, 1821. Their children were as follows: Marie Jeanne Celeste Forstall, who married Henry A. Rathbone Esq. April, 1846; Marie Louise Emma Forstall; Jean Jules Forstall, who died in 1846; Marie Louise Paulin Forstall; Marie Louise Forstall (II); Anatole Jean Forstall; Joseph Octave Forstall; Marie Adelaide Forstall; Marie Jeanne Forstall; Marie Octavie Forstall; Marie Julia Forstall. The children of Marie Jeanne Celeste Forstall and Henry A. Rathbone, Esq., were: Marie Celeste Emma Rathbone, who married John B. de Lallande de Ferriere of New Orleans; Henry Paul Rathbone; Marie Virginie Pauline Rathbone, who married Peter Labouisse, Esq., of New Orleans; Francis Henry Rathbone, died in infancy; Marie Elizabeth Rathbone, who married James de Buys, Esq., of New Orleans; Marie Louise Rathbone, died in infancy; Marie Louise Alice Rathbone, who married Marie Octavie Rita Rathbone, who married M. Edgar de Poincy of New Orleans.

The children of Marie Celeste Emma Rathbone who married John B. de Lallande de Ferriere of New Orleans, are: Juanita de Lallande de Ferriere; Marie Rubie de Lallande de Ferriere; Marie Roy de Lallande de Ferriere; Marie Rathbone de Lallande de Ferriere; Marie d'Assise Gayoso de Lallande de Ferriere. The children of Marie Virginie Pauline Rathbone and Peter Labouisse, Esq., are: Peter Rathbone Labouisse and Marie Edith Labouisse. The children of Marie Elizabeth Rathbone and James de Buys are: Rathbone Emile de Buys; James Temple de Buys; Walter Lawrence de Buys; and Lourence Richard de Buys.

From the Family tree record—Courtesy of the de Buys family, of New Orleans, La.

Old Uncle Ned

MACARTY PLANTATION
(de Marcarthy Family)

In the area that became Carrollton, the Macarty Plantation, originally the property of one of the Lafrenier family, was known as the Lafrenier plantation. The other Lafrenier plantation not very far away belonged to another member of the same family.

It is now known as Elmswood and is one of the show places near New Orleans, the old manor house having been beautifully restored. The Macarty plantation, a grant to Lafrenier and later the property of Louis Cesar Le Breton is no longer in existence. The old plantation and manor have ceased to exist, but stories of the old plantation days that have been handed down by descendants of this old family have a more or less romantic charm, and have caused interested strangers to inquire who was the beautiful, fascinating Mademoiselle de Macarty one reads about in old Louisiana Stories?

The family of Macarty was an aristocratic Irish family, who rather than submit to religious and political tyranny of the English preferred exile. Bartholomew Macarty or Marcarthey—Mactaig to give the name in its original form, which later became Marcathy—a member of the Albermarle Regiment, fled to France, where his ability was recognized. He became a Major-General of a Division in the department of Rochefort, being made a Chevalier of St. Louis before his death. He was the father of two sons, christened with French names, being born in the land of their father's adoption. These two sons, Jean Jacques and Barthelmy, the French for Bartholomew, left France for Louisiana in the year 1730, the older in command of a marine detachment, the younger brother in the same command under him. Later Jean Jacques was married to Madame Francoise Barbe Ignace Trepagnier, whose first husband was Francois Antoine Damaron, Apothecary of the King in Louisiana. Two sons were born of this marriage and the family returned to France. The two sons entered service in the King's Army; one joining the marine, the other becoming a member of the King's household troops. Jean Jacques married in New Orleans after his return, Mademoiselle Jean Chauvin, a daughter of an early Louisiana settler. His wife dying before he did, he returned to the French service and was appointed aide to the Compte d'Estaing on the Fendant. He was made a Chevalier of St. Louis and died in New Orleans in 1793. Barthelmy de Macarty, as he signed himself, to denote his aristocratic lineage, remained in New Orleans, where he married Dame Francoise Helene Pellerin and became the father of eight children. He rose rapidly from a lieutenant to a captaincy in 1732, and filled the position of Aide Major of the city four years later.

Barthelmy de Macarty left a fine military record and died

about the time of the transfer of the colony to the Spanish Crown. He left a family of four sons and four daughters. His sons were (1) Jean Baptiste Francois de Macarty, who married Mademoiselle Helene Charlotte Fazende who was a daughter of Rene Gabriel Fazende and Charlotte Dreux; (2) Barthelmy Louis de Macarty who married Madam (vieuve) Lacompte—their daughter, described by contemporaries as being very beautiful, was Delphine de Macarty who was married to Don Ramon Lopez y Angullo and who became the mother of the no less beautiful Marie Francoise de Boya de Lopez y Angullo (Borquite) who married Placide Forstall and became the mother of twelve children from whom descend the prominent New Orleans families of Forstall and Rathborne; (3) Augustin de Macarty, son of Augustin Guillaume de Macarty and Jeanne Chauvin, became Mayor of New Orleans for several terms.

The daughters of Chevalier Barthelmy de Macarty and Francoise Helene Pellerin were Francoise Brigitte, Marie Catherine Adelaide, Celeste Eleanore and Marie Marthe. Francoise Brigitte became the wife of Nicolas d'Aunoy. Marie Catherine Adelaide became the Comptesse Fabre de la Jonchere—Jeanne Baptiste Cesaire le Breton, their daughter, became the wife of Baron Delfau de Pontalba. Celeste Eleanore Elizabeth married Governor Estaban Miro, Spanish Governor to succeed Galvez.

According to the late Judge Charles Gayarre, Louisiana Historian, the Macarty Plantation had been the property of Louis Cesar le Breton, and at his death passed to his son, Jean Baptiste Cesar le Breton. In 1771 it became the plantation of Barthelmay Daniel Macarty after le Breton "had been murdered by a petted and pampered slave. Barthelmay had been the tutor of the le Breton children and the plantation has since become the town of Carrollton."

The Macarty Plantation comprised in the boundaries "as a tract of land thirty-two arpents in front on the Mississippi." The tract owned and cultivated by the Macarty family at the beginning of the nineteenth century (1808) extended from the present Monticello Avenue, then the lower boundary of the Ludgore Fortier plantation which had formerly been part of the Macarty plantation, down to the present Lowerline street—the lower boundary. The upper boundary, the line at the upper limits of the Foucher Plantation—the lands of the plantation reaching back eighty arpents. The plantation was located eight miles above the Canal (Canal Street at present), river road measurements. Only the front acreage at that date was under cultivation.

In the vicinity of Clinton Street, Carrollton, not far from the then river road is said to have been the site of the old plantation home. The first one was like the old de Marigny de Mandeville plantation home, but smaller. It is supposed to have been lost by the caving in of the land in that section. The ruins of the old sugar house—for it had been a sugar plantation—were further back from the river than the plantation house, and remained standing until 1863, when they were demolished by orders of the U. S. Government that the space and material might be used for the erection of stables.

At the death of Jean Baptiste Macarty on November 10th, 1808 the plantation, with other property, was apportioned to his three children, Barthelmay, Edmond and Marie Celeste. Barthelmay Macarty, and Paul Lanausse who was married to Marie Celeste Macarty bought Edmond Macarty's share in the estate, and later on Barthelmay also purchased his sister Marie Celeste's share after the crevasse which had occurred on May 6, 1816—purchasing it while the land was still submerged.

The great crevasse which was to mean so much to the future of New Orleans occurred in the levee at the upper section of the Macarty Plantation. All the rear section of surrounding plantations were flooded, the high water extending as far down the river as the section known today as Canal and Bourbon streets.

The entire rear area of the present New Orleans was flooded, in some places the water attaining a height of five feet. The greatest part of the flooded area cleared in a little over three weeks being carried to the Lake Pontchartrain by Bayou St. Jean and other small bayous.

The entire area around New Orleans was immensely benefitted by its outcome. When the water had entirely subsided and it was found that a rich alluvial deposit of top soil, carried in the water of the Mississippi giving it the murky color, had destroyed the crops, but enriched and revitalized the soil. Land values immediately rose to ten times their original value in some cases. Even the swamp land was somewhat filled in certain areas.

Barthelmay Macarty, as is shown by an old notarial act, had Huges de la Vergne, draw up the deed of sale of an undivided half of his land to Eleonore Mirtile Macarty, wife of Charles Barthelmay Lanausse, and another instrument deeding by sale another half jointly to Samuel Kohn and Bernard de Marigny de Mandeville.

In 1815 General Carroll, in command of a large detachment of American soldiers, encamped at the Macarty Plantation and this was a great event in that day to the people of that section.

It was on this old Macarty Plantation, and in the old plantation mansion, which according to tradition, was swallowed by the ever hungry Mississippi, lived that beautiful Mademoiselle de Macarty who used to drive in her elaborate chaise with her postillion in front, to the old de Bore plantation near their plantation, when the little negro boy, on sighting her arrival, would swing wide the de Bore entrance gates crying out—"Mamselle Macarty a pe vini"—while at a brisk pace the chaise and horses would drive in beneath the green arcade.

Mademoiselle, always attired, like Madam de Bore in a Louis XIV gown, according to numerous writers, was a beauty to behold.

Von Phul

CHAPTER XXI.

Von PHUL—CADE—DUBROCCA—ALLAIN FAMILIES

VON PHUL FAMILY.

TRANSLATION OF AN EXPLANATION TO A SKETCH IN THE OLD von PHUL FAMILY BIBLE.

Explanation of the Drawing Above the Mantle in the Entrance Hall of Bel Air.

"A" represents the figure of Mr. Wilhelm von Phul, as an American Dragoon, willing to fight for Freedom, Honor, and Fatherland; born 1739, November 14th, at Westhofen in Middle-Pflaz; came to America 1764; married in Lancaster on November 14th, 1775. B, the High Honored and Honorable Maiden Catherina Graffin, born 1757, the 6th of January in Lancaster, and reared in this happy marriage the following children: (1) George, born 1776, the 3rd of November, baptized the 6th of November; the witnesses are the grand parents of the mother's side, Mr. Graff and his honored wife. (2) Catherine, born 1773, the 6th of October, and was baptized the 11th ditto; the witness is the grandmother, Mrs. Graffin. (3) Wilhelm, born 1780, the 12th of August, and baptized the 24th, the witnesses are the parents themselves; (4) Sara, born 1782, the 15th of September, and baptized the 15th of October; the witnesses are also the parents. (5) Heinrich, born 1784, the 14th of August, and baptized the 5th of September; the witnesses are also the parents.

(6) Maria, born 1786, the 17th of May, and baptized the

25th, ditto; the witnesses are the Mr. Father, and the sister of the Mrs. Mother, Mrs. Eva Krugin. (7) Philip, born 1788, the 17th of December, and baptized the 4th of January, 1789; the witnesses are Mr. Father and the Mrs. Mother themselves. (8) Graff, born 1790, the 1st of September (in the morning half after 3 o'clock) and baptized the 25th, ditto; the witnesses are the Mr. Father and the Mrs. Mother themselves. All of the children born at Philadelphia, Pa.

von PHUL FAMILY.

William von Phul, a German of noble ancestry, came to America and settled in Lancaster, Pennsylvania, in 1764. His son Henry von Phul, later leaving Lancaster, went west and located in Kentucky, from which place he again proceeded to St. Louis, where he established himself in the general mercantile buisness. With St. Louis a growing place, it was not long before he had become a very successful business man, ranking among the leading merchants of the city, where he was also largely interested in Mississippi shipping, having one of the large boats named after him, The Henry von Phul.

His three sons Henry, Frank, and William previous to the Civil War went south to Louisiana, Henry settling on the East bank of the Mississippi River, below Baton Rouge, while William, married a Miss Mary McD. Williams, thereby became master of Poplar Grove and Bel Air plantations which had been first owned by Mrs. von Phul's grandfather and later by her father, having been in the family since the year 1820. After the Civil War in which Henry, Frank, and William served in the Confederate army, during the entire period of hostilties, the three embarked in the cotton and sugar manufacturing business in New Orleans.

Mr. Frank von Phul was educated at the St. Louis University, a class-mate of Francis Joseph Boehm, an uncle of the author, the two men being close friends about whom gathered the classmates located in New Orleans. Among them being Numa Landry who became President of the Peoples Bank, Ernest Landry, his brother, who became cashier of the Peoples Bank, Charles Conrad who became a prominent lawyer in New Orleans, Mr. Frank Webre, and Mr. Bienvenue at whose home in Royal Street these classmates often met.

Crest and Coat-of-Arms of the von Phul family.
(Courtesy of Mr. William von Phul, Sr.)

Mr. William von Phul.

Mrs. William von Phul, Sr., who later became Mrs. S. Stafford.

Mrs. Robert Cade, neé Corinne Dubroca.

Miss Lillie Dubroca

DUBROCA GENEALOGY.

Martin Milony Duralde, born in Biscay, Spain, became a Spanish officer in Louisiana, located at Post Attacapas. His wife had been Mlle. Marie Josephe Perrault, who had come from Quebec, Canada. Their daughters were: Duralde, who married John Clay (brother of Henry Clay); Clarisse Duralde, who married W. C. C. Claiborne; Celeste Duralde, who married Valerian Allain, and became the parents of one son named Valerien Allain, born 1789, and three daughters, who became Madame Ursin Soniat du Fossat. Madame Valentin du Broca, and Madame George Eustis (nee Clarisse Allain).

Their sons were: Allain Eustis, who married Anais de Semanat; James Eustis, an ambassador to France, and George Eustis, who married Louise Corcoran of Washington, D. C. Celestine Allain Soniat du Fossat, married her cousin Ursin Soniat and later went to live in an apartment in the Quartier de la Madelaine in Paris, France. Here she maintained her salon, gathering about her a coterie of distinguished poets, writers, and musicians. Louis Philippe who had been entertained by her father with other members of the Royal family was among her numerous distinguished visitors.

From the time that Madame Celestine Allain was born on her father's plantation near Baton Rouge, La., her colored maid, had been her attendant from infancy up until her marriage. Always devoted, when Madame Soniat du Fossat went to live in Paris, naturally Anna LeAndre went to the French capitol with her. Such an attentive nurse and maid did Anna prove to be during Madame's long illness that her Mistress often would tell her friends and relatives, that she always concluded her prayers by asking that God take her first, so that she might be spared the anguish of outliving her devoted Anna. The family tell of how grateful Madame Soniat was, for upon learning that in Paris there existed a branch of the "National Society of France for the Promotion of Virtue", Madame Soniat at once wrote to the Society accompanying her letter with Anna's full name and a full account of her maid's absolute devotion, with the result—that to the delight of all, Anna received a gold medal from the Society.

In the City of Paris, on the official register of that Society appears the following: "Madame Anna LeAndre, a woman of color, seventy-five years old; born in Louisiana, living in Paris. This excellent woman has been in the service of Madame du Soniat for fifty years as maid and nurse, always showing unalterable attachment. Her parents and grand parents have served the same family from father to son for one hundred and fifty years. We recompense this rare example of Fidelity by the award of a medal of honor. Paris, May 22nd, 1881".

Madame, who had witnessed the presentation and happiness of her maid, wrote her family in New Orleans telling them in detail of the presentation as follows. "The ceremony was touching and handsome. I was thrilled with emotion at seeing my dear Anna taking the arm of a young and handsome officer to go to the platform, where were thirty judges and presidents, and more than five thousand spectators to receive applause, but Anna was more warmly applauded than anyone else."

When Madame Soniat died, she was buried in beautiful Pere la Chaise cemetery in Paris, and according to Madame's wishes her Anna was left a large annuity during the remainder of her life, which was spent in Paris, she living as a boarder in a convent of that city, and at her death she was buried by the side of her old Mistress in the grave that Madame had ordered when her own was planned in Pere la Chaise cemetery.

ALLAIN FAMILY.

Francois Allain who was born in Brittany, and had fought in the Battle of Fontenoy in 1745, according to his descendants, was the first one of this distinguished family to come to America, and located at a place called at that date Post des Attakapas (now Baton Rouge, La). His children that accompanied him were four in number, two daughters and two sons. To one son, Augustin by name, who became a captain of Grenadiers, stem the New Orleans family.

George Eustis, son of George Eustis and Clarisse Allain, married Louise Corcoran, whose father gave to the nation's capitol the art gallery that bears his name. He also distinguished himself by other notable gifts to the City of Washington. George Eustis Junior's sisters are Mathilde who became the wife of an Englishman and lived abroad. Celestine, who was known as one of the most cultured women in this city during her lifetime.

Valerien Allain, brother of Clarisse Allain, Alzire and Celestine, was educated in France, spending most of his spare time in Paris. Having spent a decade there in the Bohemian colony, upon his return to Louisiana found the life of a planter unsuited to his tastes, so decided to live in New Orleans, meeting and later marrying Mlle. Armantine Pitot, daughter of the young French nobleman who while in Paris became so outraged when he witnessed the head of Marie Antoinette's close friend Madame deLamballe upheld on a pike dripping blood, gave vent to his horror, and being warned fled to America. He later became the first American mayor of New Orleans. (The name originally Pitot de Beaujardierre). The Allain home became one of the greatest social centers in the city, famed specially for its cuisine, having one of the best chefs in the state. A constant stream of guests filled this hospitable home, where many of the brilliant men of the day gathered continually.

Chapter XXII.

D'ESTREHAN DES TOURS

THE d'Estrehan family ranks among the most aristocratic in the annals of the history of Louisiana. The founder of the family in Louisiana was Jean Baptiste d'Estrehan des Tours, who served for many years under the French as Royal Treasurer of the Colony, until Governor Kerlerec had him sent back to France for being "too rich and dangerous";—the true cause, according to reliable authorities, being that Rochemore, the French Government Intendant, was a close friend of d'Estrehan who supported him in his cabal against the Governor.

Jean Baptiste d'Estrehan was born in France. He married Mademoiselle Catherine de Gauvet, whose father was an officer in the colonial troops, her mother having been a Mlle. Pierre. He became the father of six children, one of whom, Marie Margarite, became the wife of Jean Etienne de Bore, being married in Paris on Sept. 20th, 1771. Marie Margarite received her education at the Royal Convent of St. Cyr, founded by Madame de Maintenant for the proper education of the daughters of the aristocracy. Jean Etienne de Bore de Mauleon, as the full name is written, was born in Kaskaskia, Illinois, Dec. 27th, 1741. He immortalized his name by his discovery of the process of granulating sugar, thus saving the sugar industry, or rather creating it. His sugar plantation was located on the site of the present Audubon Park in New Orleans. Today no trace remains of the old house. He died in New Orleans on the 27th of December,

1741. He was given an appropriate funeral from the St. Louis Cathedral and interred in the family vault in St. Louis Cemetery No. 1 He had requested that the sum that would have been spent for a more costly funeral be given to charity.

(2) Jean Baptist Honore d'Estrehan married Felicite St. Maxent and he died on the 20th of October, 1773, leaving no children. (3) Jean Louis d'Estrehan. (4) Jeanne Marie d'Estrehan, who became the wife of Pierre Enguerrand Philip de Marigny de Mandeville, who was a son of Antoine Philip de Marigny de Mandeville and Francoise de Lile Dupart. (5) Jean Louis d'Estrehan de Beaupre, who married in 1788 Mademoiselle Marie Claude Celeste Lenore Robin de Logny, daughter of Pierre Antoine Robin de Logny and Jeanne Dreaux de Gentilly, daughter of Sieur de Gentilly (Mathurin Dreux) one of the most prominent and wealthiest land owners in Louisiana who traces his lineage directly to Robert the Fifth, son of Louis VI of France.

Jean Noel d'Estrehan became the father of fourteen children: (1) Celestine d'Estrehan was born in 1787, became the wife of Rene Trudeau, and died in 1811; (2) Guy Noel d'Estrehan, whose wife was a Miss Oliver of New York, and at her death left two children, who became respectively Mrs. Chazot and Mrs. Thophile Roussel; (3) Justine d'Estrehan married Jean Baptiste de Macarty; (4) Nicolas Noel d'Estrehan was born in the plantation home in St. Charles Parish, April 3rd, 1793. He married Victorine Fortier, a daughter of Jacques Fortier and Aimee Durel, who bore him no children, and for his second wife married on Nov. 12th, 1826, Louise Henriette de Navarre, who was born in Paris, France, on the 10th of October, 1810, and died in the state of Louisiana, October 11th, 1836. She was a daughter of Ange Louis de Navarre and Adelaide Catherine Clement Gabrielle Rose Barth. (5) Eleonore Zelia d'Estrehan was the wife of Stephen Henderson. (6) Louise Odile d'Estehan was born in the year 1802. Her first husband was Pierre Edouard Foucher; she later married Pierre Adolph Rost. From her first marriage, amongst her children, are Destours Foucher, who became a prominent character in the Mexican War. He served on the staff of General Taylor. A daughter, Louise Foucher, becoming the wife of Felix Henri Larue, the children of this marriage were George H. Larue, who left no children; Anna Larue, who married Leon

Sarpy, and left children; Odile Larue, who married Frank O. Minor and left children; Ferdinan E. Larue, whose wife was Anna Le Gardeur de Tilly, left children; Felix A. Larue, M. D., whose first wife was Lisette Rea, who bore him children. After her death he married Stephanie Levert, a prominent harpist, daughter of the late sugar planter and distinguished Confederate soldier, Colonel J. B. Levert. From this marriage there was no issue. Destours P. Larue left no children. The children by her second marriage with Pierre Adolph Rost, Louise Odile d'Estrehan Foucher Rost became the mother of five children, a son Emile Rost, who became district judge of Jefferson, St. Charles, and St. John parishes.

(7) Marie Celeste d'Estrehan, born 1808. She first married Prosper de Marigny and later Alexander Grailhe. (8) Nicolas Noel d'Estrehan was born in St. Charles Parish on April 3rd, 1793, and died there June 16th, 1848, and is buried in the cemetery given to the parish by his family. By his marriage with Louise Henriette de Navarre, he was the father of four more children. (a) Louise d'Estrehan, who married Joseph Hale Harvey; (b) Adel d'Estrehan, who became Mrs. Samuel B. McCutchon, a member of the prominent plantation family who at one time owned "Ormond Plantation" close by. (c) Eliza d'Estrehan, who became Mrs. Daniel Rogers. (d) Azby d'Estrehan, who married Rosa Ferrier.

The children of Joseph Hale Harvey and Louis d'Estrehan are: (a) Nicolas Harvey, whose wife was Miss Stewart, their children are: (b) Sallie Harvey, who married Samuel R. Stewart, with issue. (c) Henriette Harvey, who married Horace de Gruy, with issue; (d) Henry Harvey, who married Marie deGruy, with issue; (e) William Harvey, with issue; (f) Laura Harvey, who married James D. Seguin, with issue; (g) Robert Harvey, with issue; (h) Horace H. Harvey, with issue; (i) Jennie Harvey, who married J. E. McGuire, with issue. 9. Adel d'Estrehan, who became Mrs. Samuel McCutchon, left four children as follows: (a) Samuel McCutchon; (b) Amelia McCutchon; (c) Adel McCutchon, without issue; (d) Azby d'Estrehan McCutchon, whose wife was Mattie Cabaniss, with issue. 10. Eliza d'Estrehan, who became Mrs. Daniel R. Rogers, left two children: (a) Lucie Rogers, who became Mrs. Alonzo Charbonnet, with issue; also

(b) Nina Rogers, who became the wife of S. Locke Breaux, a member of the family for whom the Breaux Bridge plantation is named. (Without issue). 11. Azby d'Estrehan, who married Rosa Ferrier, and left one child. 12. Marie Delphine Louise d'Estrehan, who was first married to Dupuy de Lome, and later to Ernest Richard.

ARMS OF THE DE LA BARRE FAMILY

Field Argent, Bar, azure, Charged with three gold (or) shells, accompanied Troiseau sable. Support a lion on either side. The simplicity of the arms indicate crusade origin. A family whose name finds its origin in the town of Beauce Flanders, in 1330, and stemming beyond to the city of Ghent, where members of the family held position sovereign Baliff, of Flanders giving almost kingly powers.

THE DE LA BARRE FAMILY

The de la Barre family is of ancient origin, reaching back to the year 1330 to one Guillaume de la Barre, Chevalier et Seigneur de Chauvincourt whose wife was Mademoiselle Robine d'Orval, also of a noble house of France. Francois Pascalis de la Barre, the first of the de la Barre family to come to America and settle in Louisiana, was appointed to the responsible office of Alguazil, corresponding to high sheriff. He married Charlotte Volant, daughter of Chevalier Gregorie Volant stationed at Karkey in Louisiana, in command of the 4th Company of the Swiss Regiment. Of this union four children were born: Francois Pascalis de la Barre, Jr., Pierre Volant, Aimee de la Barre, who became the wife of Antoine Bienvenue; Marie de la Barre, who became the wife of Francois Joseph la Molere d'Orville. Francois Pascalis de la Barre, Jr., became the husband of Charlotte de Tillet; ten children were born of this union, four sons and six daughters.

CHAPTER XXIII.

HEWES.

THE HEWES—GRYMES FAMILIES

THE first part of this memorandum was found among papers of Ann Poindexter, daughter of Samuel Hewes of Boston.
Mather Cushing came from England and settled in Hingham, and married Nagarett? (Margarete) Pitcher of England. The question mark after Nagarette evidently shows doubt about that name. Their son Thomas married Deborah Thaxter and settled in Boston. Their daughter Margaret Cushing married William Fletcher, born in Surry, England, 1688, and settled in Boston. This Margaret Fletcher married Henry Newman, who came from England and settled in Boston. Their daughter Hannah Newman married John Milliquet, who came from England and resided in Boston, afterwards returned to England. Their daughter Margaret Milliquet married Deacon Samuel Hewes of Boston. Their son William Gardner of Boston married Maria Abercrombie Kent Searle of Kent, England, daughter of Sir Francis Searle and Maria Abercrombie Kent, who was a niece of Admiral Abercrom-

William von Phul, Jr., 1st Lieutenant, U. S. Army,
World War

Madame Ursin Soniat du Fossat, neé Melle. Celestin Allain. (From a miniature in the Cade family.)

Apartment house in Paris where Madame Ursin Soniat du Fossat lived.

Madame Ursin Sonia du Fossat and Anna Le'Andre.

Graves in Pere La Chaise Cemetery, Paris, where Madame Ursin Soniat du Fossat and Anna Le Andre are buried.

Mrs. Effie Cade Daniels, on the handsome stairway of Bel Air Manor. (Illustrations courtesy of the von Phul and Cade families.)

The Thomas H. Hews family, Pleasant View Plantation. (See page 184, Vol. II.) (Courtesy of Mrs. Thos. H. Hewes.)

bie of the British Navy. Their son Thomas Hewes, born in New Orleans Nov. 5th, 1823, died Aug. 13th, 1889. Married Anna Lancaster, born March 8th, 1840, died March 13th, 1902. They had a son, Charles Lancaster, born in Sacramento, California, Sept. 2nd, 1856. Anna Lancaster, born Aug. 12th, 1858, at Placerville, California. William Gardner, born in Texas, Feb. 27th, 1860. Thomas Henry, born on Grosse Tete, Louisiana, Sept. 14th, 1863, died January 9th, 1865. Miguel Tacon, born in New Orleans, Nov. 22nd, 1865. Thomas Hewes, born at Pleasant View Plantation, Pointe Coupee Parish, Louisiana, July 31st, 1868. Walter Herbert born at Pleasant View Plantation, Nov. 10th, 1870, died April 5th, 1883. Robert Edward, born at Pleasant View, July 11th, 1873. Rosina Dunbar, born at Pleasant View, June 25th, 1876. Cecil Grayson, born at Pleasant View, April 21st, 1879. Kent Searle, born at Pleasant View, June 14th, 1882.

Charles Lancaster Hewes, married Sarah Pilant June 30th 1896. She was born June, 1864—they have three children: Anna, born April 12th, 1897; Wm. Pilant, born June 27th, 1899; Charles Denis, born March 1st, 1904.

Anna Lancaster Hewes married Charles Denis, Oct. 10th, 1882. He was born in New Orleans Jan. 4th, 1886. Miguel Tacon married Aug. 5th, 1891 Elisabeth Hyams who died June 2nd, 1898, leaving two daughters, Inez Rosina, born May 21st, 1892, and Myrtle Thelma, born August 6th, 1894. Tacon married again on July 19th, 1899, Rosemary Claiborne; they have three children: Lewis Claiborne, born July 27th, 1900; Thomas Hewes, born Aug. 4th, 1901, and Fanny Tacon, born March 1st, 1904.

Thomas Hewes married Annie Laurie Grimes March 8th, 1904. They have three of their four children living: Elliot Henderson Hewes; Marie Louise Hewes (Mrs. David Miller Mims); Annie Laurie Grimes Hewes. Thomas H. Hewes, Jr., died June 19th, 1909.

Robert Edward married Dorsey Van Vleck of Ohio, Jan. 15th, 1908.

Copied by Anna L. H. Denis from a letter written to Wm. Gardner Hewes, his father, Thos. H. Hewes about 1886.

As to the Hewes and Searle families.—Samuel Hewes and Nancy Hill. Samuel Hewes, Jr. and Margaretti Milliquet.

Wm. Gardner Hewes and Maria Abercrombie Kent Searle, daughter of Sir Francis Searle and Maria Abercrombie Kent, who was a niece of Admiral Abercrombie of the British Navy.

Thomas H. Hewes and Anna Lancaster.

The Hewes family came from Wales. The first Samuel Hewes was a prominent and wealthy citizen of Boston prior to the Revolution. He was an ardent rebel and gave largely to that cause. His wife, Nancy Hill, was a high spirited little woman of whom I have heard many interesting anecdotes. They had six children, two sons and four daughters. The daughters all married prominent men, Edward Jones—Newman—Wm. Gardner. Newman and Wm. Gardner of Portsmouth, New Hampshire gave a warship to the Colonial cause. Their son, Samuel, had for his first wife Margaretti Milliquet of French extraction—their children were William Gardner, Margaret, Samuel Hill and Nancy or Ann as she preferred to call herself. The second wife was Martha Bliss and they had issue—Mary, Edward, Henry and Sarah. That Samuel was in early life a merchant engaged in the East India trade, but for the last thirty years of his life he held an office in the Boston city government. He died in 1844 and I heard a long funeral oration, delivered some weeks subsequently.

He certainly was noted for integrity, kindness of disposition and great energy. His son, Wm. Gardner (your grandfather) came to Louisiana about 1815, Margaret also came soon after to this state and married Robert Layton. She died in 1878, having survived all of her children except one son, Robert, who now lives in Monroe, Ouachita Parish. Her husband was rich and left a large amount of property. Ann married in Washington City, George Pointdexter, then a senator from Mississippi. They had no children, by his will he left all (a considerable property) to his wife. She died some eight years since.

Samuel Hewes is now about 87 years of age (according to his own letters he was ninety in 1886 which gives date of father's letter A. L. Denis) lives in Tuscola, Michigan and certainly is in full possession of all his faculties. He has a large family, none of whom I ever have met. Edward died of cholera in my father's home in New Orleans in 1832, and Mary died some fifteen years since. Henry settled in Calcutta as a merchant, and died there about the year 1851. Sarah still lives in Boston, a most refined and estimable old lady.

Your grandfather, William Gardner, was a very prominent merchant of New Orleans, and prior to 1842 had acquired a large fortune and virtually had retired from business, entrusting all to a partner. That partner with no evil intent endorsed, in the firm's name for a brother of his, for over $200,000.00. The first intimation your grandfather had of the matter, was a demand upon him as indorser, it was a panic year and property could not be sold. For instance the Orleans Cotton Press, for which he had paid $27,000.00 he sold for $17,000.00 in order to pay the debts. His struggle was fruitless, and he gave up everything and began anew. Such was his character, that offers to loan him money exceeded in the aggregate one million of dollars were made. I read those offers—but he declined all aid and when Secession he had again become worth some $30,000.00. He most warmly espoused the Confederate cause and may truly be said to have given to it all he had. When Butler entered New Orleans, he left, and died near Opelousas within a year afterwards. He originated the Water Works Co., was its first president, was president of several banks and insurance companies, and at the time of his death, was president of the Great Western and Pacific Railroad, and of the Bank of America. Like his father and grandfather he was very devoted to his family and to business, was I to believe without a vice. He had some fondness for military affairs, was Captain of the first American company ever organized in New Orleans, did duty in the war of 1812, and was granted land by the U. S. for his services. His marriage was a love and somewhat romantic affair.

Sir Francis Searle was the first to march into London at the head of a regiment to resist the threatened invasion of Napoleon. The King gave him magnificent tokens of favor (a diamond snuff box I remember well). His wife, Maria Kent, was a niece of General Abercrombie who figured in our revolutionary war on the British side. They had four children: Frank, Maria, Caroline and Frederick. Early in this century they left England for one of the British West India Islands, where he was to fill some high office. Forced by a French Fleet to find refuge in Boston, he bought a fine place near that city, but seems to have been careless in money matters, and died there much involved in debt. His widow was as remarkable for energy as for beauty and made many friends in Boston. Leaving her children in Boston she made a dangerous voyage to England only to find her husband's affairs involved so badly, she compromised and getting some $20,000.00, returned to Boston. There she married Thomas Hewes the second son of the first Samuel, and moved to New Orleans, taking the Searle children with them. But your grandfather William G. was in love with Maria, so he soon followed to New Orleans, was married, and went into business with his uncle Tom. Their first child was named William, but he died soon after the second son (myself) was born.

By her marriage wth Thomas Hewes my grandmother had one child, Fanny, who married Miguel Tacon about 1837 and went to Spain where with a large family she remained. Thomas Hewes for whom I was named, died about 1825, and his widow removed to Washington City. I have but a very indistinct recollection of my uncle Frank Searle. Fred attended West Point became distinguished in the army, was wounded during the Florida War, with the Indians, and remained paralysed from the waist down during life. He died about 1854. Carolyn (you have seen), she married John Breckenridge Grayson, an officer of the army. His mother, Loetitia Breckenridge, Aunt of Judge Breckenridge of St. Louis. You know how energetic and impulsive Caroline was. Her brother Fred was much like her. But my mother was more retiring, and more amiable and loving. She died of cholera in 1861.

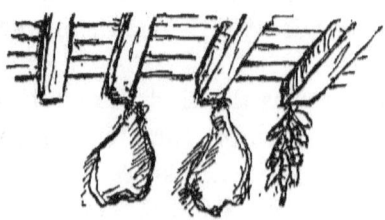

GRYMES.

Mrs. Thomas H. Hewes, nee Annie Laurie Grymes, is a daughter of the late John Collins Grymes, who was a son of William Bryan Grymes, who was born in Willamson, Martin Co., North Carolina, Oct. 4th, 1806. He married Sarah Marina Lanier in 1838. William Bryan Grymes was a large land owner in Rapides Parish and Avoyelles Parish, where his plantation before the Civil War was on the bluff known as "Grymes Bluff". John Collins

Grymes was a nephew of the late John Randolph Grymes, a lawyer, and legislator who was born in Orange County, Virginia, in 1786. He studied law in Virginia, was admitted to the bar, and in 1808 removed to the territory of Orleans, where his great ability was soon recognized. He was appointed district attorney, and in that capacity became connected with the notable Batture Case, his fee as counsel being $100,000.00. He was Andrew Jackson's counsel in the U. S. Bank case, and was opposed to Daniel Webster in the case of Myra Clark Gaines against the city of New Orleans. He fought two duels, in one of which he was severely wounded. He died Dec. 4th, 1854 in the City of New Orleans. His residence, according to old city directories, was at 122 Canal Street, New Orleans.

John Collins Grymes (Mrs. Thomas Hewes' father) was born in 1841 on his father's plantation. He was a Lieutenant of Company A, 8th Louisiana Cavalry, during the Civil War. He attended L. S. U., at that time Louisiana Military Academy at Alexandria, Louisiana, and was one of its first students. Mrs. Thomas Hewes' uncle, Lanier Grymes was a member of the first class to graduate from L. S. U. and later was a professor of Mathematics there. John Collins Grymes was married to Annie Lyme Smith, a daughter of Geo. Childs Smith of Waterbury, Conn. Her mother was Eleanor Amelia Tanner, whose wedding dress was carefully pressed and worn by Mrs. Thomas Hewes' daughter, Marie Louise Hewes, at her marriage to David Mims of Minden, La. Mr. and Mrs. Mims have one son, Thomas Dangald Mims, born Aug. 26th, 1934. Eleanor Amelia Tanner was the daughter of Robert Lynn Tanner and Marian Irion, who was the daughter of George Anderson Irion and Rebecca Hunt of Halifax County, Virginia. George Anderson Irion was a major in the War of 1812. He moved to Avoyelles, La., from Virginia, and settled where the town of Bunkie, La. now stands. Mrs. Thomas Hewes is a great niece of Judge Alfred Irion of Avoyelles Parish, who was well loved for his wit and humor. His book "Tribulations of Boaz" has won for him the reputation of being a great humorist.

Chapter XXIV.

THE FROTSCHER—KOCH—MULLER—BRUCE FAMILIES

THE name Frotscher is Scandinavian, "one who dwells by a fiord", later in Austria. About two hundred years ago, two brothers left, one settled in Leipzig, Germany, the other in France. The family is descended from the German branch and has a long line of Lutheran ministers and University professors.

The Frotscher plantation has been in possession of the family for sixty odd years—bought by Richard Frotscher from Judge Kreider. The overseer's house is still standing. It was originally a sugar plantation: name, *Apiary*—located at Fausse Point on Bayou Teche in the parishes of Iberia and St. Martin.

Richard Frotscher married Emilie Schwalm. Children: Anna Wilhelmine married Julius Koch of Stuttgart, Germany, Architectural Engineer from Karl Schule, Stuttgart; Mary, died unmarried; Emilie married Nicholas Muller of New Iberia; Helen Virgin married Charles Bartholomew! Minna married Edward Frederick Bruce, M. D. Tulane, of Pensacola, Fla. (a daughter Lydia Mary); Lydia Elizabeth, Professor of German and Head of Department, Newcomb College, Tulane University. A. B., Newcomb; A. M. Tulane; Ph.D., Chicago.

KOCHS.

1. Richard—First Bachelor of Architecture ever conferred by Tulane. Architect, born New Orleans, La., June 9, 1889; s. Julius and Anna (Frotscher) K.; B.A., Tulane University, 1910;

student Atelier Bernier, Paris, 1911-12; unmarried. Architect since 1916; member of firm Armstrong & Koch, New Orleans, 1916-35; alone since 1935. District officer Historic American Buildings Survey in La.; Chairman of Committee on Preservation of Historic Monuments of Am. Inst. of Architects; v.p. Arts and Crafts Club of New Orleans; member of board of Delgado Art Museum; member of Zoning Board of Appeal and Review; member City Park Board. Served as 1st Lieutenant Air Service, U. S. Army, 1916-18. Fellow Am. Inst. of Architects. Award: Silver medal in Architecture by Archtl. League of New York for "works of minor importance executed in local tradition", 1938. Episcopalian. Club: Boston (New Orleans). Designed traditional house for families of $2000 - $3000 income, pub. in Life, 1938. Home: 2627 Coliseum Street. Office: Queen and Crescent Bldg., New Orleans, La. 2. Julie Frotscher—A.B. Newcomb; A.M., Chicago. History Department of Roosevelt High School, St. Louis. 3. Wilhelm—Bachelor of Civil Engineering. Construction Engineer; has done much government work. 4. Minna Frotscher—A.B., Newcomb; M.S. and Ph.D., Cornell. Has done research at Cornell and in New York Botanical Gardens. 5. Emilie Frotscher—Newcomb, New York School of Social Service. Case Worker for Children's Bureau. 6. Anna Frotscher—A.B., Newcomb. Teacher of mathematics in Sophie B. Wright High School.

Architects for the Ramseys: Koch and Stone.

From Life, Sept. 26th, 1928: "Richard Koch of New Orleans is the architect Life chose to design the best traditional house for the Ramseys' wishes and pocketbook. A quiet sober hard-working craftsman, Mr. Koch has won a national reputation for skill in adapting the easy charm of old Southern homes to demands of modern living. Last April the Architectural League of New York awarded him its Medal, top award for residential design".

Among the outstanding examples of Mr. Koch's work are the following: Harry T. Howard Residence, New Orleans, La.; Boatner Reily Home, Lewisburg, La.; J. W. Reily Country Home, Bayou Liberty, La.; Donald Markle Home, Pass Christian, Miss.; Restoration of the W. W. Hall home in New Iberia, La., "Shadows on the Teche"; Restoration of the Andrew Stewart Home "Oak Alley", Vacherie, La.; Restoration of Little Theatre, New Orleans,

La.; Restoration of "Petit Salon", New Orleans, La.; Miss Matilda Gray's Home, Royal and Esplanade Avenue, New Orleans; Andrew Stewart Home, Valence Street, New Orleans, La.; Home, number 704 Gov. Nicholls Street, New Orleans, La.; Tavern at Natchez "Connelly's Tavern; and Trinity Chapel, New Orleans, Louisiana.

Every detail of the work was accomplished under the direct supervision of Richard Koch, local architect, Louisiana district officer of the Historical American Building Association, now functioning in every state in the union with funds furnished in the past by Civil Works Administration and in the future by the Emergency Relief Administration. Mr. Koch was recommended to the government for this extraordinary task by the American Institute of Architects with the assurance that he was the man best fitted for the purpose. He is chairman of the local committee for the preservation of historical monuments of the city; acting chairman of the Vieux Carré commission for the preservation of that section and chairman of the new City Park landscape planning commission.

At a banquet terminating the 70th annual convention of the American Institute of Architects which took place at the Roosevelt Hotel, New Orleans in April, 1938, Richard Koch was awarded a fellowship. Mr. Koch being honored for "his studied and charming adaptation of the distinctive architecture of his state to the needs of present-day building, and his record of sustained effort in the best interests of his profession.

HOME OF THE JULIUS KOCH FAMILY.

The handsome home of the Koch family, located in the "Garden District" was originally built for James Biddle Eustis, Ambassador to France. During his residence here it was one of the leading social centers in this city. The late John Coleman in writing of this house in his series of "Noted Old New Orleans Homes" has this to say—"In the old Eustis mansion there is an admirable blending of architectural charm with its surroundings—an edifice of stately transquility. Bright, cheerful and inviting, it is as beautiful within as without. Senator and Mrs. Eustis lived there with their family until his election to the United States Senate, when he made his home in Washington, D. C. During this time

MRS. RICHARD FROTSCHER

RICHARD FROTSCHER.
(See Chapter XXIV, Vol. II.)

MISS LYDIA ELISABETH FROTSCHER
Professor and head of German Department, Newcomb College, Tulane University, New Orleans.

MISS MARY FROTSCHER.

(Illustrations courtesy of the family.)

JULIUS KOCH,
Architect and Engineer

RICHARD KOCH,
Architect

An attractive corner of the Koch home, Coliseum Street, New Orleans.

Showing the beautiful detail of the elaborate iron-work, Koch home, Coliseum Street.

the home was leased to Mr. A. R. Shattuck, later to Mr. Ben. Oxnard, largely interested in the refining of sugar, and later again to Mr. Henry Forsythe, son-in-law of the late Bradish Johnson.

Following the death of Senator Eustis which occurred in New York City in 1898 the property was disposed of by his heirs and it was then that Mr. Julius Koch a local architect became its owner; and is still preserved by this cultivated family". Continuing—"Above all else the mansion is comfortable, with high ceilings, large rooms and exposure from every point of the compass. In the center is a spacious hallway, extending the entire length of the building, and on which on the uptown side gives access to a spacious parlour occupying on the lower floor the whole of that side of the building. On the downtown side of the hall is the reception room fronting Coliseum Street, and in the rear of this apartment is the elegant dining room extending to an octagon. The floor above is reached by a handsome staircase which winds upward. On this floor are five large bedrooms, amply supplied with bath rooms".

All of the accessory rooms to be found in a large home are found here, all of large size and well finished. The spacious garden has always been the pride of its owners, and the Koch family, all great flower lovers, see to it that the garden does not lose the reputation it has enjoyed for so many years, as one of the beauty spots of the "The Garden District". Great masses of azaleas, japonicas, roses and the one hundred and one beautiful flowering shrub one meets in an old-fashioned garden of this sort are found. The splendid lace-like iron work of this home is some of the finest in the state. Cast in beautiful patterns and planned as trellisses enclosing attractive porches hung with wisteria, bignonia and rose of montana—the home becomes an ideal dwelling place in such surroundings.

MULLERS.

1. Hans Nicholas—Bachelor of Fine Arts, Carnegie Tech., majored in Stage Design and Costume. Worked as Interior Decorator in New York for Mack, Jenny and Tyler. Later did independent work. 2. R. Frotscher—Bachelor of Mechanical and Electrical Engineering, Tulane. Married to Alma Schuler, one son, R. Frotscher. Works for Allis Chalmers Co.

BARTHOLOMEW

Helen Frotscher—married to Felix Morel: one daughter, Naomi, who teaches in Jefferson Parish Grade School.

BRUCE.

Lydia Mary—teacher in Grade School of Pensacola, Fla.; holds teaching certificate from University of Florida.

CHAPTER XXV.

THE BOEHM FAMILY

THE Boehm family is originally from Vienna, Austria, where it is listed among the ancient patrician familes of the Old Austrian Empire, and in England in Burke's Peerage. The American branch of which we are writing, came to New Orleans from the City of Metz in Lorraine, a French possession at the time, to which the family had fled from Austria several generations before while religious wars were raging.

The paternal grandfather of Francois Pierre Boehm, who came to America a century ago, was August de Belasyse Boehm who had been Burgomaster of Vienna. He was also owner of large land holdings in the suburbs of that city, a section that later became a residential area for many of the Viennese nobility. In his list of properties was a large flour mill at Dahlberg, near the old von Dahlberg Castle in Hessendarmstadt. A smaller flour mill bearing the family name is still in existence, having replaced the one mentioned on the old Burgomaster's list of his property holdings, the original mill having burned many years ago.

Burgomaster August de Belasyse Boehm was the son of Edward Boehm of Vienna who held a responsible position in the Austrian mint, who in turn succeeded his father in the position. His mother was Mathilda de Belasyse of the ancient family of that name from Rouen, France. He married Magdalina Kirkland D'Almont of another patrician family of Metz.

A son of Baron von Dahlberg, while playing about the grounds fell into the old moat of the castle and was drowned, and the Baron von Dahlberg and his family moved away, leaving his sister and her family there in charge of the lands. Baron von Dahlberg's sister married Francis Joseph Boehm I, and their daughter Anna

Maria, a noted beauty, married Pancratious Swendle, a wealthy wine manufacturer with large vineyards and wine-presses in the locality.

The von Dahlberg castle was erected in the early 1600's and according to the ancient crumbling stone tablet pictured in this article, was a memorial to the wife, born a von Flersheim, of Baron von Dahlberg MDXXX. Recorded in honor of the best and noblest." The old castle, according to records, was first badly damaged during the wars with the French by the army of Louis XIV, but had been partly restored, and was later struck by lightning and burned to the ground. Its ruins remained for many years until the town spread. A promenade was made of what had been the old moat. The ancient stone tablet was rescued and imbedded in a heavy wall which ran behind the castle. There is an ancient church where both Catholics and Protestants worship, having hand-carved woodwork on pews and altar.

"Life moves quietly in this rural community today (written before the present war) where those now occupying lands that formerly belonged to an ancient aristocracy, and for several centuries had been the seats of the Counts von Dahlberg and von Becker." This community that had been a very aristocratic one in the middle ages, contained some seventeen Knights and their families, who resided in the settlement, and who had a following of retainers who dwelt on their lands and saw to the management of their estates. The community was governed by the combined knighthood (called Gauerschaft) and consisted of members of the most prominent knights and their families at that time, and which comprised the following families: 1. von Dahlberg; 2. von Deinheim; 3. von Riedesel; 4. von Weyhers; 5. von Wallbrun; 6. von Bertolfesheim; 7. von Knebel; 8. von Becker; 9. von Dachroder; 10. von Stroem.

The descendants of Knights lost control of the country at the time of the French Revolution, the French Republic taking possession in the year 1797. The settlement was a French protectorate until Jan. 21st, 1814, and for the next two years under the Imperial Austrian and Royal Bavarian Land Administration. Finally on July 8, 1816 it was taken over by the Arch Duchy of Hessen and from 1816 to 1852 was part of the County of Alzey, then it was included in the country of Oppenheim. Part of this

BOEHM

Burgomaster August deBelasyse Boehm, paternal great-grandfather of Mrs. W. E. Seebold. (From an ivory miniature in the Seebold family.)

Magdalena Kirkland D'Almont, wife of Burgomaster August de Belasyse Boehm. (From an ivory miniature in the Seebold family.) Paternal great-grandmother of Mrs. W. E. Seebold neé Lisette Boehm.

THE OLD VON DALBERG CASTLE NEAR MAINTZ.

Built for the von Dalberg family in 1550, as a memorial to his wife, born a von Flersheim, by Baron (Knight) von Dalberg. Copied from a painting of the castle in the collection of Rhine Castles in the Coblence Museum.
(Courtesy of the Curator of Coblence Museum, 1919.)

Anna Maria von Dalberg, a sister of Count von Dalberg, a direct descendant of the builder of the castle. Anna Maria von Dalberg married Francis Joseph Boehm I, and took possession of the castle after a son of Count von Dalberg was drowned in the moat that surrounded the castle—the castle and land still being retained by the Count's heirs—after the family had moved away.

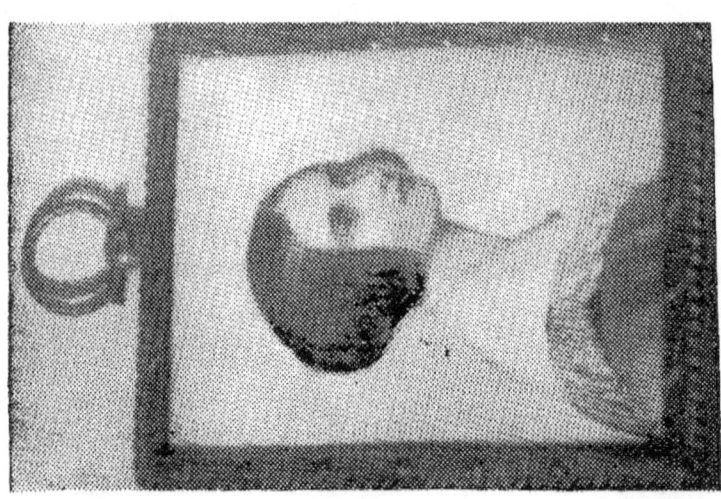

Anna Maria Boehm, daughter of Anna Maria von Dalberg and Francis Joseph Boehm I. Maternal grandmother of Mrs. W. E. Seebold, neé Lisette Boehm. (From miniature in the Seebold family.)

Mrs. Francis P. Boehm I, neé Elisabeth D'Aunoy of Metz, Lorraine, France. (From miniature signed R. M., paternal grandmother of Mrs. W. E. Seebold neé Lisette Boehm. In Seebold collection.)

land was held by the von Dahlberg family, whose castle had been partially destroyed by the troops of Louis XIV.

Francois Pierre Boehm I, eldest son of Burgomeister August Belasyse Boehm and Magdalina Kirkland D'Almont, was born in the City of Metz in Lorraine (at that time French). He attended the French Military Academy of that place, and after having graduated joined the French Army and attained the rank of a Colonel. He married Elisabeth D'Aunoy, a member of the ancient and wealthy D'Aunoy family of Metz, with large land holdnigs in the city of Nancy where other branches of the family resided. The children of Elisabeth D'Aunoy and Francois Pierre Boehm 1st, were Francois Pierre Boehm II, Elisabeth Boehm, who became a nun and another sister Margurite Boehm, who died unmarried.

Francois Pierre Boehm II was educated at the University of Jena, that date one of the finest universities in the world to include a strict military training. The Boehm family were closely related to the noted sculptor who became the protege of Queen Victoria, having been knighted by her Majesty.

On the inside of the cover of a little autograph album belonging to Francis Pierre Boehm II, and in which are the names of many of his classmates while at the University of Jena, he wrote in a fine copper-plate hand writing his name over a century ago. Many of these fellow students became distinguished later in life. His father had been an army officer, and as was customary the sons of army officers each wrote a few lines. After graduating he entered the French Army. As only men with independent fortunes could become officers in peace time, his mother, being a wealthy widow, settled on him the required amount to enable him to be independent. Shortly afterwards he married his second cousin, whose mother was Anna Maria Boehm of Dahlberg Castle, a noted beauty of her day, a member of one of the oldest and most prominent families of the Counts in the Hessendarmstadt area, their castle having been one of the seven leading ones in Hessendarmstadt.

A RELIC DATING FROM 1550.

Deeply imbedded in a heavy wall on the site of the old von Dahlberg Castle in Hessen-Darmstadt still can be seen the ancient tablet that was placed, when this memorial castle was built in

1550, for the Knight Wolf von Dahlberg. Deeply carved in the heavy stone is the following:

> *Als man zahet 1500 Jahr Und 50 darzu das nimm war Das Fundament andiesm Haus Gelect ward Gebauetaus Durch Georgen Kemmer Guaud von Dalberg Ritterlich Bekannt Sein Gemalil von Flersheim, he survived. Geboren Hat er ilium Auser koren Darum ist diese Schrift erbracht Suf dass desselum werd gedacht Renoret divich den edlin und besten.*
> Wolf von Dalberg MDLXXX.

TRANSLATION.

> *As one counts 1500 years and 50 added to it, was the foundation of this House laid.*
> *Built during the reign of the Georges—by von Dahlberg, known as knight.*
> *His Spouse, born Von Flersheim, he survived.*
> *Therefore is this writing created, that this will be remembered. Recorded in honor of the best and noblest.*
> Wolf von Dalberg. MDLXXX.

An illustration of this ancient castle of the von Dahlberg family hangs on the walls of the Historical Museum of Coblentz, Germany, along with other old castles of the Rhine Country.

The area in which was this once settlement of nobles has suffered much from constant warfare, and at present contains only the relics of its once proud castles, most of them stone memorial tablets carved deep in relief, giving family date with large coats-of-arms surmounted by family crests at each corner of the large stone tablets, that of the von Dahlberg's being one in the best state of preservation. Great arcaded Gothic chapel-like basements with walls four and five feet of stone in thickness remain partly buried in the earth to show where once these old castles stood.

The high taxes, the continual destruction of their property, and the many raids on their wine cellars by the soldiers stationed about Metz, the continuous wars in which France was involved, brought the Boehm family to the conclusion that while they still had means it was wiser to seek a place that offered a relief from these conditions and America seemed that refuge.

Upon the death of his wife's parents, Francois Pierre Boehm II with his wife and their two children, after a long journey, came to America. They settled in the City of St. Louis, Missouri, where other branches of the family had already gone. When the furniture, etc., that they were bringing to America with them had been prepared for shipment, according to old notes written by Francois Pierre Boehm II of Metz, it came by way of the Moselle River to Coblenz into the Rhine River, stopping in Cologne which was the last stop before reaching Zeeland enroute to America.

The furniture reached New Orleans in the Spring of 1841, accompanied by a brother of Mrs. Francois Pierre Boehm II, who remained with the family until they were settled in the City of St. Louis. This brother then visited the family of his brother living in New York State where they had settled, their children later marrying into the families of Maurer, Melsner, Roesch, Hebert and others. He later returned to his home in Europe to manage his vineyards.

When Mr. and Mrs. Francois Pierre Boehm arrived in New Orleans they stayed at the Old Planters Hotel, which stood on Chartres Street. On board the steamboat bound for St. Louis the family met Mr. Antoine Bienvenue and his son who was going to attend the University of St. Louis. Mr. Bienvenue persuaded Mr. Boehm to enroll his son also in the University of St. Louis, telling him that many prominent Louisiana planters sent their sons to this University. At the University of St. Louis young Boehm formed many close friendships which lasted during his lifetime. Among his friends were young Bienvenue, von Phul, Numa Landry, who became president of the Peoples Bank of New Orleans, his brother Ernest Landry of the same bank, Alfred Webre also of this city, besides a large number of young men that later became prominent citizens of the state. Francis Joseph Boehm from the first proved to be a leader in his classes, as the old university records show. Yearly he brought home the class medal, and he became a Greek and Latin scholar, as well as an apt linguist, speaking French, Spanish and German fluently. The class medals were in the shape of a shield about 3 x 3 inches made of heavy silver.

When the Boehm family reached St. Louis, the young city gave evidences at every turn of being a rapidly growing place.

The lack of homes and business places indicated that real estate would be a good investment. So, Mr. Boehm erected a number of stores, and several residences on the land that he had purchased shortly after his arrival in St. Louis. Later he bought a residence from a Mr. Girot—a two-storied brick structure which Mr. Boehm reserved for his own home. It was a house well constructed, containing a number of spacious rooms, and he purchased this large home because he expected his mother and sister to come to America and live with his family.

Shortly after purchasing this home, for most part furnished with the furniture brought from Europe, he met John Fremont, the explorer. He was captivated by the glowing stories of the West told by this interesting man, and decided to make a trip across the continent with him. Mrs. Boehm objected telling Mr. Boehm that he had promised his mother he was going to return to Europe for her once he was settled in St. Louis. Fremont came again and again, and so enthusiastic did Mr. Boehm become, that he financed a large part of the Fremont trip to California, furnishing equipment, horses and mules, and part of the provisions. Boehm wrote to his mother and instructed her about the disposal of her holdings in Metz, telling her that he would return for her and his sister after his return from California. With his family well provided for, a good income from rentals from his property, and a good home in the central part of the town, he felt safe in leaving.

In the wide hallway of this house was a large grandfather's clock in which the children would crouch when playing hide and seek, so as not to touch the pendulum. On entering the house my grandfather would put on a shelf in the clock, his chamois gloves, placing his cane in a corner of the case.

Those were hectic days in St. Louis for there were many French refugees continually getting themselves in trouble for airing their plans to help France, then in an upheaval. St. Louis was intensely French in certain sections, and as Mr. Boehm had been an officer in the French Army, his home became a rendezvous for these refugees. On one occasion one of the leading citizens of St. Louis, a Frenchman who had killed in temper his opponent, was brought by a number of the French coterie to Mr. Boehm's home where he remained until it was safe for him to leave the country. Each night after supper in the large dining-

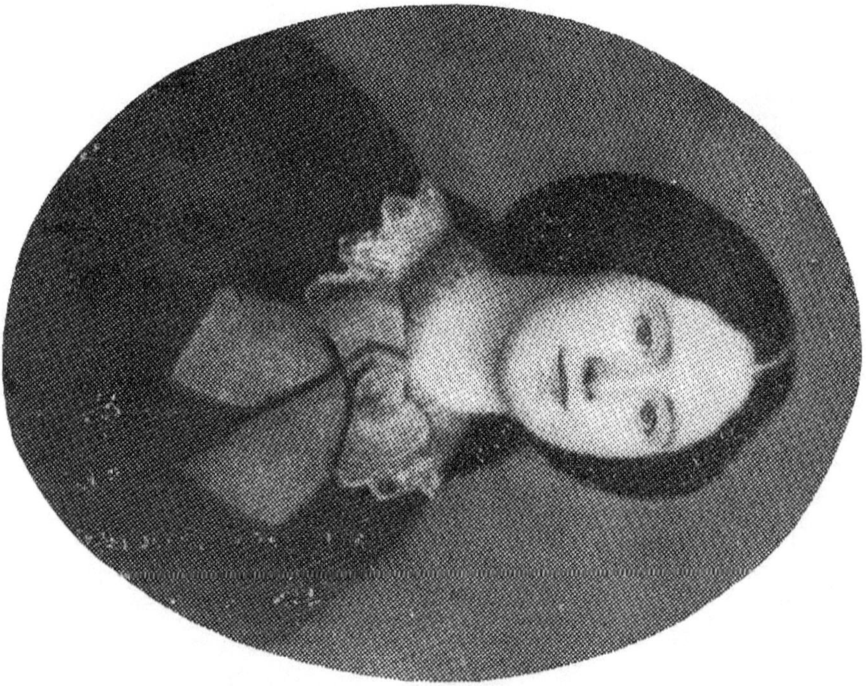

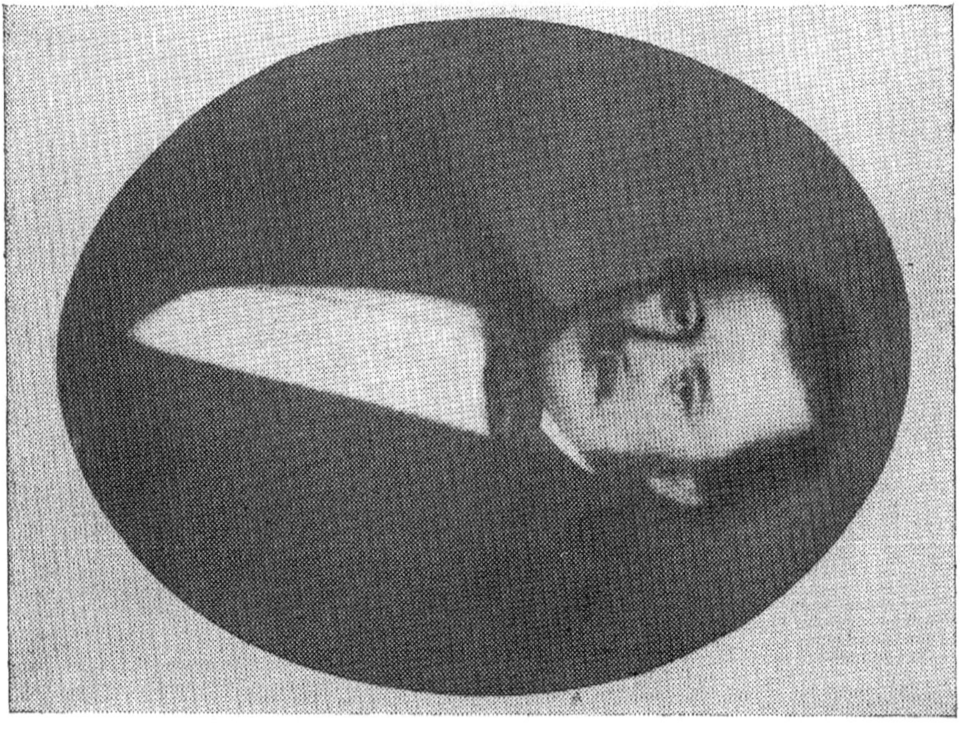

Memorial Tablet erected over main doorway to castle, at time built by Count (Knight) Wolf von Dahlberg in memory of his wife.

room in the rear of the hall would gather many from the French Colony to discuss the affairs of the day. Here, too, came Fremont night after night while planning his cross-country trip.

Mr. Boehm finally announced that he would accompany Fremont. Mrs. Boehm from what she had learned of some of the explorer's previous overland trips and hardships and of what she had heard was happening to the pioneers who were moving westward over a practically unknown wilderness filled with wild beasts and savages, realized that a spoiled son of a rich mother, a man who had had his every wish gratified, one who never left the house unless he was perfctly groomed and equipped with impeccable gloves and linen and his gold headed cane, was not the man to "rough it" on such a trip. She told him, "Certainly you would look fine with chamois gloves and gold headed cane going over the mountains!" She finally consented to let him go to California if he went by the way of Panama. It was a far shorter and less dangerous route. It was agreed that my grandfather would meet the explorer near Oroville, California, Fremont taking in Mr. Boehm's place a man by the name of Banton besides his crew.

Mr. Boehm, his business affairs in order, started for New Orleans by boat and while there visited his friend, Bienvenue, (who we know from letters written to the Boehm family in St. Louis failed to dissuade Mr. Boehm from continuing on such a hazardous journey). Reaching Panama, letters came telling that the trip was being made by pack mule. Other letters came telling that the overland trip was being made, and California eventually reached. Boehm waited for some time in Oroville for Fremont, and finally decided to invest some of his money in a warehouse which he filled with mining supplies, as there were thousands of miners all of whom seemed anxious to buy supplies. He employed several men that had been recommended highly and were anxious for positions as salesmen of miners' supplies. His choice appears to have been wise, for in writing home he told of his new business and the clerks, how all was going, how he was doubling his money, stating as yet that he had not heard from Fremont, (who from later reports had been meeting with one disaster after another). Boehm wrote that he had grown tired of waiting for the exporer, and was building a large home in Oroville, giving a description of it, telling the family how much easier it was to make a fortune in Oroville than in St. Louis. The house was a large one in the center of a square of ground with an orchard. Surrounded by beautiful trees it still stands in the City of Oroville in what is now the main part of that California city. When finished Mr. Boehm wrote his family he would come for them shortly.

Not long after getting this letter from Oroville, an epidemic of cholera swept the City of St. Louis, thousands dying weekly. So terrible was this epidemic that daily a crier went about the city calling from the street, "Put out your dead so the city carts can pick them up." The bodies were burnt, as that was the measure the health authorities were using to check the spread of the epidemic. So many of Mrs. Boehm's friends and acquaintances died that she was almost frantic. She drove to the Florisant Convent and took her daughter, Lisette, (who later became Mrs. W. E. Seebold) home. Lisette was educated at this convent, having entered when the convent had just been completed, being registered there as its fourth pupil. Her son, about to graduate from the St. Louis University was given his complimentary degree, as the University was closing owing to the epidemic. Hastily disposing of her property, the family were about to leave for New York when Mr. Antoine Bienvenue, who had come to St. Louis to get his son from the University, persuaded them to come to New Orleans. They came by the next steamer, the only route at that date.

Reaching New Orleans, Mr. Bienvenue located an etage, or apartment as the floors of the large three-storied buildings were called, in the vicinity of his own home in Royal Street at No. 188. It was in the block of old residences now occupied by the new white marble court-house. On the ground floor were located the law offices of Judge Spofford and Mr. Charles Conrad, for the French Quarter at that date was still a very fashionable residential place. Before leaving St. Louis, the health authorities told the family that they would not be permitted to take any clothing with them but the garments they were wearing and their night robes, and that all of their furniture would have to undergo a washing with lime to "kill the poison", as they classed it at that date. The house furnishings were all treated to this lime-wash before being sent to New Orleans and much of it nearly ruined by this treatment. No bedding or linen, or clothing was allowed to be sent to New Orleans. China, glassware, paintings, guns, swords and the collection of fire arms belonging to Mr. Boehm, Sr., were all given the treatment before forwarding. Much of the carved rosewood and mahogany was nearly ruined.

Owing to the haste in which the Boehm family left St. Louis, all communication with the family in Europe was apparently lost, as no address had been left with the post office department so that mail might be forwarded. Mr. Boehm's mother and sister died in the meantime, and Sister Elisabeth moved to a convent in another part of France. Although the authorities of the City of Metz advertised for a year in the St. Louis papers, no trace of Mrs. Francis Boehm's heirs being found, the estate was seized by the French government and retained by it, notwithstanding that both Judge Spofford and Mr. Charles Conrad later tried to get it for the Boehm family. Later the war between France and Germany settled forever the question of the family ever getting anything of Mr. Boehm's mother's large estate.

About the time that the Boehm family had gotten comfortably settled in the Royal Street home in New Orleans, news was brought to Mr. Francis Boehm, Jr. that his father had lost his life in a fire in the City of Oroville. From a newspaper clipping it was learned that a fire had started in a building close to the warehouse owned by Mr. Boehm at night time, and a family had been trapped in the building where the fire started. While assisting others who tried to rescue the trapped family, Mr. Boehm was overcome with heat and smoke, dying as a result. When his body was found, according to the newspaper clipping, a quantity of gold coins of large denomination were found in the money belt that he was wearing at the time of his death. Mr. Sorrenson, the cemetery sexton that buried Mr. Boehm, according to his own statement, was present when the body was found, and saw them turn over the money to the lawyer, later appointed to represent the Boehm family.

Upon receiving the news of his father's death, Francis Boehm, Jr., communicated with the authorities in Oroville. Postal facilities for California being scant, a long time was consumed in correspondence, and Judge Spofford, who handled the case seemed to get little satisfaction. So Francis Boehm, Jr. was advised to take the trip to California to find out what had become of his father's estate, but his mother would not consent to let him go, so the family waited to hear from the authorities to whom Judge

Spofford had written. Finally word came back that the body had been given a Christian burial, but that Mr. Boehm had left no estate. Mrs. Boehm, Sr. and the family then realized that they had been robbed of their inheritance.

The imminence of war and the uncertain condition of the country made taking that long trip an uncertain venture. The family reconciled themselves to their loss, as with the death of Mr. Boehm, Sr. But they knew that he had always a great deal of money on hand, and had written them in detail about the home he had built for them. The war came on with all of its loss and complications. My mother married at the close of the war, and the family busy establishing itself with children to be educated and three businesses to be kept going, the Boehm and Seebold families let matters stand until 1905.

In that year my mother and myself went to California to find out what really did happen to her father's estate. Reaching Oroville, which at that date was having a renaissance of dredging for gold, we saw large brick buildings being torn down so the ground could be dredged. We sought out the oldest resident Catholic priest who had been there many years. This priest told us of Mr. Sorrensen, who was the oldest living resident of Oroville. We found the old gentleman, some seventy-three years of age at the time, quite active for his age in full possession of his faculties, and his memory good. Mr. Sorrenson recalled the fire and stated that at that time he was the cemetery sexton. Looking up the cemetery records in order to locate the grave, he took us to where Mr. Boehm was buried. A temporary marker was placed on the spot until the headstone of white marble which we ordered could be cut.

We looked up the old newspaper files and found that there was data touching on the subject in a large number of the issues. We employed a young lady typist recommended to us who lived on Bird St., near the court house where the old files of the newspapers were kept. Miss———— of Oroville had completed several folio size sheets of data when arriving the following morning to continue the work to her surprise found that quite a number of the pages following in rotation had been removed from the files. This of course prevented us completing the record and ever finding out how my grandfather's estate was finally settled.

Undaunted we looked up the real estate title records to find

Mrs. W. E. Seebold (Lisette Boehm) at the age of 20 years. From an ante-bellum daguerreotype in the collection of her daughter, Mrs. George O. MacPherson (Stella Lisette Seebold).

Francis Joseph Boehm II, brother of Mrs. W. E. Seebold and Peter Boehm I. (From a daguerreotype taken in 1860, in Seebold family.)

Mr. and Mrs. Peter Boehm, daguerreotype taken at the time of their marriage. Peter Boehm, private, Co. I, 22nd and 23rd La. Infantry, entered Sept. 11th, 1861, Camp Lewis, Confederate Army. Honorably discharged at the end of the war. (Record at Confederate Memorial Hall, New Orleans.)

Old home of the Peter Boehm family, 124 Chartres Street, now changed to 538 Chartres Street. Built in 1824.

Dominicque Peter Boehm, in the U. S. Navy during the World War.

Philip Johnson

where Mr. Boehm had had his home. We located it in a prominent neighborhood.

We consulted a lawyer, who after looking into the case, told us that while the property was valuable (for on all sides the town was torn up in the dredging for gold) such a length of time had elapsed that to sue would cost more than we could ever hope to get out of it. The attorney stated that the early California laws were so lax in fact so elastic that a shrewd lawyer could do anything that he chose to do. I have often wondered if the sheets have been replaced in the newspaper files and if so whether they will show the outcome of the case. If not replaced, has it ever been discovered why they were removed in 1905?

Mr. Sorrenson had the white marble headstone selected by us made and put in place. The old man died after he had reached the late eighties.

Francois Joseph Boehm III came to New Orleans at the time of the cholera epidemic in St. Louis, and when the family had been comfortably located, purchased a book store at 182 Chartres St. (old number) from a gentleman who was retiring from business because of ill health. He did so on the advice of Judge Spofford who was a friend of the family. This book store was located two doors from St. Peter St., then one of the most aristocratic sections of French New Orleans, for the Pontalba Buildings housed many of the most exclusive families in the city. The lower floors of most of the buildings housed innumerable specialty shops as one finds in Paris.

Mr. Boehm replenished his stock, specializing in law, medical, and architectural books; all then in great demand. He also kept a large selection of choice literature, rare editions, fine prints and works of art, for plantation families coming to the city bought supplies for the plantation schools as well as sets of books. At once his establishment became a center where gathered the professional talent of the French section for nearby were the courts, cathedral and many other important buildings. A Greek and Latin scholar as well as a great reader, he became a favorite with the doctors and lawyers, who came to his store.

There, Judge Spofford, Mr. Frank von Phul, Mr. Webre, Mr. Charles Conrad, Mr. Bienvenue and other legal lights made it a practice to stop and read for an hour or so, in the comfortable library that Mr. Boehm had fitted up in the rear of his store.

The Boehm family at that date consisted of Mr. Francois Boehm's mother, his sister Lisette (who became Mrs. W. E. Seebold), a younger brother named Peter, and himself. Francois Joseph Boehm married Miss Isabella Adrian, and became the parents of a daughter named Isabella who died unmarried.

Lisette Boehm married W. E. Seebold and became the parents of eight children. Peter Boehm married Miss Harriet Pier, whose mother was a Miss Christine Collot, a member of the plantation family of that name located in St. Martin Parish, La. Miss Christine Collot and the father of Mrs. Numa Landry whose husband was the President of the Peoples Bank of New Orleans, La., were brother and sister. Miss Christine Collot married Andrew Pier whose ancestors lived in Lorraine, France, and who became planters in the vicinity of St. Martinsville, La. when they were married.

After his marriage Peter Boehm and his wife lived in what is now the French Quarter, later buying the then handsome three-storied brick structure which had originally been built for Louis Joseph Dufilho, as a residence and Pharmacy shortly after 1823, old number 124, new number 538 Chartres Street. For many years, through a mistake of Henry C. Castallanos, in his "New Orleans as it Was" it was always referred to as the "NAPOLEON HOUSE". It was stated in his book that this house had been built for Napoleon Bonaparte by the Emperor's admirers who planned to rescue him from the Island of St. Helena and bring him to America.

The Boehm family lived in this home many years, and reared a large family within its ancient walls. The home remained in the family during the lifetime of both Mr. and Mrs. Boehm, and was sold by the family shortly after Mrs. Boehm's death, as most of the children had married and were living in their own homes. Owing to the fact that it was supposed to have been built for the "Little Corporal" the house was visited by many distinguished personages, as well as others interested. Since deserted by the Boehm family it has served many uses, and struck by a storm a few years ago it has gradually become a ruin, now being but a shell. The great brick facade has been partially restored preserving its handsome architectural lines, but nothing else has been done further about repairs. Its neighbor at the corner of St. Louis Street, since Stanley Arthur cleared up the question about the Boehm house being built for Napoleon, is now advertised as the "OLD NAPOLEON HOUSE". The old friends of Mr. Boehm's brother Frank who had been at the St. Louis University with him often took visitors to the place, so did Judge Charles Gayarré who was a close friend of the family, his grandfather's home in olden days being close by.

Peter Boehm, second son of Francois Peter Boehm II was born in the city of St. Louis, and later educated in New Orleans. Under age at the outbreak of the War Between the States he served in the Home Guard of the City of New Orleans. After he had purchased the home at 124 Chartres Street, he opened a stationery store, also carrying newspaper publishing supplies, and the paper on which the newspapers were printed. He also maintained a store across the street from his residence where he carried sporting goods, billiard tables, etc. The children of Mr. and Mrs. Peter Boehm I are: Julia Boehm, who became Mrs. Marvo, no children; Theresa Boehm, who married Dominicque Barbé who before his death many years ago was secretary of the Irish American Club. Amelia Boehm, who married John J. Burke, long associated with the Southern Pacific Railroad before his retirement. Their children are as follows: Mary Henrietta Burke, a teacher in the New Orleans Public Schools; Joseph Edgar Boehm Burke (named for the famous sculptor relative Edgar Boehm) a merchant; Amelia Mary Burke, who married Cyril Prattin; Edward Boehm, who married Emily Mathews.

Peter Boehm, Jr., who married Hortonce Swertz, their children are as follows: Dominicque Peter Boehm, an adjuster for Emery Kaufman Ins. Co. of New Orleans; Henrietta, who married Albert Sidney Johnson, their children are as follows: Peter Boehm Johnson; Philip B. Johnson, a medical student at Tulane University; Julia Boehm; Josephine. Josephine Boehm married Emile Swertz, their son Joseph is a professor at the Warren Easton High School of New Orleans, La. Of Peter Boehm II's children are Louis Boehm, Isabella Boehm, William Boehm, and John Boehm, all dead. From the marriage of Louis Boehm and Leonora Bernard are two boys, Edward Boehm and Andrew Boehm.

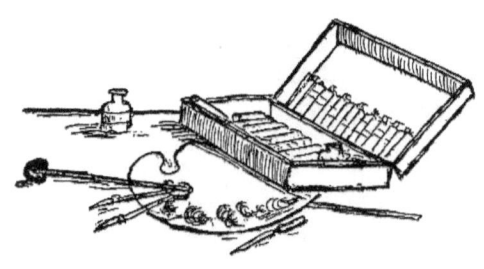

CHAPTER XXVI.

THE SEEBOLD—deBACHELLÉ—de VILBISS de BEAULIEU—de MARCONNAY KONZELMAN FAMILIES

SEEBOLD

(SEEBOLD von dem BRINK)

Of Huguenot ancestry, the motto of the Seebold, Siebold or Seeboldt von dem Brink Family is

"FIDEM QUINPER DIT QUO IN RELIGIUM"

The crest shows a gorgiere and ducal helmet full face Pierced a coupt rampant argent griffin displaying crossed arrows—a baron's crown surmounting all. The mantle, gules et argent, enveloping the arms of the Seebold and von dem Brink, quartered alternately Argent griffin, displaying crossed arrows, on a field or gules et argent alternate cheverons, indicates crusade origin of high rank.

The motto of the Seebold family is a fitting one for a family that for many generations became ministers of the church, and married into families the heads of which were church dignitaries. A name listed high in the records of the ancient patrician families of Hanover and Prussia, some members of which were united in marriage with the Warvel family close to the Polish throne. Such is the family from which Frederick William Emile Seebold, founder of the New Orleans branch of the Seebold family, stems.

The youngest son, Charles August Herman, born in Stockheim, March 6th, 1843, died unmarried on April 26th, 1912, in

John Charles Fremont, Explorer.
(From a miniature in the Seebold family.)

The annual Firemen's Parade, 1872, from the painting by Paul Poincy, picturing the gathering at the Henry Clay Statue which formerly stood at St. Charles and Canal Streets. Many of the elite are among the firemen in the painting.

Mantle and over mantle from Boboli Palace, near Rome; ceiling mural a signed Tojetti.

Crest and Coat-of-Arms of the Seebold von dem Brink family. The Seebold quartered with the von dem Brink family.

Ancestral home and estate of the Seebold Von Dem Brink family. Now a suburb of the City of Hanover (Prussia.)

the City of Hanover, where he is buried with other members of the family.

An older sister, after the death of her father, became a deaconess in the Lutheran Church. Another sister married Charles de Beaulieu—Marconnay, son of General Charles de Beaulieu de Marconnay. The old feudal castle of the de Beaulieu de Marconnay family is still standing in the midst of its estate near the City of Pothiers, France. Another sister married an important church dignitary in the Lutheran Church, their son becoming a minister, their son's son also becoming a minister, a daughter marrying a minister and her son at present studying for the ministry.

Frederick William Emile Seebold, better remembered in New Orleans where he was a prominent figure in art circles as W. E. Seebold, was born in the City of Lachem on Sept. 15, 1833. He was educated at the University of Goettingen, where an uncle, Francis Joseph Pauli, the celebrated surgeon and world famous anatomist, held the chair of anatomy while Professor Langenbeck was dean. W. E. Seebold was educated for the ministry, but was not enthusiastic for the cloth, and completing his education came to America in 1852.

Seebold's boyhood home was located on the outskirts of the City of Hanover. The house was a large one with extensive gardens enclosed in a great park. A large plantation-like farm was attached to the estate, which was worked by German peasants whose homes were scattered about the large grounds. The lands were rented out much as the plantations of the South are today. This estate was located midway between the royal castle of Hanover (Hanover at that time being a Kingdom) and the forest land where the King of Hanover had a shooting lodge where in his earlier years he used to hunt.

Reverend Herman Seebold, who was head of the Lutheran Church of Hanover, was once asked by the King to reserve a rest room in the parsonage, that he might rest between walking to and from the shooting lodge to the castle. His physician had prescribed the lengthy walks to reduce the Kings' weight and avoid diabetes, with which his majesty was threatened. Of course Reverend Seebold was honored and delighted to oblige his King and render him this service. As related by members of the family, the King, who did not wish to be annoyed, was always simply garbed, wearing a broad somewhat slouched hat and large black glasses. He was accompanied by some one equally simply dressed from the castle. A small salon was reserved for the royal visitor, so that his privacy would be not intruded on during his resting period, which he usually took on his return walk to the castle according to memoirs of Deaconess Louisa Seebold.

This little parlor where the King rested was always immaculate and fresh flowers were daily arranged on a table by the lounge. A large engraving of His Majesty hung above the mantel, and another engraving portraying the royal family hung on the wall by the lounge. This lounge was a large one of Empire design of maple wood inlaid with ebony stripes, but devoid of brass mounts. On this divan the royal visitor often rested an hour at a time before returning to the castle, and at no time was any question asked any member of the family or those attached to the household about their regular visitor.

During the period that the king was taking the walking exercise prescribed by his physician, an incident occurred that greatly embarrassed the wife of Rev. Seebold and almost caused her to collapse from mortification. Some one had stolen a set of military drawings containing fortification secrets of the German Army Office Headquarters. A general check up was being made of the surrounding country where it was reported the thieves were in hiding. Those in charge of the case, who did not recognize the King, suspected that it was his Highness and his companion. It had been noticed that two gentlemen regularly entered a carriage a short distance from the Castle of Hanover, and when they dismounted from the carriage a short distance away, were seen to be wearing dark glasses and slouched black hats. It was the King and his companion who had assumed this disguise so that they would not be annoyed by the populace who were always anxious to see their King. Furthermore no one who was questioned as to who these two persons might be, could or would give any information.

So the two disguised gentlemen were followed and were found to visit a small lodge in the forest where they remained a short while, and noting that they were being followed, came out of the lodge, closed the door and walked back towards the parsonage some distance away. Seeing no traces of those who were following them, the King and his companion, without knocking entered by a small side door which opened from the garden.

When the intelligence officers who had followed the King and his companion without knowing who they were questioned the maid who answered the door, and were told that no one in the house but the minister and his wife knew who the two gentlemen were, it only increased their suspicions. The two officers demanded to see either the minister or his wife at once. Reverend Seebold, being out at the time, Madame Seebold came into the side hall and inquired of them what it was they wished to know. When she was questioned by them as to who these two men were she said that she was pledged not to reveal their identity. She immediately was told that if she did not turn them over to the police at once, the entire household with them would be imprisoned. All this time the King and his companion were unaware of what was happening. Suddenly one of the men forced his way into the room where the King was resting, and seeing his Majesty without his slouched hat and dark glasses, and his portrait on the wall above the lounge on which he was reclining, he immediately recognized the King and realized that they had made a great mistake. They were profuse in the apologies to all concerned. However, the King took it good naturedly saying, that the men had only done their duty, for how were they to know it was the King of Hanover that was wearing the disguise?

In the days that Hanover was still a Kingdom, it was customary in large German households for some of their daughters to live with prominent German families, in order that they might become efficient housekeepers and learn to be self-dependent. Daughters in the higher circles, at that day classed as the lesser nobility, as well as the haute-bourgeoise, followed this custom, for the daughters of the higher nobles became attached to royal houses.

According to Rev. Herman Seebold's daughter, there was always a list of young ladies awaiting the opportunity to be apprenticed to this home of Rev. Seebold. At no time were they looked upon as servants or treated as such, but thought of as today we look upon a student of domestic science. If any of the neighbors ever knew that it was their King who came incognito to the Seebold home, they never by word or sign indicated it. It may have been because of the many entertainments during the year that so many young ladies made application for training here for the opportunity of meeting distinguished people.

The home of Reverend Seebold was a large one, and his poistion in the community was such that much entertaining was done. This took the form of garden parties, fetes champetre, etc., at which times the garden grounds and lawns were decorated with many attractive booths at which important members of the community presided over the tables of beverages and booths of trinkets usually found at such affairs. Chinese lanterns hung from festoons of greenery, illuminating the grounds. The object of these affairs was usually charity for some church, school, hospital or orphan asylum. Religious tableaux were at times presented. During the time that Hanover was still a Kingdom, these affairs were under the patronage of the Royal Family, whose presence always assured a gathering of the aristocracy of Hanover and surrounding country. The bazaars, sponsored by these patricians, always proved a great success. Although the estate belonged to the Seebold family, and was not church property, the church being near by, many of the plants and shrubs came from the castle gardens, for the Crown was anxious to have the grounds at all times as attractive as possible for these festal occasions.

The furnishings of the Seebold home were conservative, the furniture of the main rooms being of choice pieces of fruit wood and maple inlaid with ebony devoid of gilt mounts. Much of the furniture is still in the homes of descendants of the family. There was a handsome silver service of many pieces including three sizes of silver plates, a number of large platters, three large vegetable dishes with containers below for hot water, a tea set, a coffee set, fruit epergnes, and many other pieces. This handsome solid silver table service was a gift of the City of Goettingen to the father of Reverend Seebold when he was Burgomaster of that city. All of the silver is still in the family, having been divided between the different members.

Burgomaster
John William Seebold.
Portrait painted while he was Burgomaster of Goettingen, before he became a minister.

John Fredrick William Seebold, who became a banker in Goettingen.

Originals of both paintings in home of Charles de Beaulieu de Marconnay—Villa Vellure, near Lucerne Suisse.

Countess Johanne Henriette de Bachellé, born in Brauchhausen castle in the year 1752, (great grandmother of W. E. Seebold). Became Lady in Waiting to her Royal Highness of Hanover.

Sophie Louisa Julia Seebold, oldest daughter of Rev. John William Herman Seebold, who became a Deaconess in the Lutheran Church. Authoress of Seebold family record.

Rev. Superintendent John William Herman Seebold, born Jan. 14th, 1801, died Feb. 22, 1887.

Sophie Henrietta deBachellé Munchmeyer, wife of Rev. J. W. H. Seebold. (Reproduced from a painting in the Seebold family.)

MRS. W. E. SEEBOLD
At the age of 80 years. (Portrait by Andres Molinary.)

W. E. SEEBOLD
Art Collector and Conoisseur. (Portrait by A. Molinary.)

After Rev. Herman Seebold became head of the Lutheran Church of Hanover, twice yearly he entertained the chief Lutheran ministers of the Kingdom and their wives at a banquet, at which time old friendships were renewed just as today conventions bring groups together. Christmas Day was always a big day for all families, but three days after Christmas in the home of Rev. Seebold was *the* big day for that family. On that day the Royal Couple dined at their home and with them those persons of the City that the Crown had honored during the year. On these occasions the younger members of the family were not present, their seats at table being taken by those the King chose to honor. The reason for this honor being paid Rev. Seebold was that the Court of Hanover was so rigid that it would have caused embarrassing situations had honored guests among the civilians been seated in a way other than that which their rank demanded at a table as guests of the Crown. But as Reverend Seebold's guests all were at their ease, court etiquette was not violated.

Reverend Herman Seebold was a musician of ability, and treasured an ancient spinet with double key board which had always been kept in good repair. One of his greatest pleasures was to spend part of his leisure time playing airs from Mozart, he having penciled many sheets with copied selections from the compositions of Mozart, Handel and others whose music was written for the quill-plucked instrument. Often a friend accompanied him on a flute or cello. Several times a year musicales at which times chamber music was played were given. These were regularly attended by the Duke of Cumberland while he was in Hanover.

Rev. Herman Seebold at his death left a scholarship open to any one wishing to study for the ministry at the University of Goettingen. This Seebold stipendium was still in existence in 1914.

For generations members of the family of Seebold (vondem Brink) have been clergymen of high standing in their communities. In a family whose eldest sons for generations have been clergymen, there is little use for armorial bearing, and the "vondem" has gradually been eliminated when writing the name. But this does not mean that they lost their pride of family according to the grand-daughter of Rev. Superintendent Seebold, Clara Bremer de Beaulieu de Marconnay, who lived in her grandfather's home while attending school in the City of Hanover. At no time was she permitted to visit school-mates unless those homes appeared on the list that had been made by the head of the institution and submitted to her grandfather. School circles were strongly select in Europe of that date, and her aunt, the wife of Rev. Gustave von Meyer, was most careful to select for her companions girls of patrician families, telling her that she was too little to know and understand these things. In Germany of that date class distinctions were quite marked, and in the smaller towns where the family sojourned in the summer time, this class distinction was even stricter.

According to the notes on the record of the SEEBOLD family furnished by Deaconess Louisa Seebold, eldest sister of W. E. Seebold, "The mother of Christopher Seebold was Octavie Civellé, daughter of a Huguenotte family of a border town of Lorraine, who married Pastor Seebold, father of the Seebold of which the given name appears on the family record."

SEEBOLD, (von dem BRINK.)

Christopher Seebold of Waldeck, a minister of patrician birth and Huguenot ancestry married Anna Margaret von der Knabenbeck, a member of the old nobility of Hanover, whose family record is chronicled by the Hof Calender of Gotha. Rev. Seebold was a minister and professor of Theology of the University of Goettingen, and later in the University of Hanover. Their son John Frederic Seebold, born May 28th, 1731, married April 20th, 1751, Kathryn Marie Kamm, born March 17th, 1728 and died Nov. 26th, 1810. John Frederic followed in his father's footsteps, graduated from the University of Goettingen studied for the ministry, became a pastor in the Lutheran church, their children were as follows: John William Seebold, born Jan. 10th, 1753; John Frederic Seebold, born Dec. 24th, 1755; Katherine Wilimine Seebold, born Aug. 17th, 1758; John Conrad Seebold, born Sept. 6th, 1761, died July 15th, 1787; Johanne Katherine Seebold, born July 20th, 1764.

John William Seebold, born Jan. 10th, 1753, was educated for the ministry, but inheriting a large interest in a military-uniform factory in Hamburg, delayed becoming a minister until he could dispose of his factory satisfactorily. He was chosen the Burgomaster of the city of Goettingen for a number of years, finally becoming a minister later in life, holding a pastorate in that city until his death on April 16th, 1850. On June 5th, 1781 he married Caroline Dorothea Frederica Scharf, daughter of Christopher Scharf, a prominent citizen of Goettingen. While he was Burgomaster of that city he was presented with a solid silver table service. Their children were seven in number as follows: (1) Willemine Dorothy Elisabeth Seebold, born June 12th, 1784; (2) George Christian Frederic Seebold, born Nov. 22nd, 1786; (3) John Frederic William Seebold, born Nov. 16th, 1789; (4) Harduika Elizabeth Margaret Seebold, born Jan 5th, 1794; (5) Dorothea Katherine Margaret Seebold, born June 13th, 1797; (6) John William Herman Seebold, born Jan. 14th, 1801; (7) Frances Elisabeth Seebold, born Jan. 2nd, 1805. George Christian Frederic Seebold, born Nov. 22nd, 1786, went into Russia in the War of 1812 with the rank of Sergeant-Major—he died at the age of 26, in March 1815, and was buried in Goettingen. John Frederic William Seebold, born in Goettingen April 16th, 1789, became a leading banker of Goettingen, married Julia Kuhlman, daughter of Sergeant Henry Kuhlman, of the 3rd Landwehr Battalion, and Wilhemine Koch of Harburg. Children: Sophie Regine Seebold, born May 25th, 1814.

Reverend John William Herman Seebold, born Jan. 14, 1801, in Waldeck, was a son of Burgomeister of Goettingen, John William Seebold, who later became a Lutheran pastor and Elizabeth Scharf. In 1863 was decorated by the King of Hanover at which time he was knighted, and on the 18th of July 1865 was decorated by King George V with the Guelp Order of Hanover, and on the 26th of May 1875 celebrated his golden jubilee as pastor of the Lutheran church, having become head of the Lutheran church of Hanover. The loving cup presented to him on this occasion is now in possession of his grand-daughter, Mrs. George McPherson (Stella Lisette Seebold).

Rev. J. W. Herman Seebold died in his eighty-sixth year, Feb. 22, 1887. He was a graduate of the University of Goettingen. In 1829 being ordained a minister in the New State Church of Hanover. On the 8th of October 1830, he married Sophie Henrietta de Bachelle Munchmeyer, daughter of Reverend Superintendent August Conrad Munchmeyer and Louise Charlotte de Bachelle Volkenhauer. Louise Charlotte de Bachelle Volkenhauer being the daughter of Countess Johanne Henriette de

Bachelle, born in 1752, daughter of Gideon Davis de Bachelle and Eleonore Amalie Charlotte von Oeffener, daughter of Christian Frederic von Oeffener, First Lieutenant stationed at Hattorf.

SEEBOLD

American Branch

Frederic William Emile Seebold, better known as W. E. Seebold, oldest son of Rev. John William Herman Seebold was born Sept. 15, 1833. Having graduated with honor, he came to America in 1856, taking the tour as a part of finishing his education as was customary at that date. Travelling through a number of states in a leisurely manner, he visited his sister Antonia, who had married Charles Baron de Beaulieu de Marconnay, at that time living in Philadelphia, Pa., a noted fresco artist who has left much of his work in the principle churches of that city. W. E. Seebold finally reached New Orleans in 1861. Being of an artistic temperament it was not long before he made the acquaintance of Francis J. Boehm, who had a book and art establishment at 182 Chartres Street. Shortly afterwards he visited Mr. Boehm's home where he met his mother, his brother Peter Boehm, and his sister Lisette. Later an attachment sprang up between Lisette and young Seebold and they became engaged to be married.

The war fever was raging at this time, and W. E. Seebold having met Judge Spofford and Mr. Charles Conrad, was introduced by them to a number of the members of General Scott's First Louisiana Cavalry. Being a fine horseman and noting that many of his newly made friends were enlisting, he joined that company. He was among the first to enlist from this city, and took part in various engagements. He was seriously wounded when his horse was killed under him. He was taken prisoner and kept on Johnson Island for nine months, not being permitted to receive any mail, deprived of his money and made to suffer the indignities that those imprisoned there were made to endure. He later became a close friend of Generals P. T. G. Beauregard, de Trobriant, Francis T. Nichols, President Jefferson Davis, and other famous men who wore the Confederate uniform. Being an able linguist he became a valuable member of his command where he frequently acted as interpreter. At the cessation of hostilities, he was paroled and honorably discharged. Returning to New

Restored Reception Salon from the Royal Chateau de Bercy, favorite retreat for French Royalty. Boiserie rebuilt in the New Orleans home of Dr. and Mrs. H. de B. Seebold.

Front view of the drawing-room in the home of Dr. and Mrs. H. de B. Seebold.

Old home of the William Henry Kinney family, Wichita, Kansas.

Orleans, he married Miss Lisette Boehm, who had not heard from him for many months while he was imprisoned, but had not given up hope of his return. A large number of his Confederate friends attended his wedding.

For a short while he was an assistant to General Beauregard, who was doing survey work in the state. A little later he opened an art store with books and engineering supplies on the site where the Loew's Theatre on Canal Street now stands. The Boehm family had built a house directly opposite the new St. Joseph Church on Tulane Avenue, at that date Common Street, where there were a number of newly erected homes, and the short-lived promise of becoming a new residential neighborhood.

After the fall of the City when the Federal authorities were searching the homes for weapons, Mrs. Boehm became frightened because Mrs. Seebold's father, having been a collector of fire arms, had swords, guns, pistols, and other articles of this kind buried deep in the back yard. It is doubtful if any of them ever have been removed, although many were of great value. The fact that he came from a military family made him a connoisseur of weapons, the nucleus of the collection having been received from his father.

After a long life in the community in which he had helped to develop art seriously, at the advanced age of eighty-eight years, W. E. Seebold (Frederic Emile Seebold) died on June 25, 1921. He outlived most of the old crowd of co-workers in the art movement in this city, but a newer and younger crowd continue the good work done by their predecessors, filling the French Quarter with their studios, establishing that section as an art center recognized throughout the country. He died in New Orleans and was buried with honors due an American citizen and a Confederate Soldier who had served loyally throughout the war. A resident of the city of his adoption, he took an active intrest in civic affairs and was always ready to assist any movement for the City's and State's benefit when sponsored by the proper element. During his lifetime he was a loyal friend to his less fortunate Confederate companions and was always ready to assist them. His funeral was attended by members of the Army of Tennessee of which he was a member, along with other prominent Confederates, and representative citizens, among them the artist colony of which during so many years he had been so prominent a part. All came to pay a last tribute to their old friend who lay in a Confederate Flag-draped casket, where with military honors accompanied by a long line of old comrades and Confederate Guard of Honor his body was laid away, while his lifelong friend, Rev. Mathew Brewster, read the funeral service ending with "Going Home". Taps were sounded as his coffin was placed in the family tomb.

The MEMORIAM from the Association of the Army of Tennessee of which he was a member reads:

New Orleans, La., July 12th, 1921.

The taps have sounded for another of our Comrades, William Emile Seebold, who died June 25th, 1921. Comrade Seebold was born in Lachem, Kingdom of Hanover, Sept. 15th, 1833, entered the service of the Confederacy Oct. 15th, 1861, joining Co. I, 1st Regiment, 1st Louisiana Cavalry, Col. Jno. S. Scott. Served in all the engagements that this Command was engaged in, until captured in 1863 in Kentucky, confined as a prisoner of War at Johnson's Island and Point Lookout, Md.; exchanged May 11th, 1864, then rejoined his command; served till the end of the war, and was paroled May 20th, 1865 at Demopolis, Ala.; elected a member of our Association Sept. 12th, 1882.

This is the brief Military record of a volunteer of the Southern Army, a graduate of the famous University of Gottingen, who emigrated to this country, and after visiting the principal cities of the North finally attracted by the Citizens of this State, where at that time Chivalry prevailed, adopted Louisiana as his chosen state, and when the Call to Arms was made to protect her rights, Gallantry joined the ranks, giving all his ability and energies to the Cause, serving faithfully throughout the war.

After the war was over, comrade Seebold returned to this City, opened an art business and became the dean of art dealers, and a Charter member of the Art Association, and was an authority in questions of the arts. Of a retiring, modest disposition, he never sought the limelight of publicity, but was a genial and courteous gentleman to all who approached him.

He married and is survived by his wife, two daughters and three sons to whom this unblemished record of a gal-

lant soldier of the Southern Army is bequeathed, something that they can point to with pride and glory in the knowledge, that he was their ancestor.

Wherefore be it resolved, That in the demise of our late Comrade William Emile Seebold, our Association has met with an irreparable loss, the State a true and faithful Citizen, his family, a devoted husband, father and friend. Further resolved that these resolutions be transmitted to his afflicted family to whom we tender our deepest sympathy in their great loss they have sustained, and a copy inscribed on the Minutes of our Associaiton.

Respectfully submitted,
F. Ernest
John K. Renaud
M. Mallet.

For nearly half a century Mr. Seebold had been one of the leading rosarians in the state, his large garden on Canal Street containing hundreds of the finest specimens of rose bushes. The great quantities of beautiful flowers at his funeral were a tribute of the high esteem in which he was held by the city he loved so well. His wife and devoted companion of so many years, Lisette Boehm Seebold was born in the city of Metz in Lorraine(when that country was a French possession) on the 19th of March, 1837, where her father's and grandfather's families for a century had their residence—her father and grandfather both being officers in the French Army. Mrs. Seebold did not survive her husband long, dying after a short illness on August 29th, 1923, at the age of eighty-six years. She had been a moving spirit in the art world, an authority on art and connoisseur of fine china and crystal of which she had a large collection. Unostentatious in her charities which were many, of a deeply religious nature, she was always interested in church matters until old age prevented. She had been educated by the nuns of the Florisant Convent, being a resident pupil. St. Louis at that time was intensely French and while living in the convent had been required to speak French at all times outside of classes with the result that she spoke and wrote French like a native Parisian, for the Nuns of this convent prided themselves on the purity of the French as taught there. Always a great reader and seeker after knowledge, she would remain up until the early morning hours when interested in a subject. The nuns at the convent, discovering that she was a good reader with a clear, distinct voice, appointed her to read to the class during the time when the class had an hour of sewing. Finding that she had become so proficient in French, she was often called upon by the nuns to take charge of the advanced French classes, to her delight for her father had told the head of the convent that he did not want her to spend her time doing fancy work, but insisted that she learn to speak, read and write French correctly. They fulfilled their duty, as the Convent of Florisant to this day prides itself on the accent of its French pupils. Mrs. Seebold's passing was marked by a similar tribute from her friends as that which marked her husband's a short while before.

Their children are: Marie Madeleine Seebold, who married Andres Molinary; William John Seebold who died March 25th, 1868; George Sandford Seebold, who died Dec. 25th, 1880; Walter Emile Seebold, who died March 15th, 1914; Stella Lisette Seebold, who married George Ossian MacPherson; Randall Hunt Seebold, who died Sept. 1st, 1927; Herman Boehm de Bachelle Seebold, M. D., 1st Lt. M. C., 6th Field Hospital, 2nd Brigade, U.S.A. Silitian Expedition, A. O. Married Nettie May Kinney March 15th, 1922. Francis Semmes Seebold, who died Jan. 29th, 1934.

Mrs. Andres Molinary—nee Marie Madeleine Seebold is a painter and a restorer of paintings. Born in New Orleans she is the eldest daughter of Lisette Boehm and William Emile Seebold, Art Connoisseur and Collector. Her mother was a cousin of Sir Joseph Edgar Boehm, R. A., a protege of Queen Victoria, who designed many of the figure monuments in the City of London and other English Cities. As a small girl while attending school at the Cenas Institute, she would go after lessons to the studio of George Coulon near by, where her early Art education was begun. Later she was enrolled at the popular select school for young ladies conducted by the Misses Huger, where she finished her education, studying French and German besides her native tongue. Some years later Paul Poincy opened a Studio over the Seebold Art Store and asked her to come into his classes, where she worked for several years.

When the Art Union came into existence and Andres Molinary conducted classes in painting there, she enrolled as one of his pupils—and later she worked as his pupil at the Art Association's

Herman Boehm deBachellé Seebold, M. D., 1st Lieut., M. C., U. S. A., 6th Field Hospital, 2nd Brigade, Silesian Expedition, World War—Army of Occupation.

Crest and Coat-of-Arms of the MacPherson family.

Crest and Coat-of-Arms of the deBachellé family.

Crest and Coat-of-Arms of the MacPherson family.

Mrs. John Donald MacPherosn
(Katherine Mooney)

James MacPherson, of Iverness Scotland
Gaelic scholar; son of Donald MacPherson.

Mrs. Geo. Ossian MacPherson, neé Stella
Lisette Seebold.

George Ossian MacPherson

Hallway in Seebold Home from Hamilton Palace, Lanarkshire, Scotland.

Mrs. H. deB. Seebold (Nettie Kinney.)

School of Art. She also studied with William Chase in New York. Miss Cora Townsend was the first woman member of the Artist Association, Marie Seebold the second. By preference she paints flowers, but she frequently paints portraits and landscapes as well as still life.

During his lifetime she frequently helped her husband when large orders for restoration came his way. He had done much of this while a student at the Academy in Rome, and as it is a slow, sometimes hazardous task, was glad to have younger eyes work under his direction.

MAC PHERSON.

John Donald Mac Pherson of Iverness Scotland married Kathrine Mooney of Dublin, Ireland, and came to America between 1852 and 1853. During the Civil War they came to New Orleans. Their children are as follows: 1st, Agatha, who married John Nolan, former Supt. of the Southern Pacific Railroad, N. O.; 2nd, William Oscar; 3rd, George Ossian, who married Stella Lisette Seebold; 4th, Harry L., who married Theresa Ford; 5th, Annette, who married Felix McGivney; 6th, Katherine, who married J. F. Galloway, notary and lawyer of Gulfport, Miss.; 7th, Helen (Nell), who married Edward Douglass McNair; 8th, William, who married Marguerite Delery.

The maternal grandfather of this family was John Mooney of Dublin, Ireland, who owned a large ranch in Tulamoore, Ireland, where he bred race horses which were shipped to the various large racing centers of the world. The paternal grandfather was Donald Mac Pherson, who was a professor of Gaelic, and translator of Gaelic into English.

His sons are Ossian Mac Pherson, Oscar Mac Pherson, William Mac Pherson, James Mac Pherson, and John Donald Mac Pherson, all of Iverness, Scotland.

De BACHELLE

Countess Johanne Henriette de Bachelle married Rev. Henry Frederic Ebehard Volkenhauer in the chapel of Brauchhausen Castle Aug. 10, 1779. Their daughter Louise Dorothea de Bachelle Volkenhauer, born Oct. 20, 1785 in Kirch-Wohlingen, was married Jan. 6, 1806, in Sinsdorf, to Rev. John August Conrad Munchmeyer, who died April 7, 1809 in Linden. Their daughter, Sophie Dorothea de Bachelle Munchmeyer, born June 7, 1809 in Hanover City, married in Great Berckel, Nov. 10, 1830, Rev. John William Herman Seebold, born Jan. 14, 1801. Among children were: Sophie Louisa Julia, born Aug. 4, 1831, in Lachem, died Feb. 8, 1919, in Hanover; and Frederick William Emile, born Sept. 15, 1833, died in New Orleans, June 25, 1921.

(1) Mangin de Bachelle married Marie Evrand, was notary and counsellor, secretary of the city of Metz 1556, Zwischem 1593 and 1599. (2) Israel de Bachelle married Ida Provot in 1585, who was born in Metz in 1565. (3) Paul de Bachelle, born Jan. 11, 1591, married Marie de Duchas, 1513; a member of the French nobility. (4) Gideon de Bachelle, born Jan. 19, 1677, counsellor of Baillage, married in 1642, Marie Goffin. (5) Gideon David de Bachelle, born Sept. 17, 1752, married Eleonore Amalie Charlotte von Oeffener, daughter of First Lieutenant in charge of the Infantry of Army Engineers and members of the German aristocracy. (6) David de Bachelle, born April 7, 1734, married Susanne Hedwig de Gauvin, daughter of General Lieutenant de Gavin 1721. Over Lieutenant stationed at Wurtemberg 1733 in charge of his Infantry troops, (French Army of Occupation). (7) Gideon David de Bachelle, born —————, died 1752, married Elenore Amalie Charlotte von Oeffner, daughter of Christian Frederick von Oeffener, First Lieutenant at Hattorf, Klinkowstrom. (8) Johanna Henrietta de Bachelle, born 1752, was married in 1779 in Bruchhausen Castle, to Pastor Henry Frederick Eberhard Volkenhaar.

De BACHELLE'
Arms and Quarterings

*Ecastiti An I d'or a troi canards au naturel
An II d'azur a la band d'or accompanie de trois
etoiles de meme, un enchef et deux en pointe
An III d'azun au lion controune d'or
An IV d'or a une plant sur une terrasse de sinople, de
laquelle sortent de quintefeuilles on roses de gueules
accastus deux Cryozoses au naturel.*

The fifes, or extensive land holdings, in the area of Metz where the Chateau de Bachelle was located were among the most ancient ones in that part of France. The deBachellé family, originally "le Bachelle", were a patrician family from the town of Mettis, as Metz was first called. In 1648 Jacques le Bachelle, a great warrior, was one of the leaders who secured for France the City of Metz by the peace of Westphalia. A part of the family later settled in Paris, where the family tomb can still be seen in the Pere La Chaise Cemetery.

Many of the family were killed during the French Revolution during which time the "de" was cut off of the name on the family tomb—the outline of the "de" still being visible. On the old rolls of officers' names of the French Army this name is found often.

Countess Johanne Henriette deBachellé was born in Castle Brauchhausen in the year 1752 and later became lady in waiting to her Royal Highness of Hanover. She was a direct descendant of the celebrated warrior Jacques de Bachelle, the saviour of the city of Metz, and whose life was a succession of successful combats. It was mainly through his efforts that Metz became a French possession. Jacques de Bachelle, the second of that name, a member of that ancient noble house joined Francis III, Compte de la Rochefocault, Prince de Marellac (1531-1572) one of the leaders of the Protestant party who caused the banner of the Calvinists to float along the whole coast from the river Cheriante to the river Gironde.

"ARMORIAL GENERAL DE FRANCE" d'HOZIER.
Archives of the Chicago Public Library

Jacques de Bachelle, Knight of the Military Order of St. Louis, ancient Lieutenant Colonel of the Regiments of Bressei, and since reformed in the one of de Desgrigni, was conformed and maintained in the possession of his nobility, and ennobled again in so far as needed with his children and his posterity, male, and female, born and to be born in legitimate marriage, by patented letters in form of gifts of Charles given at Versailles in the month of April 1732 and addressed to the Courts of Parliament: "Chambres des Comptes and Courts of Aids at Metz, in consideration of the services that the said Sieur de Bachelle had rendered without discontinuation since the year 1675, that he entered, then fourteen years of age, in the Regiment *de le Ferte* until 1714, that his wounds and infirmities forced him to retire."

These letters make mention that the said Sieur de Bachelle was at the battle of Saverne under Marshal de Luxembourg, at the Siege of Trebourg, at the capture of the Forts of Strasbourg where he was wounded; at the Siege of Luxembourg, and the one of Philisbourg where he was also wounded. He was employed in 1689, under the orders of the Marquis d'Asfeld, in the defense of Bonne where he was again wounded, and sent in hostage to the enemies then of the first capitulation.

After this he served under the Marshal de Catinat in Piedmont, and then found himself at the Siege of Veillane, de Carmagnole, de Suze et Montmeliand, where he was crippled at the attack of "contre - escarpe", following this at the battle de la Marsaille,

CHATEAU FLEUR de LYS.
Home overlooking the Hudson River, built for Dr. and Mrs. H. deB. Seebold. Much of the historic panelling was removed for the second time to the present New Orleans home of Dr. and Mrs. H. deB. Seebold.

Carved Door and Door Frame from private Library of Catherine de Medicis in Chenaceau Chateau in Tourainne. Removed when Chateau was purchased by Mr. Terry in 1901 at which time Chenaceau underwent extensive repairs. Now a door leading to a bedroom in the Seebold home, 2617 St. Charles Avenue. Purchased through the late Blasford Dean of New York City. Medici Arms in center panel.

Mrs. Jack Kinney Moore, neé Noville Mock.

Crest and Coat-of-Arms de Wartegg family.

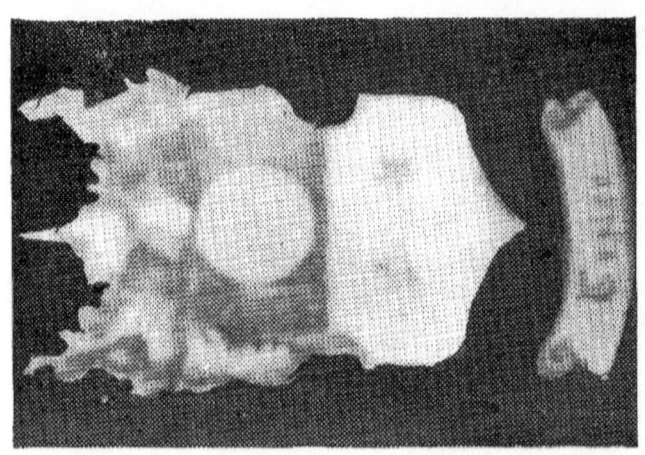

Irish Register Office of Ulster King of Arms.

Crest and Coat-of-Arms of the Taylor family. (Irish branch.)

Coat-of-Arms of the de Vilbis (Velbiss) family.

Minnie Hauk (Baronne de Wartegg) as Marguerite in Faust.

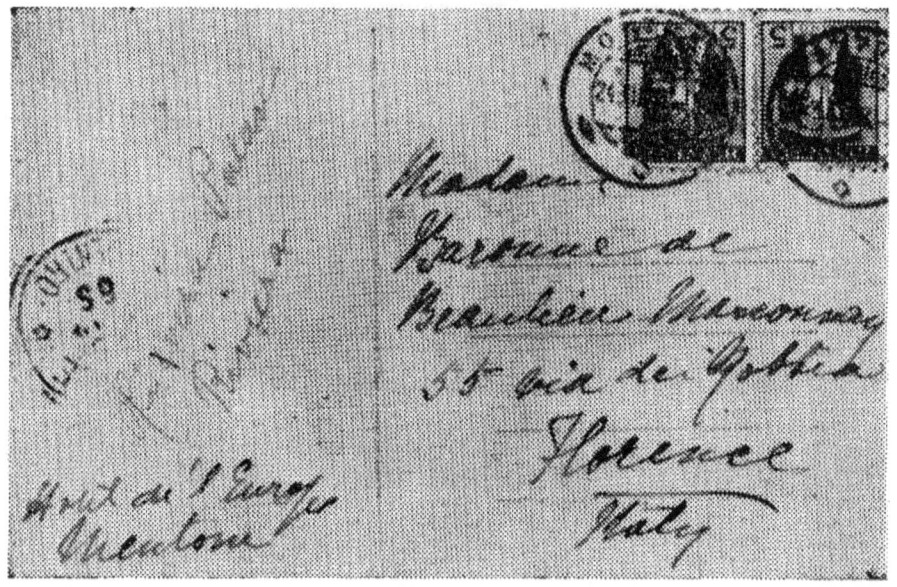

A post card from Minnie Hauk to the Baronne de Beaulieu de Marconnay.

Baron and Baronne de Wartegg in front of Villa Triebchen, their home, originally the home of Richard Wagner.

Mrs. William Henry Kinney, mother of Mrs. H. deB. Seebold, and Mrs. John Hawkins Moore. (From an ivory miniature.)

William Henry Kinney, father of Mrs. H. deB. Seebold

J. Kinney Moore, vice-president of the Wichita Flour Mills. Son of Mrs. John Hawkins Moore.

Mrs. John Hawkins Moore (Jennie Kinney.) Sister of Mrs. H. deB. Seebold. (From an ivory miniature in the Seebold family.)

and at the combat of Staffarde, after which, having been commanded with four hundred men to present himself in front of Saluces, this place rendered itself to him with fifty men of regulated troops who were in the Chateau. He also made several Campaigns in Flanders under the orders of the Marshals of Luxembourg, de Villeroi and de Bonflers; appeared with distinction at the Sieges d'Hui and of Namur where he was wounded heading the Grenadiers, and under the eyes of the late King Louis XIV, from whom he received a gratification; then at the Battles of Steinkerque and of Newinde, at the capture of d'Hasnon, to the one d'Ostie, and at the Battle de Luzara, Ect.

As for his family it was of the most ancient noble ones of the City of Metz, and his ancestors had been successively associated with the Sovereign Magistrature of that city, even from the time that it was a dependent of the Empire. In 1556, Mangin de Bachelle, his great, great grandfather, signed the Ratification of the Treaty of Cession which was made of the same city to the King Henry II. He was depositary of the public acts, Receiver general, one of the Thirteen and Counsellor at the "Grand Council" of the Master Echevin. Jean de Bachelle, his son, who succeeded him in the Charges d'Aman, and Receiver General, was father of Jacques de Bachelle, Aman, and one of the Thirteen that was publicly deputed to the late King. Paul de Bachelle his son, and father of the one who gives honor to this article had also the quality of Aman, and was the first one named by order of His Majesty, to the Magistracy of the said City (Metz), like Echevin; and that like the family of Sieur de Bachelle had always lived in a noble manner and possessed Fiefs that could be held only by nobles.

D'Azur, une Fasce d'argent,
chevronne de deux pieces, et
surmonte de deux Etoiles d'Or;
le Casque de profil.

THE DE BACHELLE' FAMILY

From "L'archives de cette Huguenotte famille de Bachelle" pouvoia obtenir a la Bibliotheque Nacional a Paris, France (a la familli d'ancienne Nobless de Lorraine, France.) Armorial de France a Pierre d'Hozier. Bibliotheque Nacionale, Paris, France.

The deBachelle family, originally a French family of Catholic faith, many branches of which still adhere to the Roman Church. Jacques deBachelle, the celebrated warrior, who had won fame by his continual victories over his opponents, became the saviour of the City of Metz in Lorraine, which had been a fortified fort from its earliest days. Originally a Roman camp that had been abandoned and allowed to revert to forest, its location on the strategic point of the river caused Jacques deBachelle to seize the site for the King of France.

During the early days of Calvinism, several members of the deBachelle family embraced the new faith, being ardent followers of Martin Luther. Among those who were close to the King in his efforts to spread the new faith, was Mangin le Bachelle, an able notary and King's Counsellor of Metz, who married (1556) Mademoiselle Marie Everand in that city and was enobled by the French King Henry II in the year 1549 for his faithful services. In 1539, when Henry II and his mother, Catherine de Medici were at Loche Castle and threatened with bodily harm, the father of Mangin leBachelle saved their lives and for this act the family were further enobled with full privileges of the greater nobility.

After the death of Francis I of France, with the accession of Henry II to the throne, the Protestant party that had been gaining headway in spite of Francis I, an ardent Catholic—spread rapidly and Mangin deBachelle rose to great height between the years 1547 - 1559, becoming strong politically. Mangin deBachelle became a strong ally of Henry II. By 1560 following the death of Francis II Catherine de Medici, in order to suppress the Duc of Guise, who had risen to great power, seeing that the Protestant power politically endangered the French throne, formed an alliance with the Catholics of the Guise party to betray the Huguenot party, as the French Protestants were called. A trap was set to ensnare the leaders of the Huguenots. The date set for the massacre, was St. Bartholomew's night, when fearful scenes were enacted. "An order was issued from Paris directing the people at the sound of the tocsin to fall upon the religionists and kill them like so many mad dogs. They called it hales la grande levriere (setting on the hounds)."

At last when the heads of the Huguenot party in France were trapped, the interior of the Chateau of Ambroise was arranged as if for a fete, and great rows of seats appeared on all sides of the spacious courtyard for the accommodation of the Royal party —King, Queen and Nobles. Around the wide space where the executions were to take place, with the Royal family in the iron grille enclosure of the balcony were seated special guests. On the 30th of March immediately following the banquet that had been served them, a long line of fifty gentlemen was conducted to the base of the scaffold, all chanting "Clement Maroti", metrical version of the LX VIth psalm.

Dieu nous sort doux et favorable—Nous benissant par sa bonte et de son visage adorable—Nous fasse luire la clarte.

On horseback could be seen the Cardinal close to the scaffold, and the young King, sickly pale between the young Queen, Mary Stuart, his wife, who later was to share the same fate—equally pale—forced to attend the gruesome spectacle by Catherine de Medici. As the signal was given the Duke of Conde took his place beside the Queen and the group below saluted their silent Captain. Conde returned the salute. The first name was called, and the first head laid on the block, followed by the second and a third and so on, until the chanting of the hymn growing fainter and fainter—until the very end when the last one, the Baron de Castelnau Chalosse, was heard "Dieu nous sort doux er favorable". The headsman raised his axe, the Cardinal gave the signal and the last head fell. Then off they rode to Chenoceau, where music, dancing and a great feast made them forget it all.

Taylor Crest and Coat-of-Arms—Irish branch of family.

GENEALOGY OF THE de VILBISS FAMILY

Christopher de Vilbiss and his brother came to America from Lorraine (the city of Metz). Christopher settled in Maryland and his brother, in Pennsylvania. Chirstopher de Vilbiss married Catherine. Their children: Michel C., born June 7, 1799, died May 14, 1863; Henry; Eliza; Joshua, Jasper. Michel de Vilbiss married Jane Taylor, Nov. 22, 1822. Their children were: Catherine, born Nov. 11, 1823; James Taylor, born Nov. 19, 1825; Harriett Ann, born Dec. 4, 1829, died Aug. 13, 1897; Elizabeth Jane, born Nov. 3, 1831, died Jan. 14, 1913; Mary Elizabeth, born Jan. 28, 1833, died May 27, 1848; William Andrew, born April 13, 1837, died Aug. 27, 1860; Alfred Newton, born July 24, 1840; Albert Taylor, born June 30, 1843, died Nov. 6, 1844.

Catherine de Vilbiss married Jonathan Hauk, their children, Jennie and James, twins; Ella and Eva, twins; Rose, Lida. Harriet Ann de Vilbiss married Ira Cook, Jan. 29, 1852. Their children, Edward Willis, Katie, Mary, Emily, Alfred Newton.

DE VILBISS.

Eliza Jane de Vilbiss, married Louis Henry Summerl, Feb. 7, 1855. Their children: Estelle, born Dec. 6th, 1855; Cora, born March 16th, 1858, died Feb. 6th, 1860; Hattie, born Jan. 10th,

Dorothea Gertrude Agnes Seebold who married Rev. Superintendent Gustave von Meyer.

Rev. Superintendent Gustave von Meyer.

lara Bremer de Beaulieu de Marconnay (Mrs. red William Konzelman).

Frederick W. Konzelman, Manager of the Interior Decorating Department of the L. C. Tiffany Co., New York City.

Mary Baronne de Beaulieu de Marconnay, née Mary Mason Beacham, wife of Charles Baron de Beaulieu de Marconnay.

Entrance gate to estate "Villa Velure" Lucerne Suisse, country home of Baron de Beaulieu de Marconnay family.

Minnie Hauk (Baronne de Wartegg) as Carmen.

Crest and Coat of Arms of the de Beaulieu de Marconnay family.

Chateau de Beaulieu de Marconnay near Poitou, France, Ancestral seat of the de Marconnay family.

1862; Minnie Kate, born Oct. 28th, 1864, died Sept., 1904. Alfred Newton de Vilbiss married Susie Crossing, Jan. 27th, 1864—no children.

Estelle Summerl married Florence A. Getz, May 12, 1887. Children: Charles E., born June 27, 1888; Louis C., born June 7, 1890, died Aug. 27, 1890; Hattie May, born July 22, 1891, died Feb. 16,, 1892; Delmer de Vilbiss, born July 20, 1897; Raymond Howard, born Oct 2, 1912. Hattie Summerl married Walter Steverley, Sept. 10, 1890—Minnie, born Feb. 24, 1894. Minnie Kate Summerl, married Charles Henry Finley, June 12, 1895. No children.

The deVilbis, deVillebiss, deVillebois family from Metz, Lorraine, is a tree of many branches, having limbs stemming throughout France into England as the Ogle deVilbiss family who came to America in 1665, a member, Samuel was thrice governor of the Province of Maryland. Another was Thomas deVilbiss, who founded the deVilbiss Manufacturing Company, and built the magnificent group of buildings, the Thomas deVilbiss High School, Toledo, Ohio. There are innumerable members of the same name scattered throughout the United States, where the name has been known for two hundred years.

In Hozier's Armorial in the Bibliotheque Nationale, Paris, appears the genealogy of the French branches of this family originally deVillebiss, deVillebois, one Sieur Henry deVillebois, ecuyer deVillebis en deVillebois.

Mrs. H. deB. Seebold's mother was Jennie Hauk, daughter of Katherine de Vilbiss and Jonathan Hauk, uncle of Minnie Hauk, the celebrated grand opera singer, whose interpretations of Carmen made her famous shortly after her debut in the Old Grand Opera House which stood in Canal Street, where is now the Maison Blanche Building.

A dainty souvenir of the celebrated singer of a day now passed, who obtained a part of her early musical education in New Orleans, when her parents brought her South following an overflow of their land in the West, is a post card sent Mrs. Seebold by the Baronne deBeaulieu Marconnay, a cousin by marriage of Dr. Seebold's who was a close friend of the opera singer and her husband, the Baron de Wartegg. Baronne de Marconnay and her husband often visited the deWartegg's while they lived in Lucerne, and attended many of the musicales given at their villa Tribschen, the one time home of Richard Wagner, where many of his famous opera scores, such as Tristan and Isolde had been written.

The post card shows a picture taken at a date when the Baron and Baronne deWartegg were still in their prime. To the greetings the Baron and Baronne deWartegg both affixed their autographs.

The picture is of Wagner's old home with the singer and her husband standing in the doorway. In this house Litz and all the contemporary musical notables gathered during Wagner's life and later during the deWarteggs's lifetime.

Minnie Hauk, the grand opera singer, made her debut in the Old Grand Opera House on Canal Street between Dauphine and Burgundy Streets, New Orleans. She later married Baron deWartegg and they made their home in Lucerne, living in the Villa Triebchen, the former home of Richard Wagner. In this house Minnie Hauk (Baronne deWartegg) held her salon, gathering noted musicians and singers about her, making her home as Wagner had done during the years he lived there, one of the most interesting meeting places in Europe for persons of culture. Here she lived with her husband, Baron deWartegg, surrounded by hundreds of souvenirs from music lovers. She outlived Baron deWartegg and died at the advanced age of eighty-six years a few years ago.

In her "Memoirs of an Opera Singer" she affectionately recalls the years spent in New Orleans, and of her return time and again to see her old friends and share with them the joy of her triumphs, after her notable success in her interpretation of Carmen, which placed her in the first ranks of the opera singers of her day.

* * * * *

MEMORIES OF A SINGER (BARONESS DE WARTEGG)

Minnie Hauk was one of the greatest dramatic artists of her age. Her influence in Opera has been immense, for in creating the role of Carmen as it has been played for forty-five years all over the world, she at the same time revolutionized the dramatic side of opera, introducing real acting in place of the conventional gestures previously em-

ployed. She was, moreover, a woman of vivid personality and charm; and has much to tell about her friendships with royal personages and celebrities such as Wagner, Gounod, Litz, Patti and Henry Irving.

A. M. PHILPOT, LTD., 69 Great Russel St., W. C. I., London.

* * * * *

KINNEY.

William Henry Kinney, founder of a chain of flour mills in the states of Kansas and Oklahoma, was the son of James Kinney of Zanesville, Ohio, who owned a flour mill at that place. He married Margaret Barton of English descent, whose family owned one of the early clipper ships out of Boston plying between Boston and England, the family settling in Maryland. William Henry Kinney married Jennie Hauk, daughter of Jonathan Hauk, and Katherine de Vilbiss, a Huguenot family of Metz, Lorraine. Jonathan Hauk was a brother of the father of the celebrated Opera singer, Minnie Hauk, whose interpretation of Carmen made her an outstanding Grand Opera singer of her day. The children of William Henry Kinney and Jennie Hauk are: Nettie May Kinney who married Herman Boehm de Bachelle Seebold, M. D.; and Jennie Kinney, who married John Hawkins Moore, issue Jack Kinney Moore, president of the Moore Lowry Flour Milling Co., Kansas City, Mo., who married Noville Mock, issue, Mary Ellen Moore, Evelyn Moore, Jack Kinney Moore, Jr., and Dianna Moore.

MOCK GENEALOGY.

William Charles Wasson, married Emelia Pruitt, issue, Thomas Mattox Wasson, who married Margaret Schultz, who was the daughter of John M. Schultz, and Frances Lewis (Paternal). Mock married Frances Shoemaker, issue, William Henry Mock, who married Mary Ellen Beeman, daughter of Mary Ann Meeks, and Martin Beeman, their one son was Thomas Mock.

SEEBOLD FAMILY—Continued

Sophie Louisa Julia, born Aug. 4th, 1831 in Lachem, died Feb. 8th, 1919; Elise Antonia Seebold, born April 6th, 1836 in Lachem, died in 1876, in the city of Philadelphia where she is buried. Dorothea Gertrude Otille Agnes Seebold, born May 14th,

1841 in Stockheim, died March 20th,, 1926, buried in Hanover city in the family plot. Elisie Antonia Seebold, born April 6th, 1836, married Charles Baron de Beaulieu de Marconnay, son of General Charles de Beaulieu Marconnay of the French Army, and later chief Forester of the Kingdom of Hanover, and his wife, **Julie Baroness von Egloffstein.** Charles Philip de Beaulieu de Marconnay was born in 1832 at the family chateau, Chateau de Marconnay in Poitiers, France, and died in Wilmington, Delaware; is buried in Mount Vernon Cemetery, Philadelphia. Their children are: Clara, born Feb. 1864; Charles Baron de Beaulieu de Marconnay, born Jan. 16th, 1865; Baron Albert de Beaulieu de Marconnay, born Jan. 16, 1874; Clara de Beaulieu de Marconnay married Frederic W Konselman Jan. 17th, 1881, issue two sons.; Charles de Beaulieu de Marconnay, born Feb. 15th, 1882; Albert Somers, born Feb. 15th, 1894.

Herman Albert de Beaulieu de Marconnay, married Mary Elisabeth Hill; one son, born Nov 10, 1895, died 1923; named Carl de Beaulieu de Marconnay, buried in Mount Vernon Cemetery, Philadelphia. Frederick W. Konselman, who married Clara Bremer de Beaulieu de Marconnay was until his death, manager of the decorating Department of the Louis C. Tiffany Art Glass Co. of New York City. His son, became manager of The Handel Glass and Lamp Co., with offices in Fifth Ave., New York City. Herman Albert de Beaulieu de Marconnay's second marriage after the death of his first wife was to Marian Nichols, daughter of William Wallace Nichols.

NICHOLS GENEALOGY

William Wallace Nichols, engineer, writer and business man, was born in New York City, Nov. 17, 1860. In his early youth he went to Colorado where he taught in the public schools of Denver. He was graduated from Yale in 1884. He was vice-president for a time of the Allis-Chalmers Company. In 1916 he was appointed chairman of the American Industrial Commission to France.

Mr. Nichols belongs to many organizations in which he has been prominent such as the United States Chamber of Commerce, American Academy of Political and Social Science, American Iron and Steel Institute and so on.

William Wallace Nichols is the son of Edward Erastus and Anna Maria (McAuley) Nichols. Nichols traces his lineage from

Elise Antonia Seebold, wife of Baron Charles Philip de Beaulieu de Marconnay II.

Baron Charles Philip de Beaulieu de Marconnay II, son of Baron Charles de Beaulieu de Marconnay I. of the French Army.

Baron Charles de Beaulieu de Marconnay III, son of Baron Charles Philip de Beaulieu de Marconnay II.

Baronne Mary (Mae) Mason Beacham de Beaulieu de Marconnay, wife of Baron Charles de Beaulieu de Marconnay III.

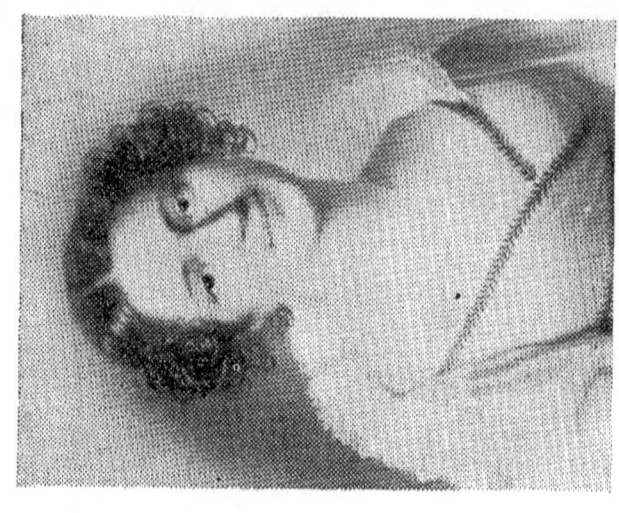

Baron Charles de Beaulien de Beaulieu de Marconnay I., a General in the French Army, later Chief Forester of the Kingdom of

Julie Baronne von Egloffstein, wife of Baron Carl Philip de Beaulieu de Marconnay.

King Robert Bruce of Scotland (1334), the continuous line being as follows: Robert Bruce of Clackmanan; Sir Edward Bruce; Sir Robert Bruce; Sir David Bruce; Sir George Bruce of Carnock, father of Margaret Bruce who married Francis Nichols, Sr., of Ampthill, Bedford County, England. The Nichols lineage also is distinguished, originating with Robert Nichols of London, who died about 1548. His eldest son, Thomas, left large estates to his heirs and also made liberal bequests to various charities. His second son was Anthony, who married Margaret Bruce in the latter part of the Seventeenth Century. Of their several children two attained special distinction, Richard and Francis, known as Sergeant Francis Nichols. The family was evidently in royal favor, Richard having participated in the (English) Civil War. In 1664 he joined the forces serving as colonel of James, Duke of York, commanding the fleet at the time Dutch New York surrendered to the English. He served as the first English Governor of New York for three years and died in 1672, in subsequent battle with the Dutch. His brother, Francis, also held military offices in the royalist armies. On that account he was forced to leave England to which he never returned. He was the first of the Nichols family to come to America. His military skill was recognized in Stratford, Conn., where he settled in 1639, and was assigned to train and discipline the men in military affairs.

Of Sergeant Nichols' four children, Isaac was ancestor of succeeding generations as follows: Ephraim, Ignatius, Ephraim II, David, Jesse, Wallace, and Edward Erastus. The latter, father of William Wallace Nichols, was born Dec. 15, 1829, and died Oct. 26, 1905.

Frederic W. Konselman, a member of a prominent Philadelphia family, studied art at the Academy of Fine Arts of that city, and became a mural artist of distinction. In the "Gay Nineties" splendid mansions were springing up in the larger cities of the North, East and West, and his work was to be found on the ceilings of many of these splendid mansions, some still in evidence. He became associated with Charles de Beaulieu de Marconnay, the fresco painter, and married his daughter, Clara. Their two children are Charles de Beaulieu Konzelman and Albert Somers de Beaulieu Konzelman.
Later Frederic W. Konselman became manager of the art decorating department of the Louis C. Tiffany Co. of New York City.

Among the notable achievements of that company under his supervision are: the splendid Tiffany decorating exhibit at the Paris Exposition of the 1890's, the Tiffany Chapel of mosaic glass now in the crypt of the Cathedral of St. John the DIVINE, New York City, and the decoration and mosaic work of the Chicago Public Library. The beautiful interior decorations and murals of the Carneige, the Harriman, the Tiffany, the Vanderbilt, and other mansions too numerous to mention were executed under his supervision.

Dorothea Gertrude Otille Agnes Seebold, born in Stockheim, May 14, 1841, married Rev. Gustave von Meyer on Nov. 23, 1865, issue: Rev. Herman von Meyer, born Sept. 23, 1866; Marie, born Aug. 9th, 1868; Werner, born July 18th, 1870; John, born Aug. 13th, 1873; and Gottfried, born Feb. 29th, 1876. Rev. Herman von Meyer married Sept. 21, 1892 Sophie Rath, born Nov. 18, 1867, died Nov. 10, 1930. Marie von Meyer married Pastor Henry Hedenhausen, who died Oct. 22, 1918, issue: Magdelen, born June 1893; Marie, born Aug., 1895, became a deaconess.

Charles de Beaulieu Konselman married June 15, 1905, Cornelia Zimmerman, issue two children: Charles de Beaulieu Konselman, and Cornelia Helen, born June 18, 1911, who married Marvin Clark.

Charles de Beaulieu de Marconnay, born Dec. 9th, 1865, educated at Dickerson College, Carlisle, Pa., married May, daughter of Mary Mason Beacham, her grandfather being the reason of Mason Dixon Line fame, and her father, Henry Beacham, a judge of Baltimore. Charles de Marconnay and May Beacham were married in the chapel of Glengariff Castle, County Cork, Ireland, a relative of the Beacham family owning the castle. The European homes of the de Beaulieu Marconnay family are in the suburbs of Lucerne, a country place Villa Vellure, and another No. 2 Konigenstrasse, Munich. The family are buried here in their handsome family mausoleum, in the main cemetery of that city. Albert Somers Konzelman married Josephine Morton.

MORTON.

Josephine Morton is a daughter of Edward Morton, whose father was John Morton. Edward Morton's mother's name before her marriage was Minerva Sims of Kentucky, while the Mortons were natives of Pennsylvania.

The mother of Josephine Morton was Cora Phillips, and her father was David Phillips who came from Ohio. Her maternal grandmother's name was Adelia Welch, all of the original branches of the family have been in America previous to the American Revolution.

Crest of de Beaulieu de Marconnay family.

CHATEAU DE MARCONNAY.

The Chateau de Marconnay in the Province of Poitou in France was built about the year 940. Its site was originally an old Roman Fort. The feudal castle with its accompanying acreage became the seat of the ancient feudal family of de Beaulieu de Marconnay in the early part of the 12th Century. Of massive construction and still in good state of preservation, the Chateau remained in the de Beaulieu de Marconnay family until the year 1859, when it was sold to the Comptess de l'Abonnier in whose family it still remains. Among the oldest of the noble families in the district of Poitou in France, is that of de Beaulieu de Marconnay with family records dating from the twelfth century. There were three sons of Louis II of MARCONNAY, whose line began in 1287 with Jehan.

After the Edict of Nantes (1685), the second son remained and carried on the title of Marquis, which still exists, as de Beaulieu de Marconnay. The descendants of the youngest son Oliver I de Beaulieu de Marconnay, for three generations carried the title of Master of the Hounds in the Austrian service of the Court of Weimer (1811 - 1889) Carl Oliver.

During the days of the TERROR, friends of the unhappy Queen Marie Antoinette used the chateau de Beaulieu de Marconnay as a meeting place to discuss plans for rescuing her. When this was discovered the family had to flee from France, and at this time a large part of the chateau was demolished and part of the land was confiscated.

During this period distinguished noblemen escaped being murdered by hiding in underground secret chambers whose location is indicated on the family charts in many of the ancient chateaux of France, these families knowing where they could find refuge should occasion demand it.

Albert Baron de Beaulieu de Marconnay.

Baronne Albert de Beaulieu de Marconnay, neé Marian Nichols.

William W. Nichols, father of Baronne Albert de Beaulieu de Marconnay.

Carl Baron de Beaulieu de Marconnay, son of Albert Baron de Beaulieu de Marconnay, Air Corps World War.

Mary Elizabeth Baroness de Beaulieu—Marconnay.

William Lorain Hill, father of Mary Elizabeth Baronne de Beaulieu-Marconnay

Villa Velure near Lucerne—Summer home of Baron and Baronne Charles de Beaulieu de Marconnay III.

Mrs. Charles de Beaulieu Konzelman, née Cornelia Helen Zimmerman.

Charles de Beaulieu Konzelman.

Albert S. de Beaulieu Konzelman.

Mrs. Albert S. de Beaulieu Konzelman née Josephine Morton.

Charles de Beaulieu Konzelman, Jr., and Cornelia Helen Konzelman (Mrs. Marvin Clark).

Mrs. Charles de Beaulieu Konzelman Jr., née Marcia Rolf.

Marvin Clark.

Chapter XXVII.

THE WALTER PARKER FAMILY—THE PITKIN FAMILY
GENEALOGY OF THE PARKER FAMILY

THE Burrs, maternal side of the Walter Parker family, are of English extraction, coming to New England in 1635, and founding Hartford, Conn. The grandfather of Walter Parker (maternal) came South on a flat boat as a young man and was wrecked at the present site of Memphis, Tenn. He remained there and was prominent among those that helped to found that city.

"On my father's side," said Mr. Parker, "The dominant strain was Huguenot. The families were large. When anything happened to the men the women carried on and took their places."

The founder of the Huguenot side of his family was Bartholomew Dupuy, a captain of Dragoons, who escaped from France when the Treaty of Nantes was repealed, coming to America in 1700. The story of Dupuy is a lengthy romance. In it one is taken to the residence of a gentleman of Virginia, in Prince George County, a Huguenot who fled from France. In that home is still to be seen Dupuy's sword, an ancient relic triangular in shape, with a spear-like appearance. Its own scabbard was lost, its present one was picked up from the battle field of Guilford. "It drank the blood of more than one enemy of the American cause", according to the story.

The family tree of the Parker family, one of the largest, judging from ramifications of its endless branches, has among the many names those of the Huguenots that fled to Virginia, including the Flournoys, Meauxs, DuVals Maryes, Boudoins, Latines.

VIRGINIA

Our true chronicle is told; and we need not pause to comment on it here, or point the spirit and moral. Long years afterwards in Monican-town, on the banks of the noble James River, in Virginia, an aged soldier lay upon his death-bed, with a kneeling woman weeping at his side, and children watching the pale face through tears. "Don't cry, Susanne," said Messire Dupuy, "I am only going home, whither you, true wife, will follow me. Do you know what we said in the woods of Germany?" I waited patiently for the Lord, and he inclined unto me, and heard my cry. Blessed be his name! In him and the blessed Jesus is my trust—I who have lived and now die a true Hugenot."

The faint voice faltered, and a ray of sunlight falling on the snowy hair, lit it up gloriously. "And to you, my children," continued the dying gentleman, "I bequeath an untainted name, which you in turn should bear worthily."

"Jacques," he continued, addressing the eldest, "Take my old sword there, and make use of it in a good cause only; it has never been drawn in a bad one. Fight for your country and your faith, so God shall bless you. Imitate your godfather, Jacques de la Fontaine, of noble memory. And now, my children, take my blessing." They knelt with sobs, and the hand of the dying soldier rested in turn upon every forehead. As the last words were uttered he fell faintly back, and only a slight sigh marked the passage of a true gentleman from earth to heaven—from time to eternity.

It was the bright sunshne of Virginia, the new land, which rested last upon his forehead; but this was his home now, loved and cherished like the old, old home in France.

He died as he had lived, a true Huguenot. No better epitaph is needed.

WALTER PARKER

Walter Parker, the immediate subject of this sketch, is a native of Memphis, Tennessee, the eldest son of Walter L. Parker and his wife Ella Burr Parker. Almost half the residents of Memphis were relatives, and when he reached 21 years of age he bequeathed his share of the town to his many cousins and moved to New Orleans. He developed as a newspaper man and writer; was war correspondent for the Times Democrat in Cuba in 1898; served the United States government in the first World War, first as assistant to the Secretary of Commerce for inland water transportation, and framed the policies under which the federal barge line was developed; later during the war he served President Wilson in Europe. He organized the Mississippi Valley Association for the protection of the Mississippi Valley economy, and organized the Jefferson Highway Association which promoted the building of a paved highway connecting Winnepeg, Canada and New Orleans.

In 1905 he obtained the enactment by Congress of the federal quarantine law, which put an end to "shot-gun" quarantine in the South in yellow fever years, and under which the federal government was empowered to eliminate bubonic plague. For many years he was general manager of the New Orleans Association of Commerce. In more recent years he has been economist for the national firm of Fenner and Beane, and the author of many treatises on economics, flood control, river regulation and kindred subjects. As chairman of the National Committee on Safety at Sea he was instrumental in bringing about the enactment of several desirable laws for the safety of vessels and passengers on the high seas. He has held many honorable positions. In 1940 he was president of Taxpayers of New Orleans, Incorporated, and a member of the Board of Curators of the Louisiana State Museum.

PITKIN GENEALOGY.

William Pitkin, the progenitor of the family in America, came to New England from London in 1659, and was attorney-General of Connecticut in 1664. The records of Hertfordshire, England bear witness that the name Pitkin is an honorable one and has been prominent from the Thirteenth Century, many having held appointments under the several sovereigns. The Royal borough of Berkhamsted, appears to have been homestead of the family at an early date. In 1766 a William Pitkin was governor of Connecticut. Although a member of the Church of England when the first William Pitkin came to America, he became a member of the Puritan Church in East Hartford, Conn., into which Church some one hundred Pitkin children have been baptized and about a hundred and fifty of the same name received into membership. In war as in peace the Pitkins filled a conspicuous place in the beginning of the American nation. They fought in the Revolution and later wars. In 1791 fourteen Pitkins were granted a charter as an Artillery company.

William Pitkin's sister, the beauteous Martha, was born in London in 1638 and followed her brother to the New World in 1661, to urge his return to England, not once supposing he intended to remain in the "wilderness".

An interesting poem by Charles Knowles Bolton, "The Wooing of Martha Pitkin", attests to the popularity and charm of Miss Pitkin who married Simon Wolcott and became the mother of Governor Roger Wolcott. Her grandson, Oliver Wolcott was a signer of the Declaration of Independence, and was governor of Connecticut for ten years. A second Oliver Wolcott, son of the former, succeeded Alexander Hamilton as Secretary of the Treasury. He was in the cabinets of Washington and Adams. He declined the proffered place at the head of the First United States Bank.

Martha Pitkin Wolcott was also the great-grandmother of Governor Roger Griswold and ancestor of Senator Edward Oliver Wolcott of Colorado and Lieutenant-Governor Roger Wolcott of Massachusetts. One of the early American histories was written by Timothy Pitkin, who was the grandson of the then President Clapp of Yale University. The history was published in two volumes in 1828. Frederic W. Pitkin was Governor of Colorado in 1878. He was honored by the incorporation of the town of "Pitkin" in 1879; the Pitkin Bank, the Pitkin Hotel, "Pitkin Progress" (its newspaper), all of which testifying to the popularity of Governor Pitkin.

Horace Tracy Pitkin is the subject of a tribute on a large bronze plaque at Yale where the Pitkins were educated. Horace Pitkin lost his life in the Boxer Rebellion. On the distaff side he was descended from Thomas Yale founder of the Yale family in America. His sister married Charles Eliot, son of President Eliot of Harvard in 1888. Horace Pitkin while a student at Yale studied for the Ministry in Union Seminary and became a great influence in the missionary field. A Memorial of Horace Tracy Pitkin by Robert E. Speer gives account of a noble life consecrated to Christ. Another prominent member of the Pitkin Family is Walter B. Pitkin, Professor of Journalism at Columbia University; author of "Life Begins at Forty" and numerous other books. Mr. Pitkin was a former associate editor of the Encyclopedia Britannica.

Mrs. Christian Schertz (Helen Pitkin). From the life sized oil portrait by Allen St. John. Among the art treasures of Mrs. Schertz's Home.

William Willings Wells, Grandfather of Mrs. J. Alphonse Prudhomme II.

Much of the states cotton was shipped to England by way of New Orleans.

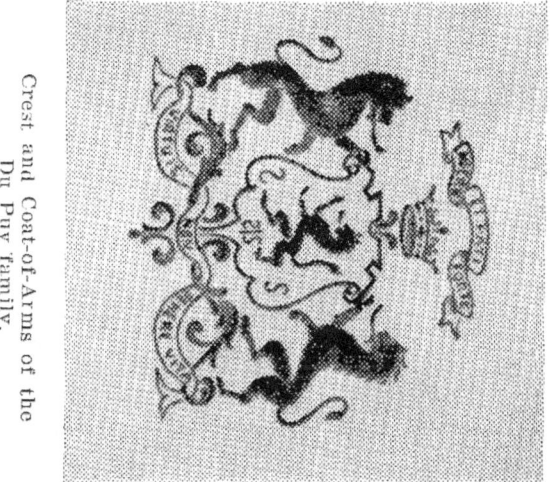

Crest and Coat-of-Arms of the Du Puy family.

WALTER PARKER

Mrs. Walter Parker (Anita Hernandez)

Miss Ester Hernandez

Samuel Fuller, close relative of the brilliant Margaret Fuller, Countess Ossoli was another relative on the distaff side. The late John Robert Graham Pitkin was Minister Plenipotentiary to the Argentine Republic, a lawyer, noted orator and statesman. The mother of J. R. G. Pitkin was Adeline Graham, only child of Commodore Graham, U. S. Navy. The mother of Helen Fearing Fuller, mother of Helen Pitkin Schertz, was Helen Gilroy Fuller, Mogridge.

CHAPTER XXVIII.

THE LEVERT—WARE—PRUDHOMME FAMILIES

LEVERT.

FROM this old Louisiana family, General J. B. Levert is selected as the one to represent its numerous members. Among the representative men of his era none stood higher in the annals of this state, and specially in connection with plantations (sugar) which forms the basis for the data of this work.

The late General John B. Levert's father was Auguste Levert, a native of this state, and his mother, Eulalie Mire of St. James Parish. Auguste Levert was born in St. James Parish in 1803, and having completed his education became a sugar planter, remaining one until his death. He was the owner of Saint Delphine, Golden Ridge, and Willow Glen plantations, all of them located on the Mississippi River and fully cultivated. For a period of his life he resided in Lafourche Parish, but removed in 1831 to Iberville Parish, here he remained until 1880. As he advanced in life he removed to the parish of West Baton Rouge where he lived until his death in 1886. He was one of the important sugar planters of his era, prominent in the affairs pertaining to the advancement of the sugar industry and other important matters of this state. He was a staunch Democrat, and throughout his lifetime he made a fine record as citizen, father, husband and friend. At his death he left a fortune in fine plantations for his descendants, who have continued as he would have wished them to do.

General John B. Levert, son of Auguste Levert, was born on Golden Ridge Plantation in Iberville Parish, La., in 1839. Finishing his commercial education, he matriculated at St. Mary's College at Emmetsburg, Maryland, and there continued his studies until war was declared. At once he abandoned his studies and volunteered as a member of the 1st Louisiana Cavalry, one of the first regiments to leave for the theatre of war. During the entire duration of the struggle he followed his regiment ever encouraging his men and sharing their hardships thus endearing himself to each and every one of them, having rendered valiant and meritorious service. On retiring to civic life, he first entered the Western Produce Co., then Henry Grable Co., which followed because of his association with Colonel Louis Bush. For a long period it was one of the leading firms in the sugar industry, which later was succeeded by the firm of J. B. Levert & Co. Several others later became interested in the firm, among them Henry Tremonlet, who owned Helvetia Plantation in St. James Parish, La., and later J. M. Burguieres known as Levert-Burguires. This was succeeded by the later firm known as J. B. Levert and Co., Ltd., which includes the different members of the family of the third generation.

JAMES ANDREW WARE

James Andrew Ware, prominent Confederate Veteran, was born on a plantation nine miles southeast of Marshall, Harrison County, Texas, in 1847. He was the son of Henry Ware and Martha Everett, both natives of the State of Georgia. Two of Mr. Ware's uncles served in the Continental Army during the Revolutionary War, and one of these uncles attained the rank of Brigadier-General. In 1866 Mr. James A. Ware was sent to New Orleans to attend law lectures, but in 1868 he abandoned his law career to go into the sugar and cotton business. He was one of the organizers of the Cotton Exchange as well as the Sugar Exchange. He was one of New Orleans' representative citizens.

James Ware's father, Henry Ware, was a New Orleans capitalist. As a result of the war in 1868 he became the owner of John Andrew's handsome plantation and splendid home with its magnificent contents. Having amassed a fortune and becoming enamoured with the plantation life of Belle Grove, in 1879 James Ware purchased the plantation from his father, where he lived for the remainder of his life. During his occupancy, most of the plantation of 7,000 acres was kept under cultivation. He also purchased Celeste plantation near White Castle, and became one of the largest plantation owners in the state. He also displayed a leaning towards politics. In Reconstruction Days he became a potent factor in the Democratic Party, both in Iberville Parish and in the state. He was a delegate to the Democratic National Convention at Chicago in 1884, and served on the staff of Governor Murphy J. Foster and Gov. Wm. H. Heard.

James Ware married Miss Mary Eliza Stone, daughter of Dr. P. R. Stone, an eminent physician and wealthy large planter of Iberville Parish. Dr. Stone's grandfather, Colonel John Stone, was a prominent figure in Colonial Days and a near relative of William Stone who was Governor of Maryland Colony about the middle of the Seventeenth Century. The Ware family descend from a notable aristocratic English family, among whose descendants was George Reade who came to Virginia in 1639, and became the great-grandfather of General George Washington. Another George Reade of the same family signed the Declaration of Independence, hailing from Delaware. Miss Penelope Lynch Adams of a family of soldiers and statesmen was the mother of Mrs. Ware, whose chic costumes, educational accomplishments, and gracious personality, made her one of the most famous hostesses of her day in the entire South. Her magnificent plantation home, Belle Grove, palatial in size, construction and furnishings was ever brilliant with a continuous series of splendid hospitalities, for both Mr. and Mrs. Ware loved to entertain. Even when the Civil War Reconstruction Days had practically ended the old plantation life, Belle Grove continued its usual routine of gay hospitalities. In New Orleans at the St. Charles Hotel where the Wares had a large suite, they entertained each winter on a large scale.

Dr. Stone Ware, born March 26th, 1870, graduated in 1893, married Miss Carmilite Gourrier, daughter of Dr. Gourrier of Plaquemines, La.

PRUDHOMME

(Meaning Wise Man).

Among those who sailed from France with Bienville in 1699 was one Emanuel Prudhomme, a surgeon in the French Army. Emanuel Prudhomme, a direct descendant of Dr. Emanuel Prudhomme, was the father of Pierre Phanor Prudhomme who was born June 24th, 1807 and died 1825. A daughter of this union, Adeline Catherine Prudhomme, was born March 6th, 1836, and married in the year 1856 Winter Wood Breazeale, who died March 10th, 1896, aged 69 years. He owned and operated large cotton plantations and spent most of his life in the Parish of Natchitoches.

Old maps of the vicinity of Natchitoches in 1722 show the Prudhommes as owners of extensive lands. With the French Army of Occupation in early days had come Jean Baptiste Prudhomme, who bore the title "Docteur du Roi", and who had received from the King of France a large land grant on the banks of Red River. On this river which later became known as "LaCote-Joyeuse", his sons on this estate began the first experiment of growing cotton on a large scale. Its success was in a measure partly responsible for the "Golden Era" of wealth which extended from 1795 to the Civil War. A portrait of one of these sons, Emanuel Prudhomme, painted in Paris, quite appropriately represents him with a boll of cotton in his hand. The house at 530 Jefferson Street, in Natchitoches was built by one of the first owners of land on the "Cote Joyeuse".

Branches of the Family

Rosalie Meullion married 1798, William Willing Wells, born 1776, died 1808, reared at the plantation Wellswood at Meeker, La. He was a brother of Samuel Levi Wells. Rosalie Muellion was a daughter of Dr. Ennemond Meullion and his second wife, Janette (Pairet) La Mathe. Dr. Meullion was born 1737 and died 1820. His wife Janette, born 1752 and died 1835. Their daughter Rosalie, born 1782, married three times—1st to William Willing Wells; 2nd, to Dr. John Sibly; 3rdly to William Marshall. She had children by the first and third husbands, and from them are descended the Branch, Tanners, Alason, Pearce and Marshall families of Rapides Parish. William Willing Wells and Rosalie Meullion had four children as follows: Benjamin, Emily, Desiree, and Meullion Sidney.

Desiree married Branch Tanner. They had several children. One daughter, Rose Meullion Tanner, born 1840, died 1903, married Dr. James Elise Keater, born 1822, died 1908. Their third son, Meullion Sands Keater, married Mabel Lucille Blake of St. Louis, Mo. Their only child, Rosalie Lucille Keater, married James Alphonse Prudhomme II, of Bermuda, La. J. Alphonse Prudhomme and his wife have five children: I. J. Alphonse III; Kenneth, Meullion, Keater and Rose Vivian.

Reviving as it were the gala days of the "Cote Joyeuse" the old plantation mansion of the Prudhomme family, Bermuda Plantation, was recently a scene of brilliancy and gayety to celebrate the Golden Wedding Anniversary honoring Mr. and Mrs. P. Phanor Prudhomme. A great throng filled the rooms of the ancient plantation home where the large reception was held.

Masses of golden blooms of all sorts mingling with fern banked every available space, creating a veritable bower of loveliness in the drawing-rooms and banquet hall, long famous for endless hospitalities in olden days. The great gilded framed mirrors reflected a scene of happiness as the impressive wedding ceremony was re-enacted at noon, where twenty-seven years ago a similar golden-wedding anniversary was celebrated—that of Mr. and Mrs. J. Alphone Prudhomme, parents of those honored on this occasion. The bride of a half century ago attired in a handsome gown of black brocaded velvet worn with a corsage of golden ranuculus was stately. Mr. Prudhomme entered with his eldest son, Alphonse Prudhomme, and met the bride at the altar placed below the wedding-bell that has served for over a century for many family weddings and anniversaries. Immediately following the ceremony a large banquet was held as is customary. Toasts were drunk and during the reception hours the house and grounds were filled with hundreds of their friends and relatives, who came bringing gifts and good wishes.

Mr. Alexander Cloutier presided and congratulated the honored couple. He sang the same sweet songs "Dearest" and "I Love You More", that he sang at their wedding fifty years ago. His voice then magnificent and strong with the full volume of youth, now fainter and a little tremulous with age but none the less sweet, having the charm and pathos of a treasured spinet.

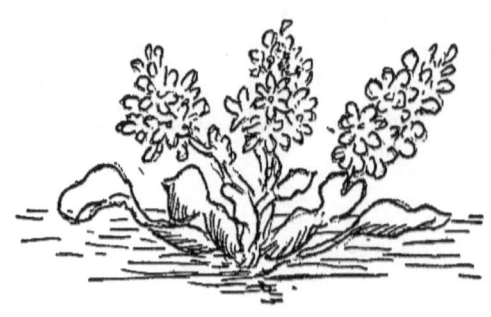

CHAPTER XXIX.

WAKEFIELD, OAK GROVE AND THE MYRTLES

WAKEFIELD MANOR.

"WAKEFIELD" was named for Oliver Goldsmith's Vicar of Wakefield, by its original owner Lewis Stirling, son of Alexander Stirling, noted soldier whose grave and that of his wife Ann Stirling in Beechwood Plantation cemetery are pictured in Vol. I of this work.

The old manor house "Wakefield" has a rather unusual history. Originally an imposing old plantation home, a great center of gracious hospitality in olden days it has continued as such on a lesser scale since ante-bellum days.

When the house was finished in 1833 it was furnished in an elegant and costly manner, most of the furniture for which was purchased in London, much of it still to be seen in the present home.

Mrs. Stirling, a member of the prominent plantation family that built "Rosedown" and many other lovely old plantation houses, was a Miss Sarah Turnbull. Lewis Stirling died in 1858, and his widow lived until 1875, and at her death it was learned that the heirs shared alike in the estate, but a clause in the will indicated that "Wakefield Manor"—the house itself be divided into three parts. Instead of selling the house and dividing the proceeds the building itself was divided.

The present chatelain of "Wakefield" plantation home is a granddaughter of Mrs. John Lobdell, who inherited the portion of

Andrew Stewart, of Oak Alley Plantation

A Bedroom at Oak Alley Plantation

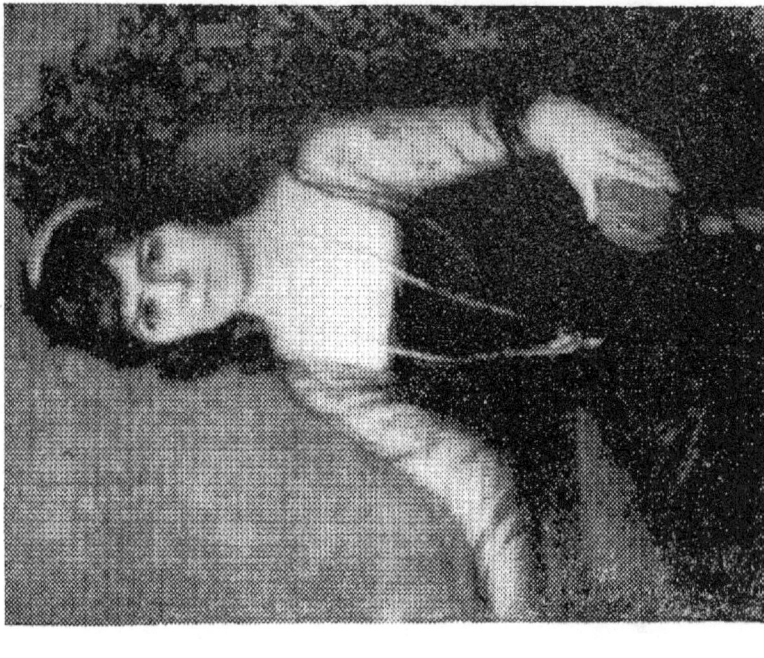

Mrs. Andrew Stewart (Josephine Armstrong) of Oak Alley Plantation. (By Edith Duggan.)

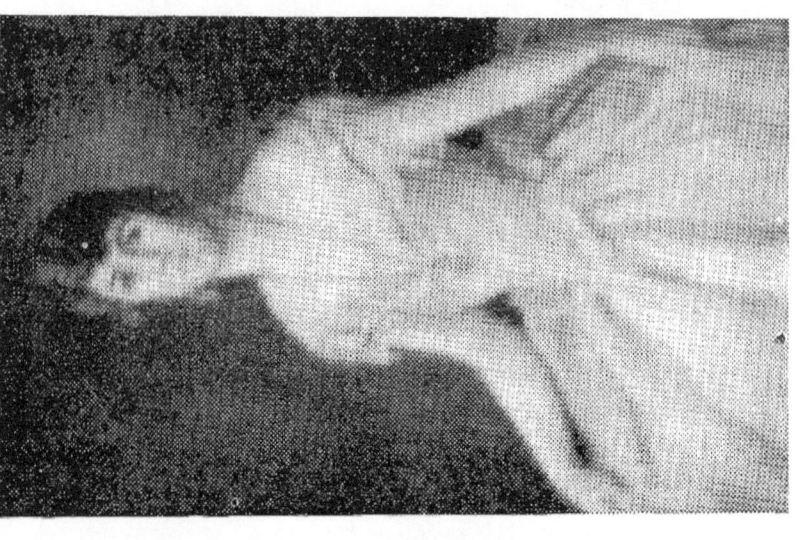

Mrs. Allard Kaufmann (Julia Armstrong.) (By Edith Duggan.)

the manor which we see today after it had been roofed, appearing as it does in the illustration.

The present plantation home known as "Wood-Hill Farm" was constructed for Dr. Rufus G. Stirling from his part of the house and which he used to build this home in 1879, the material coming from parts of the second floor of "Wakefield Manor". In the grounds of Woodhill Farm one finds the old workshop by "The Doctor's Spring", where Audubon and Dr. John B. Hereford spent hours together studying birds.

Another plantation home was built from the third section of "Wakefield Manor", but it was destroyed by fire many years ago. A short distance away now forming part of the lands of Beechwood plantation lies "Rosale" Plantation, originally called "Egypt", laid out for Alexander Stirling, father of Lewis Stirling, original owner of "Waverly". In 1844 David Barrow of Afton Villa bought "Egypt" plantation and manor house which he enlarged and redecorated as a wedding gift to his daughter Mary, who married Robert H. Barrow II. The home and plantation was rechristened "Rosale," the mansion later destroyed by fire in 1885 (see page 267, Vol. I).

OAK GROVE PLANTATION.

"Oak Grove" manor (Page 260, Vol. I) was originally built for Dr. John B. Hereford in 1828, he being a native of Virginia who settled in West Feliciana Parish. Later it became the home of a branch of the Butler family. Burnt in 1930, however, much of interest remains—the two beautiful pigeonnaires that flanked the old home, the ancient school-house of the plantation, and a number of ante-bellum out-buildings making a visit to this plantation worth while.

Another interesting plantation home close by is "The Cedars", the country home of the Misses Sarah and Mamie Butler of New Orleans, which is most attractive in its beautiful setting. A grove of fragrant cedars and oak trees enclose a lovely garden, both of the Misses Butlers being well versed in floriculture and important members of the Garden Society. Japonicas, a large assortment of roses and azaleas, jasmine and other fragrant shrub mingle with dogwood, rosebud and holly that brighten the beech woodland in front grounds that are beautiful with blooms most of the year.

Further on towards St. Francisville we find "The Oaks" the quaint and lovely home of the Thomas Butler family. Its garden is very attractive—and the long oak avenue leading to the unpretentious home is inviting.

Here dwelt the author of "Catalpa Memoirs", surrounded by lovely mementos of her happy girlhood depicted by this gracious lady. Ancestral portraits by Sir Thos. Sully, Amans and others equally notable, much fine rosewood and mahogany furniture, rare ornaments and crystal-ware inherited from the Forts, Stewarts, Randolphs and the collection of "The Cottage" are all greatly prized and cherished by this charming family.

THE MYRTLES.

Still another interesting unpretentious old plantation home "The Myrtles" home of much charm, is located in a beautiful grove of century-old oak trees. Built for a branch of the Stirling family close to the plantation home of the Edward Butlers. Its entrance is on the left side of the highway as one faces Woodville, Miss., having a sign at the gateway bearing the name of the plantation.

The house, a story and a half structure somewhat long in front, has a very wide verandah encircling the building embellished by a frame of ornamental cast-iron work greatly enhancing its appearance. It is a very comfortable house one can see at a glance, for room and light of the top story appears assured by the many spacious dormers that pierce the roof.

The darkies of the vicinity tell tales of the ghost of the place in the form of a little old lady wearing an emerald green colored cap that haunts the guest-room, and unless a lighted candle or lamp is left in the room—she will visit the room at midnight and gently raise the mosquito bar and peer into the face of the sleeper. So even today a small light is left in the room occupied by guests.

WILKINSON FAMILY

The Wilkinson family, prominent in America since Colonial days, comes of distinguished ancestry, stemming to Welsh forbears who were prominent members of the commonwealth of Wales. They were related by marriage to the Glen Owen who traces to Owen Glydwr.

The father of James Wilkinson, was Joseph Wilkinson, who left England in 1729 and located on a land grant in Calvert County, where he married Miss Skinner, and the issue from this marriage was a son who was named Joseph Jr., who was born in 1751. This son married Althea Heighe, and they became the parents of two sons, Joseph III. and his younger brother James, who was to become honored with the rank of brigadier general in the Continental Army at the age of twenty-one.

James Wilkinson's father died when James was but seven years of age, and his mother sent him to school in Baltimore. He proved an apt pupil, and was a leader in his classes. He was well educated in English, Latin and Mathematics, and studied medicine after completing his studies in Baltimore, entering medical school while a little over seventeen years of age and graduating in medicine at the age of nineteen.

At this time he enlisted as a private in Richardson's company, and his record shows that he fought at the Battle of Bunker-Hill. Later he was promoted by General Washington to a Captaincy, and later again promoted by Major General Gates as Adjutant General. He was one of Gates' representatives at the surrender of Burgoyne, and at the time had the reputation of being one of the best drill masters in the American army. On Nov. 6th 1777 he was promoted to the brevet rank of Brigadier-General.

General Wilkinson married Ann, daughter of Joan Biddle of the prominent Philadelphia family. Going to Kentucky at the termination of the War of Independence, in 1784 he founded the town of Frankfort, and also became active in Indian Warfare, where he gained the admiration of General Washington, who sent a special message to Congress in 1791. In 1796 General Wilkinson was made Commander-in-Chief of the U. S. army. Later in 1803 jointly with Governor W. C. C. Claiborne he was appointed by President Thomas Jefferson to be the Commissioner to receive Louisiana from Napoleon.

At the end of a long and active military career General Wilkinson became a planter in Louisiana and lived on his Plantation Live Oak, located twenty-five miles below New Orleans.

The three children from his marriage to Ann Biddle were sons, the 1st. named John, who died in his fourteenth year, the 2nd. James Jr., born 1784, died in 1813, the 3rd., Joseph Biddle, b. December 4, 1785 and who died in 1865, leaving a widow, Catherine Andrews Wilkinson. Captain James Wilkinson Jr., was killed in action in Mobile harbor in 1813, leaving a wife (née Miss Coleman) and a son, Theophilus, born 1811, who also followed army life, becoming an artillery officer in the U. S. army.

The second wife of General James Wilkinson was Célestine Trudeau, a daughter of the surveyor general of Louisiana, Charles Trudeau, member of the prominent Louisiana family of that name. Two daughters were born of this marriage; Maria Isabelle, who died in infancy and Elizabeth Stephanie, who became Madame Toussaint Bigot, wife of Professor Bigot. Issue: Charles A. Bigot and Theodore F. Bigot neither leaving issue.

Robert Andrews Wilkinson, better known as R. A., eldest son of Joseph Wilkinson and Catherine Andrews was killed at the Battle of Manassas, 1862. He had married Mary F. Stark of Mississippi, a daughter of Col. Stark, a Revolutionary officer, whose descendants have occupied almost as prominent a place in the annals of Mississippi as have the Wilkinsons in Louisiana. The children of Robert Andrews Wilkinson and Mary F. Stark were six in number as follows:

Robert Andrews Wilkinson; Horatio Stark Wilkinson; the daughters being Katherine, who became Mrs. Carroll W. Allen; Rose who became Mrs. Simeon Toby; Isabelle; and Mollie (Mary).

J. Biddle Wilkinson, M. D., second son of Joseph B. Wilkinson and Catherine Andrews, became a sugar planter in the Parish of Plaquemines. His wife was Josephine Stark of Mississippi—their children ten in number as follows — J. Biddle Wilkinson, whose wife was Lydia Duval; Theodore S. Wilkinson, whose wife was Pauline Spyker; R. Andrew Wilkinson, whose wife was Lucy White; Horace Wilkinson, whose wife was Julia Merwin; James Wilkinson, whose first wife was Mattie Spyker, and second Cecelia Peters; Ernest Wilkinson, who died young; Elizabeth, who died in childhood and Josephine Wilkinson, who became Mrs. Thomas Worthington.

Andrews Wilkinson, son of Dr. J. B. Wilkinson, was born in Plaquemine Parish on his father's plantation and was educated at the Washington and Lee University at Lexington, Va. He became a prominent journalist, and like the rest of the family was quite brilliant as well as genial.

Other notable members of the Wilkinson clan are the sons of Andrews Wilkinson, J. Biddle Wilkinson, Jr., Maury Wilkinson and Philip Wilkinson; the sons of Dr. Clement P. Wilkinson-Maunsell White Wilkinson and Edward M. Wilkinson; the sons of James Wilkinson — James Wilkinson, Jr.; Leonidas Wilkinson; and Hugh M. Wilkinson; the son of Ernest Wilkinson — Commander Theodore S. Wilkinson U. S. N.; Biddle Wilkinson; and the late Carroll W. Allen M. D., prominent surgeon whose early death was greatly lamented by a large clientele and host of friends; Robert W. Allen, Henry W. Allen, sons of Katherine Wilkinson Allen.

In the year 1825 General James Wilkinson died of a fever contracted in Mexico. He had gone to that country and while pressing the claims of his clients, a number of New Orleans merchants that he expected to be compensated by land claims, he was stricken with fever, and notwithstanding his rugged constitution, died shortly afterwards.

He was buried on December 29th in the Baptist Cemetery of the capital of Mexico with the honors due a noted soldier.

ANDREW STEWART

Andrew Stewart, owner of Oak Alley (Bon Sejour) Plantation, stems from a distinguished sugar planters family, his mother being Josephine Pharr, a member of the Louisiana family of that name who owned large sugar plantations in this state. His father, Andrew Stewart Sr., a cotton broker was descended from the Stewarts of Lisky — near Straban in the North of Ireland, which Lisky is still standing owned and occupied by members of the Stewart family, having been in the Stewart family for over six hundred years.

Mrs. Andrew Stewart (Josephine Armstrong) and her sister Mrs. Allard Kaufmann (Julia Armstrong), on their mother's side stem to James K. Polk, and the Nealy Family of Tennessee, and the Armstrongs and Readys of Tennessee on their paternal side—all families prominent in the social and business affairs of their communities.

Mrs. Allard Kaufmann has three children by her first marriage—Zeb, Julie and Jacqueline Mayhew, descending from Governor Thomas Mayhew of Martha's Vineyard and Nantucket and Elizabeth Iles and James Fennimore Cooper on their grandmother's side.

Mr. Allard Kaufmann of New Orleans is descended from an old Creole family of Louisiana, numbering among its members many who were not only noted for their very beautiful voices, pulchritude and ability as linguists, but who also possessed great charm and personality which made them outstanding members of the social world in New Orleans of which they formed such an important part. The Castellanos home in the French Quarter of New Orleans before the family scattered, was a veritable cage of song-birds. Mrs. Delos Mellon (Corinne Castellanos) possessed a voice pronounced by able critics "as being of the highest order; that her singing was full of soul and her phrasing exquisite." Being a radiantly beautiful blonde Creole she was acclaimed as one of the city's most beautiful daughters. So too with the other members of this talented family. All possessed great tact as well as ability and were most generous in assisting their friends in their entertainments and the various charities of the city when sponsored by musicians.

Dr. Castellanos, a "gentleman of the Old School," enjoyed the love and esteem of a large clientele, and was considered one of the brilliant Doctors of his era. Born in New Orleans — educated in the East and later graduating in medicine in this city, he became a professor of Medicine and later was one of the founders of the Medical College of this city that evolved into the Medical Department of Tulane University of Louisiana.

NOTES ON OAK ALLEY PLANTATION BY MRS. ANDREW STEWART

Oak Allee Plantation which has been restored in recent years by Mr. and Mrs. Andrew Stewart of New Orleans was originally owned by I. T. Roman, brother of André Roman, second Governor of Louisiana.

Mr. Roman built the house with mostly slave labor in 1837-39 on the west bank of the Mississippi, fifty-eight miles above New Orleans in what is known as "The Sugar Bowl" of Louisiana. Only thirteen hundred and sixty acres remain of what was once a princely estate noted for its beauty and hospitality.

The house is the Greek revival type of architecture with twenty-eight Doric columns eight feet in circumference, and double galleries going all around the house. It is seventy feet square, built of brick, plastered over, and painted a soft creamy pink. The railing of cypress which looks like wrought-iron, and the shutters are painted the green, valled "Vert Antique."

The columns are also of solid brick, plastered over, and all the windows on the first and second floors, except the back are French with small pane glass in the upper half, solid wood below, and transoms overhead. The fine Colonial entrance doors are repeated front and back, and on the second floor.

The columns are draped in vines gracefully trained to the tops of such old favorites as honeysuckle, ivy, Star, or "Confederate" jasamine, Lady Banksia, Marechal Niel, Lamarque, and pink Cherokee roses, morning glories, and "Cadena d'Amour" (chain of Love), the Antigonon Leptopus, generally called "Rose of Montana."

Old kettles once used for boiling sugar in the "open kettle molasses" days are now water-lily and water-hyacinth pools in which gold fish swim colorfully.

There are forty-one magnificent old live oaks near the house, and its two guest houses, a magnolia grove, orange grove, and many enormous pecan trees, and tall persimmons, cedar and camphor trees. The avenue of twenty-eight live oaks meeting overhead extends almost a quarter of a mile from the porch to the levee and river.

The spread of branches from outside tips across the arch to outside tips measures a hundred and ninety-seven feet, and eighty-seven across the arch from trunk to trunk, forty feet apart in a row of fourteen on each side. The largest tree is twenty-one feet in circumference five feet from the ground, and the others vary from fifteen to nineteen feet. The grass grows luxuriantly, under these trees making a green carpet for the play of light and shadow.

It is not known by whom the garden was laid out, and very little remains of it except a fine old Magnolia fuscata tree. But the avenue of Oaks are said to have been planted and to have been flourishing for some years before the house was built.

The entrance drive was bordered with Crepe Myrtle trees which were destroyed long ago. These and the fig, orange and fruit groves have been replaced by the present owners, who have added an avenue of bamboo, Dondrocalamonns Litifolus, and one of bananas, parkinsonia trees with oleanders planted between them, and large plantations of evergreen and flowering trees and shrubs with a tree hedge around the entire grounds of ligustrum and Magnolia Grandiflora.

There are eighty-seven people living on the plantation, seven white families and the rest negroes, making a little community in itself. The "Quarter" houses are some distance from the "big house," and are "planted out" with evergreens. Each one has its own garden attractively planted.

Plan of Garden

The garden is oblong square enclosed by a tall hedge of yuccas on three sides and opening on to the east side of the house and is in fine proportion. Against the yucca hedge the wide borders are planted with native evergreen winter flowering shrubs, and plants. These borders are separated from the rose beds by brick walks, and a box hedge borders the generous grass plat in the center. Eight clipped box bushes in pairs form entrances from the brick walk to the center grass plat. The brick walks are bordered with violets, and the entire rose beds covered with pink oxalis.

END OF VOLUME II.

INDEX

INDEX TO VOLUME II.

Afton Villa, 76.
Aime, Francois, 17
Aime, Valcour, 17.
Albermarle Co., Virginia. 97, 98.
Allain genealogy, 178.
Allain, Valerian, 177.
Allen, Mrs. Evelyn Parlange, 37.
Almonaster, Micaela, 135.
Alston genealogy, 152.
Augustin, James - George, 17.
Autreuil, Marthé, 1.
Avard de Solesne, Catherine, 1.

Baker family, 150.
Bayle, family, 150.
Bayou Road, 141.
Bayou St. John, 141.
Barrow, Dynasty, crest and coat-of-arms, genealogy, 75.
Barrow, Alexander, U. S. Senator from Louisiana, 79.
Barrow, Cordelia Johnson, 81.
Barrow, Bartholomew, 81.
Barrow, Martha Hilliard, 77.
Barrow, Robert Hilliard I, 77.
Barrow, Robert Hilliard II, 81.
Barrow, Robert Ruffin I, 81.
Barrow, Robert Ruffin II, family, 81.
Barrow, Wyley Macajah, 80.
Barrow, David of Afton Villa, 78.
Bermudez de, family, 29.
Bienville de, Governor of Louisiana, 3.
Birdwood Manor, 97.
Boehm, genealogy, crest and coat-of-arms, Sir Joseph Edgar, 195.
Bowman, family, 157.
Bowman, James Pirrie, 77.
Brent, General Joseph Lancaster, 85.
Brierre de, Paul, Mrs. Paul (Ida Theresa Van Vrendenburh), 38.

Brierre, Paule (Mrs. W. C. Parlange), 37.
Bringier, crest and coat-of-arms, Dynasty, genealogy, 83.
Bringier Emmanuel Marius Pons, 83.
Bringier, Ignace, 83.
Bringier, Louis Amadée, 84.
Bringier, Pierre, 83.
Bringier, Miss Trista, 86.
Burke, family, 207.
Burthe, Judge Victor, 56.
Butler, crest and coat-of-arms, genealogy, 52.
Butler Dynasty, 52.
Butlers, (The Fighting), 52.
Butler, Fitzwalter, 52.
Butler, the Misses Sarah and Mary, 57.
Butler, Mrs. Thomas Butler, (Mary Fort), 56.

Castallanos Family, 253.
Castellanos, Henry C., 5.
Catalpa Plantation, 63.
Castle Dublin, 12.
Cedars, The—Plantation Home of Butler family (T. W.), 57.
Chateau de Bachellé, 225.
Chateau de Beaulieu de Marconnay, 235.
Chateau de Chantilly, 27.
Chateau de Freneuse, 22.
Chateau de Mont l'Evecque, 135.
Chateau de la Vergne, 18.
Chateau St. Aubin, 22.
Chauvin (de Charleville), 1.
Chauvin (de la Frenier), 1.
Chauvin (de Lery), 1.
Chauvin (de Beaulieu), 1.
Chretien family of Chretien Point, 151.
Claiborne, Gov. W. C. C., 40.
Colonial Country Club of New Orleans, 2.

Concorde Plantation (de la Vergne), 19.
Crevasse de Macarty, 5.
Cruzat de, Marie Josephine (Mrs. Edwin X. de Verges), 50.

D'Arensbourg, Chevalier, 142.
D'Auberville, 22.
D'Auvergne, Baron Douradou, 83.
Damoiseau (de Verges), 46.
D'Arensbourg, Marguerite, 12.
D'Estrehan des Tours family, 180.
D'Estrehan genealogy, 182.
de Bachellé genealogy, 222.
de Bachellé, description of crest and arms, illustration, 222.
de Bachellé Chateau, 222.
de Bachellé, Jacques—Countess Johanne, 222.
de Beaufort Domitile, 39.
de Beaulieu (Chauvin), 1.
de Beaulieu de Lombard, 21.
de Beaulieu de Marconnay, 232, 236.
de Beaulieu de Marconnay Chateau, 235.
de Beaulieu de Marconnay, Baron Herman Albert, 232.
de Beaulieu de Marconnay, Marian Baronne, 232.
de Beaulieu de Marconnay, Baron Charles Philip, 232.
de Beaulieu de Marconnay, General Charles of the French Army, 232.
de Beaulieu de Marconnay, Baron Charles Philip II, 232.
de Beaulieu de Marconnay, Mary Beacham Baronne, 232.
de Beauregard, General P. G. T., 145.
de Beauregard, Touton family, 145.
de Beauregard, Touton genealogy, 145, 146, 147.
de Beauregard, Mrs. P. G. T. (Laure Marie Villere), 146.
de Belair, Ignace Robert, 1.
de Bellecastle Saunhac, 2.

de Brierre genealogy, 38.
de Brierre, Hayacynthe, 38.
de Brierre, Paul, 38.
de Brierre, Paule (Mrs. W. C. Parlange), 38.
de Buys, genealogy, 160.
de Buys, crest and coat-of-arms, 160.
de Buys, Gaspard Melchior, 160.
de Buys, Madame N. E., 163.
de Buys, Walter; James; Lucian; Dr. Lawrence Richard, 163.
de Buys, Mrs. L. R. (Miriam Duggan), 163.
De Cuzot, le Chevalier, 38.
de Dreux de Bréz, Mathurin, 20.
De Fréneuse de St. Albins, genealogy, 22.
de Fréneuse Chateau, 22.
de Fréneuse, crest and arms, 18.
de Fréneuse, Charles Alexander Landry, 22.
de Fréneuse, Mr. and Mrs. Henry Landry, 22.
de Fréneus, Henri Jacques Landry, 22.
de Forez, Count, 21.
de Gournay, Perrine Therese, 21.
des Islet de Lery (Chauvin), 37.
de Jan, Eulalie, 161.
de la Barré family, 183.
de la Barré, description of crest and arms, 183.
de la Candelaria, Delphine Lopez Anguila, 14.
de la Chaise, 26.
de Lafayette, 27.
de la Riviere, 21.
de la Ronde, crest and coat of arms, genealogy, 132.
de la Ronde, Sieur Pierre Denis, 132.
de la Ronde, Louise (Madame Almonaster), 135.
de la Ronde, Pierre Denis II. Sieur, 136.
de la Ronde Avenue of Oaks, and Mansion "Versailles", 136.

de la Source, Marie Genevieve, 4.
de la Vergne, genealogy, crest, and coat of arms, 19.
de la Tour, 3.
de la Vergne Chateau, 19.
de la Vergne, Plantation (Concord), 19.
de la Vergne, Count Pierre, 19.
de la Vergne, Col. Hugues Jules, 19.
de la Vergne, Count Bony, 20.
de la Vergne, Countess Bony, (Marguerite de la Vergne), 20.
de la Vergne, Home in New Orleans, 26.
de la Vergne, Country Home, 19.
de Lino de Chalmet, crest and coat of arms, Martin, 49.
de Livaudais, genealogy, 3.
de Livaudais (Dugue de) crest and coat of arms, 3.
de Livaudais, Jacques Esnould, Count, 6.
de Livaudais, Countess Jacques (Marie Celeste de Marigny de Mandeville), 6.
de Livaudais Plantation, 5.
de Luzeib, Charles de Hault de Lassus, 39.
de Macarty, Crevasse, 175.
de Macarty Genealogy, crest and coat of arms, 170.
de Macarty, Mademoiselle, 174.
de Marigny de Mandeville genealogy, 131.
de Marigny, Pierre Philippe, 131.
de Marigny, Bernard, 131.
de Marigny, Antoine Marie (la perle), 131.
Denis, Arthur; Henry; Louise (Mrs. Charles Parlange), 137.
de Reggio, Helen Judith, 146.
de Reggio, Francois Marie Chevalier, 146.
d'Estrehan, genealogy, 180, 181, 182.
de Vaudreiul, Marquis, 2.

de Verges de St. Sauveur, genealogy, description of arms, 47.
de Verges, Chevalier Bernard, 48.
de Verges, Plantations, 51.
de Verges, Mrs. Edwin X.
de Verges, Garsie Arnaud, 46.
de Verges, Philip M. D., Edwin X., 50.
de Vezin, genealogy, 42.
de Villbiss, genealogy, crest and coat of arms, 228.
de Villeré, genealogy, crest and coat of arms, 141.
de Villeré Etienne Roy, 141.
de Villeré, Joseph Roy, 141.
de Villeré, Jacques Philippe Roy, 142.
de Villeré, Jules, 144.
de Villeré plantation 'Conseil", 144.
de Wartegg, Baron, Baronne, (Minnie Hauk), 229.
d'Otrange, Count Berham Joseph, 24.
du Bourg, Louis Guillaume Valentine (Archbishop), 90.
du Bourg, M. Pierre, 89.
du Bourg, Pierre Francis, 90.
du Bourg, Aglae (Madame Michel Duradou Bringier), 91.
du Bourg, genealogy, crest and coat of arms, 89.
du Broca family record, 177.
du Broca, Madame Valentine, 177.
du Fossat—Soniat genealogy, 1.
du Fossat—Soniat Chateau, 2.
du Fossat, Chevalier Guy de Soniat, 2.
du Fossat-Soniat, Charles, 2.
Dugué, de Livaudais, 3.
Dugué, Robert G., Robert Jr., 2.
Dugué, Amalie (Mrs. J. N. Roussel), 14
Dugué, Robert, Mrs. Robert (Robin Brown), 14.
Dugué, Lucille (Mrs. Lucian de Buys), 14.

Dugué, Mrs. Randall (Susan Glover), 14.
Dugué, (Mrs. Emile de Buys), 14.
Dupuy, genealogy, crest and coat-of arms, 236.
Durand, Marie Francoise, 83.

Ellis genealogy, 65.
Ellis, Abram, 65.
Ellis, Eugene, 65.
Ellis, Mrs. Eugene (Marguerite Butler), 65.
Ellis, Miss Anna B., 65.
Ellis, Eugene, home of, 66.
Eustis, George, 177.
Eustis, Mrs. George (Clarisse Allain), 177.
Eustis, James, 177.

Farwell genealogy, 29.
Farwell crest and coat-of-arms, 29.
Farwell, Miss Nellie, 35.
Farwell Manor, 35.
Farwell, Charles A. I., 29.
Farwell, Charles A. II, 33.
Farwell, Charles A. III, 33.
Farwell, F. Evans, 34.
Farwell, Mrs. F. Evans (Lynne Paxton Hecht), 35.
Faubourg St. Germaine, 136.
Faubourg de Marigny, 2.
Fazende de, Jeanne Henriette, 20.
Forstall Genealogy, Dynasty, 11.
Forstall, description of crest and coat-of-arms, 11.
Forstall, Nicholas Michel Edmond, 12.
Forstall, Edmond John Plantation, 13.
Forstall, Placide, 62.
Forstall, Edward Pierre, 13.
Forstall—Rathbone Home, New Orleans, 14.
Forstall, Melle. Celeste (Madame Henry Alason Rathbone). 14.
Forstall, Madame Edward Pierre Charles (Celeste de Lavillebeuvre), 13.

Fortier, Francois, 16.
Fortier genealogy, 16.
Fortier, Alcée, 18.
Fremont, John the explorer, 200.
Mr. and Mrs. Richard Frotscher, 190.
Frotscher, Lydia Elizabeth, 190.
Fuselier, de la Clair, 150.

Galbreath, Pinkney, 38.
Gautreaux, Madame, 44.
Gayarré, Charles (Louisiana Historian), 1.
Gayoso, Felicite de Beauregard, 82.
German Coast, 143.
Gentilly, Commune of, 140.
Gordon, Martin, 85.
Gottschalk, 24.
Green, Sir Thomas, 119.
Greenwood Plantation (Barrow), 82.
Grymes, William Bryan, 188.
Grymes, John Randolph, 189.
Grymes, Annie Laurie (Mrs. Thos. H. Hewes), 188.

Hauk, Jonathan, 229.
Hauk, Minnie (Baronne de Wartegg) Opera singer, 230.
Haunted House (de la Chaise), 5.
Heraford, 96.
Hewes genealogy, 184.
Hewes, Thomas H., 185.
Hewes, Elliot Henderson, 185.
Hewes Plantation (Pleasant View), 185.
Hicky family, 164.
Hicky, Col. Philip, 164.
Hicky plantation diary, 164.
Hincks, Hon. J. W., 24.
Hincks, Louise Heléne Leda (Mrs. Charles Edouard Schmidt) noted musician, 24.
Hope Estate (Plantation of the Hicky family), 164.
Huguenot Society, 36.
Humphries, Ethlyn (Mrs. A. A. Poirson), 38.

Jefferson, Thomas, 85.
Jenkens, Mrs. Matilda, 104.
Jesuit Plantation, 2.

Kaufmann, Allard, 253.
Kaufmann, Mrs. Allard (Julia Armstrong), 253.
Kenner, Hon. Duncan Farrar, 85, 87.
Kenner, Rosella (Mrs. J. L. Brent), 185.
Kinney family, 231.
Kinney, William Henry, 231.
Knox Hall, Montgomery, Ala., 105.
Knox, Myra Eulalie (Mrs. Thos. J. Semmes), 108.
Knox, William, 105.
Koch, Julius, 190.
Koch, Richard, 190, 191.
Koch, William, 191.
Koch, Minna Frotscher, 191.
Koch, Emilie Frotscher, 191.
Koch, Anna Frotscher, 191.
Koch, Julie Frotscher, 191.
Konzelman (Councilman) family, 233.
Konzelman, Fred William, 233.
Konzelman, Charles de Beaulieu, 234.
Konzelman, Albert S. de Beaulieu, 234.
Konzelman, Charles de Beaulieu, Jr., 234.

Lafrenier, 1.
Lanaux, Louise Valentine (Mrs. John Coleman), 148.
Lanaux, George Charles, 148.
Lanaux, genealogy, 147.
Larendon, Mrs. Charles A. (Laure Beauregard), 146.
Larendon, Laure Beauregard, 146.
Larendon, Charles A., 146.
Lavigne, Voisin, 4.
Lavillebeuvre, Fannie, 14.
Le Andre, Anna, 177.
Lee, Mrs. Lilian Parlange, 37.

Levert family, General J. B. Plantation, 242.
Lind, Jennie, 136.
Lisky Manor and estate, 253.
Liszt, Franz (name spelled wrong in book), 231.
Livaudais de Dugue', crest and coat of arms, genealogy, 3.
Livaudais de Dugue', plantation, 5.
Livaudais de Marquise, letters to and from the King of France, 8.
Lyons, Henry E., 157.

Macpherson family, 221.
Mahew family, 253.
Mandeville, La., 131.
Marigny de Faubourg, 2.
Marigny de, genealogy, crest and coat-of-arms, 131.
Marigny de Marquis, 132.
Marigny de, Bernard, 131.
Marigny de, Marie Celeste (Marquise de Livaudais), 132.
Marigny, Antoine (la perle), 132.
Matas, Dr. Rudolph, 114.
Mather, James (1807), 4th Mayor of New Orleans, 167.
Matthews family, 156, 157.
Mays, family J. R., 81.
Mellon, Mrs. Delos (Corinne Castallanos), 253.
Melpomene, 92.
Milliken, Richard Allen, Mrs. Richard Allen (Debora Farwell), 28.
Milliken Memorial Hospital, 28.
Mock family, 231.
Morton family, 234.
Molinary, Andres, Mrs. Andres, (Marie Madeleine Seebold), 220.
Muller, Hans Nicholas, 193.
Muller, Richard Frotscher, 193.
Myrtles, The, 250.

McCutchon, 55.

Newcomb, Sophie—Women's Dept. of Tulane University, New Orleans, 23.
Nichols Genealogy, 232.
Nichols, William Wallace, 232.
Nichols, Marian (Baronne de Beaulieu de Marconnay), 232.
Northumberland, Earl of, 68.

Oak Alley Plantation notes, 254.
Oak Grove Plantation, 249.
O'Reilly, Count, 143.
Ormond, Duke of, Earl of, 53.

Parker, Walter, genealogy, 237.
Parlange, Col. Charles of the French Army, 36.
Parlange, Hon. Charles, U. S. District Judge of Louisiana, 36.
Parlange, Mrs. Charles (Melle. Louise Denis), 36.
Parlange, Mrs. Walter Charles (Paule Brierre), 36.
Parr, Katherine, 119.
Percy, John Hereford, 71.
Percy, genealogy, 67.
Percy, Dr. Thomas B., 70.
Percy, Robert, 70.
Pharr, Josephine, 253.
Pipes, genealogy, 59.
Pipes, David, Mrs. David (Miss Anna Key Fort), 61.
Pipes, John, 59.
Pipes, Randolph Windsor, 61.
Pipes Town House, Plantation Home Beech Grove, East Feliciana, La., 62.
Pipes, David W. II., 61.
Pipes, Sarah Randolph (Mrs. Walter J. Crawford), 61.
Pipes, William Fort, 61.
Pirrie, Eliza, 157.
Pitkin, genealogy, William, Gov. of Connecticut, Horace Tracy Pitkin, 239, 240.
Pitkin, Helen (Mrs. Christian Schertz), 240, 241.

Pitkin, Walter B., 240, 241.
Plauche, Alexander, Genealogy, Plauche Urbain, 72, 73, 74.
Plauche, Mary (Mrs. Henry Dart 1), 74.
Plauche, (General Jean Baptiste), 74.
Pocohontas, Portrait, 127.
Pontalba de, Celestin, Micaela Baronne, 135, 136.
Pontalba, Baron, Buildings, New Orleans, 136.
Portrait, a famous, 44.
Poujard de Juvisi, Barons of, 148.
Prudhomme, family (Golden Wedding), 245, 246.

Quartier de la Marmalade, 90.

Randolph, Gov. Mann of Virginia, 35.
Ranlett, A. Sidney Sr., family, 113.
Ranlett, Mrs. A. Sidney Sr. (Cora Semmes), 113.
Ranlett, David Low, 113.
Rareshide, Genealogy, crest and coat-of-arms, 149.
Rareshide, Charles Alfred Lanaux, 149.
Rathbone, crest and coat-of-arms, genealogy, 158.
Rathbone Mansion, 14.
Rathbone, Henry Alason, 14.
Rathbone, Samuel, 14.
Rathbone, Melle. Stella (Mrs. Gaspard de Buys), 15.
Reggio de, family, 146.
Revolution, French, 171.
Reynaud, Louis, 38.
Rosebank Manor, 77.

Sargent, John Singer, 44.
Schertz, Mrs. Christian (Helen Pitkin), 241.
Schmidt, Charles Edward, 23.
Schmidt, Mrs. Charles Edward (Louise Helene Leda Hincks), 24.

Schmidt, Gustavus, 24.
Seebold, crest and coat-of-Arms, genealogy, 209.
Seebold, American Branch, 216.
Séghers, genealogy, 25.
Séghers, Dominicque, 26.
Séghers, Julius, 25.
Semmes, genealogy, 104.
Semmes, Hon. Thos. J., 104.
Semmes, Mrs. Thos. J. (Myra Eulalie Knox), 103-108.
Semmes, Raphael, Dr. Alexander J., 104-106.
Semmes, America (Mrs. Rice W. Payne), 106.
Sieur de Gentilly, 2.
Sloo, Mrs. Thomas (Nanine Maria Brent), 88.
Smyth, Dr. John, Dr. Andrew, Mrs. John (Jean Sully), 114, 115, 118.
Soniat du Fossat, Charles, genealogy, 1, 2.
Sparks family, 80.
Sparks, Thomas, 80.
St. Aubin Chauteau, 23.
Stauffer, Isaac, family, 102.
Stauffer, Mrs. Walter R. (Betty M. Taylor), 86.
Stauffer, Mrs. Isaac Hull (Myrthé Bianca Taylor) 86.
Stewart, Andrew Family, 253.
Stewart, Mrs. Andrew (Josephine Armstrong), 253.
Stewart Plantation (Tignal Jones), 63.
Stirling, Alexander, 154.
St. Louis Cathedral, New Orleans, 142.
St. Marlo, Corsair of, 4.
St. Paul (St. Pol), crest and coat-of-Arms, genealogy, 21.
St. Paul de Hugues Cage, Mrs. Hugues Cage (Leda Hélene de la Vergne), 21.
St. Paul de John, 21.
Sully, genealogy, 119.
Sully, Sir Thomas, artist, 119, 123.

Sully, Thomas, architect, 119, 120, 121.
Sully, Matthew, artist, 121.
Sully, Julia (Miss), 122.
Sully, Jean (Mrs. John Smyth), 118.

Taylor, Betty (Mrs. W. R. Stauffer), 86.
Taylor, Lieut. General Richard, 86.
Taylor, Myrthé Bianca (Mrs. I. H. Stauffer), 86.
Taylor, seal ring heirloom of the Taylor family, 85.
Taylor, Zachary, President, 85.
Taylor, crest and coat-of-arms, Jane (Mrs. Michel de Vilbiss), 228.
Tchoupitoulas Reservation, 2.
Totness plantation, 85.
Trianon plantation (Chevalier Bernard de Verges), 51.
Trist, crest and coat-of-arms, genealogy, 96.
Trist, General Hore Browse, 97.
Trist, Julien Bringier, 85.
Trist, Nicholas Philip, 85.
Trist, Rosella, 85.
Tureaud - Trudeau, 84, 85.
Turnbull, Sarah, 157.

Van Vrendenburh, William H., 38.
Vaudreuil Marquis de, 2.
Versailles Plantation and Oak Avenue, 136.
Villeré de, genealogy, crest and coat-of-arms, 141.
Villeré de, Jacques Philippe, Governor, 146.
Villeré de, Joseph Roy, 143.
Villeré de, plantation home (Conseil), 144.
Vogluzan, Marguerite de, 70.
von Dalberg Castle (von Dahlberg), 195.
von Dalberg (Dahlberg), Knight Wolf, 198.

von dem Brink - Seebold, 209.
von Grabow, Ernest Romanus Guido Roudolph, Baron, 102.
von Phul family, 176.
von Phul, Bible record, 176.

Wagner, Richard, 231.
Wakefield Manor, 248.
Wakefield Plantation, 248.
Walmsley genealogy, 110, 111, 112.
Walmsley, Robert Miller, 110.
Walmsley, Sylvester Pierce I, 111.
Walmsley, Mrs. S. P., Sr., (Myra Eulalie Semmes) home, 112.
Ware genealogy, 244.
Ware, Jas. A., 243.
Ware Plantation Home "Belle Grove, 244.
Ware, Mrs. Jas. A. (Mary Eliza Stone), 244.
Wavertree Plantation, 129.
Wells, William Willing, 245.
White Hall Plantation (Maison Blanche), Vol. I, 83
Wilkinson Family, 250.
Wilkinson, James, 250.
Wogan, Angele Charles, 38.
Wogan, Victor Bienvenu, 44.
Wood family, crest and coat-of-arms, 99.
Wood, Captain Peleg, 99.
Wood, Col. John Taylor, U. S. A., C. S. A., 101.
Wood, Robert C., 95.
Wood, Bringier Trist, 101.
Woody, Nelson, Mrs. Nelson (Edith Brierre) 38.

www.ingramcontent.com/pod-product-compliance
Lightning Source LLC
Chambersburg PA
CBHW020636300426
44112CB00007B/132